SOFTWARE METRICS: ESTABLISHING A COMPANY-WIDE PROGRAM

SOFTWARE METRICS: ESTABLISHING A COMPANY-WIDE PROGRAM

Robert B. Grady
Deborah L. Caswell

Hewlett-Packard Company

Prentice-Hall, Inc.
Englewood Cliffs, New Jersey 07632

Library of Congress Cataloging-in-Publication Data

Grady, Robert B.
    Software metrics.

    "August 9, 1986."
    Bibliography: p.
    Includes index.
    1. Computer software--Development--Management.
    I. Caswell, Deborah L.   II. Title.
QA76.76.D47G73   1987   005.1'068   87-2266
ISBN 0-13-821844-7

Editorial/production supervision and
    interior design: Tracey Orbine
Cover design: Photo Plus Art
Manufacturing buyer: Gordon Osbourne

Printed in the United States of America

10 9 8 7 6 5 4

ISBN 0-13-821844-7   025

Prentice-Hall International (UK) Limited, *London*
Prentice-Hall of Australia Pty. Limited, *Sydney*
Prentice-Hall of Canada Inc., *Toronto*
Prentice-Hall Hispanoamericana, S.A., *Mexico*
Prentice-Hall of India Private Limited, *New Delhi*
Prentice-Hall of Japan, Inc., *Tokyo*
Prentice-Hall of Southeast Asia Pte. Ltd., *Singapore*
Editora Prentice-Hall do Brasil, Ltda., *Rio de Janeiro*

Dedicated to
Jan, Sean, and Erin Grady
and
Dave Caswell

CONTENTS

FOREWORD

One Monday morning in the early 1970s, traders on the American Stock Exchange were surprised to learn that the country's third largest software company had suddenly gone belly-up. The company's mainstay business had been building of Management Information Systems. It solicited this business with cute little ads about "pin the tail on the donkey" management. These ads poked fun at company executives who try to run their businesses blind, i.e., without adequate management information.

The officers of the company learned of the precipitous decline of their fortunes by the fact that the bank had seized their payroll account. Sensing from this that something might be amiss, the President called for an emergency accounting of company finances. As he told the assembled employees later that day, "When the figures came in I was shocked."

I've always thought of that as one of the Great Moments of Data Processing. And the President's quote hangs in a place of honor over my desk, a constant reminder of the marvelous illogic of our industry. Imagine, the very people who were known for exquisitely precise quantification of other people's business had failed to quantify their own.

As software developers, we are deeply involved in quantification. We build software that measures any and all aspects of our user's business. But measurement of our own business, of the software development process itself, is a rarity. The picture is particularly grim at the project level, where there is little meaningful quantification *even after the fact*. (It's one thing that we can't always estimate in advance how much a project is going to cost; it's inexcusable that we can't usually say after it's over how much it actually cost.) We're not even enough aware of this problem to be suitably self-conscious about it:

> "How many bugs did you take out of that program before you delivered it?"
> "Well, far too many."
> "What productivity did you end up with?"
> "Not as high as we'd hoped, but probably better than some of our earlier projects."
> "How big a system was it that you finally built?"
> "Hyoo-Mongous!"

Real measurement is hard work and it might point up some scary results, so many organizations simply don't do it. Their metric philosophy is more or less "Hear no evil, see no evil, speak no evil."

Fortunately there are at least a few examples of sensible approaches to measurement, and one of the most compelling of these is described in *Software Metrics: Establishing a Company-Wide Program*. The book tells of one company's need for a measurable controllable software process, and of the very professional effort the company mounted to meet that need. If the effort had been less ambitious, this book would have ended its days as a long memo, of interest only within the author's company. But the approach was so broad and so multi-faceted that it covers most of the ground necessary to set up such a program in *any* company. It tells of the metrics chosen, the tools used to collect and digest them, the selling job to get people involved, the forms, the training sequences, the documentation, the results and the costs.

Bob Grady and Debbie Caswell were not just passive observers of the program they describe, they were right in the thick of it. Their experience is germane, their advice is informed and heartfelt, and their enthusiasm is catching. The story they tell is useful preparation for anyone setting out to collect and use software metrics.

Tom DeMarco
The Atlantic Systems Guild
Camden, Maine

ACKNOWLEDGEMENTS

This book is the result of a great deal of work by a large number of people in Hewlett-Packard. The HP metrics program and this book would certainly not be possible without the support and encouragement of numerous HP managers at all levels. We are particularly grateful to Chuck House, HP's Director of Corporate Engineering, for his enthusiasm regarding the project of writing this book.

We are grateful to the hundreds of people (data collectors, data analyzers, reviewers, editors, ...) whose work provided substance for the book. We wish to pay special thanks to Wendy Schilling for her help in preparing the graphics and editing much of the text which became the manuscript. Thanks to the HP Software Metrics Council, especially to Sally Dudley, Mike Gourlay, Jan Grady, Gail Hamilton, Dave Kenyon, Lee Lebowitz, Kathy Osborne, Brian Sakai, and Chuck Sieloff for contributing material and reviewing our manuscript. And thanks to all of our colleagues in HP's SEL who supported and believed in us.

Of our non-HP reviewers, Tom DeMarco provided valuable suggestions that we feel have improved our book a great deal. To Tom, also, our thanks for agreeing to write a foreword for the book.

Our families deserve special mention for their support and patience. They are special people to give up much of their time with us so that we could chronicle this work that we believe in and want to share with others.

1

MEASURING THE BEGINNING

This book is about measuring software and software development. We believe that such measurements lead to substantial benefits for reasonable costs, and that by reading about the software metrics experiences at Hewlett-Packard you will be convinced of these benefits. The book is divided into three parts: background and history of the HP Software Metrics Council (Chapters 1–7), what we have achieved so far (Chapters 8–15), and a strategy for the future (Chapters 16–17).

> **A Proposal:** Software metrics will help you to develop better software in your organization. Analyze our approach to software metrics implementation and decide which metrics are most appropriate for your development process and implement them. Expect some immediate benefits at the project level, and anticipate the difficulties we describe. Plan on collecting and analyzing data for at least three years before you have sufficient data for measurable trends for an entire organization.

Why start with a proposal? It is difficult for us to guess what you expect to get from this book. By stating a proposal to start with, we hope to help shape your expectations to what we feel we can best provide.

Some of the things we describe here will sound quite easy. Realistically, though, establishing a successful company-wide software metrics program takes a great deal of hard work. When we say that you must wait at least three years before broad organizational trends are available, you get some idea of the scope of such an effort. We also realize how difficult it is to plan software projects which take that long.

During this book we will talk a lot about HP's Software Metrics Council. Before we tell you what it is, let us describe some interesting research one of the members of the council performed [1]. The division he represented had detailed project records which went back many years, so he decided to do some "archeology." The records did not contain much data which related to the metrics of software development, but they did report project estimates and actual results. What he discovered was a "software estimating wall." In many years of data, there were virtually no projects which estimated completion more than two years from the point of estimation. There was a cluster of estimates around the two-year point, although the actual completions for these projects were spread before, and mostly after, the two-year mark.

This phenomenon is not unusual for software estimating, and it illustrates an example of what kind of information you can expect to learn by investigating and using software metrics. We don't want you to believe that a software metrics program is a "standard," bounded software project. It represents a long-term management commitment to understanding and managing software development more effectively. By definition, a project has a fixed completion and a well-defined delivered result. A software metrics program is *part of the process of managing software development*, and it must evolve as management and development techniques change. Your first job is to convince your management that a software metrics program is not a software project and should not be expected to be completed within two years.

1.1 A PRODUCTIVITY FRAMEWORK

About a year and a half after we initiated the widespread use of software metrics at Hewlett-Packard, we were asked to participate in presenting software training courses to HP managers in Europe. This was an excellent opportunity for us to get the European labs more involved in collecting software metrics data, so we set about planning our trip with these two objectives in mind. We calculated how much effort was necessary at each location with different groups and how much time was necessary for travel between the sites, and we determined whom we had to contact to best achieve our objectives.

It is interesting that in planning a trip, we immediately started thinking in terms of metrics of time, distance, and communications. We are so used to thinking in such terms in many activities that we don't realize that is what we are doing. We are about to depart on another journey in this book, and you might think about the metrics of the process. There are eighteen chapters with 144 illustrations. The *cost* to read a book is in the form of *time*.

Complex material or a poor *environment* in which to read can affect your efficiency and require more time. The *value* is gained from the *number* and *quality* of concepts which are learned and "usefully" applied. The relationship of these terms is presented in Figure 1-1 in a variation of a productivity model we first saw presented by Victor Basili of the University of Maryland [2]. It suggests the major elements of a software metrics program (or any type of metrics program, actually). Productivity is measured as a function of output divided by input, or value divided by cost.

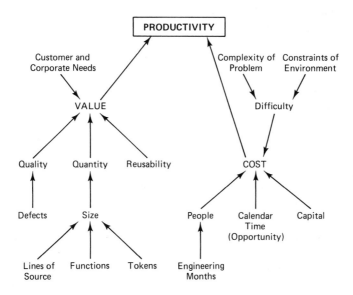

Figure 1-1   Software productivity model.

1.1.1 Our Objective in Writing this Book

To describe the history of the software metrics program at HP through the use of many graphic examples. To meet this objective we explain the common terminology and usefulness of software metrics as a means to understand development processes. We also outline the effort necessary to establish such a widespread program and some of the problems we encountered along the way. Finally, we describe the enthusiasm for the long-term effectiveness of this approach within HP and describe reasonable expectations for a group getting started with software metrics.

1.2 WHAT ARE SOFTWARE METRICS?

A *software metric* defines a standard way of measuring some attribute of the software development process. For example, **size, cost, defects, communications, difficulty**, and **environment** are all attributes. Examples of attributes in the physical world are mass, length, time, and the like. "Kilo-lines of executable source" illustrates one metric for the **size** attribute. Metrics can be primitive (directly measurable or countable, such as counting lines of code) or computed (such as noncomment source statements/engineer/month).

To many project managers at HP, software metrics are a means for more accurate estimations of project milestones, as well as a useful mechanism for monitoring progress. Estimates are more accurate when accurate historical records for projects of similar size, application, and complexity are available. Plotting weekly or monthly progress provides trends that can predict problem areas early enough that action can be taken.

In this book we do not attempt to exhaustively discuss all software metrics used throughout industry. Where relevant, we will relate HP's results to others, although the state of software metric collection everywhere is immature and imprecisely defined. Where we have seen inaccuracies that resulted from different interpretations of definitions, we will also tell why there were different interpretations and whether we were able to resolve these differences.

1.3 COMPANY BACKGROUND

Hewlett-Packard is a manufacturing company which sells instrumentation and computation products. It has 85,000 employees and there are 66 product divisions. There is a great deal of variation from one division to another, and in many ways HP consists of multiple companies. Divisions have many things in common, however, which should be described in order for anyone outside HP to understand the relevant issues in establishing a software metrics program elsewhere.

Divisions are run as profit centers, each having its own research and development, marketing, and manufacturing capabilities. R&D departments typically range in size from 40 to 150 engineers. Product decisions are primarily driven by R&D, although decisions are generally made by consensus with other functional areas. All engineers have the same title: "Member of Technical Staff." They are organized into projects within sections of a lab. Engineers are frequently exposed to many different areas of operations, and a feeling of teamwork is encouraged which goes beyond the bounds of one's own department.

Hewlett-Packard designs and manufactures scientific instruments, small to medium-size computers, and medical and analytical instruments. During the past fifteen years these components have been increasingly designed for, and used in, systems which solve complex problems. In the 46 years since its founding, HP has grown until today its research and development for new products is carried on in 25 decentralized locations scattered throughout the United States, Europe, Japan, and Australia.

The first HP computers were introduced in 1966 and 1967. The HP2116A computer and the HP9100A desktop computer (or calculator, as it was initially referred to) were designed for totally different markets and produced by two geographically separate divisions. Each contained HP's first substantial efforts into the software field, and both product lines quickly expanded. Since this beginning, the rapid growth of systems software development in autonomous divisions has raised awareness of the need for tighter coordination.

1.4 THE ROLE OF TASK FORCES

Within HP, we are highly conscious of quality and have a well-deserved reputation for quality products. Despite this reputation, there has been a great deal of consideration given to how we could produce software products as well as we produce hardware products. This has led to numerous task forces and councils whose recommendations are considered carefully. Task forces represent an important mechanism for responsible change within HP, for the members of the task force are frequently asked to carry out the task force recommendations, or to consult until progress is achieved.

The start of widespread usage of software metrics at HP was the result of a task force focused on software quality and productivity which recommended the establishment of software project teams to address short-term productivity improvements through tools, as well as long-term improvements through the establishment of a common development environment. These recommendations led to the creation of our organization, the HP Software Engineering Lab (HP SEL). One of the first major tasks we tackled was the creation of the HP Software Metrics Council.

Our objectives for initiating the Software Metrics Council were twofold. First, we felt that the very act of measuring the software development process in HP would lead to short-term improvements in our productivity. Second, we wanted to establish a measurement foundation against which the tools we planned to develop or purchase could be evaluated to determine their effectiveness.

1.5 GATHERING SUPPORT

The Software Metrics Council came up with a set of proposed metrics standards which will be discussed in detail throughout this book. Establishing support for a program such as the Software Metrics Program at HP is described quite well by two quotations from *In Search of Excellence* [3].

> People . . . like to perform against standards — if the standard is achievable, and especially if it is one they played a role in setting.

> There is no way that such programs will ever take hold without the unstinting support of the whole top management team.

Such a level of agreement and participation takes careful planning and continuous attention to be successful. The first quotation was satisfied through the council itself and its ability to identify with the broad cross section of HP software developers. The second was achieved through numerous presentations and training courses which spanned the entire management structure of the company.

1.6 SUMMARY

We began with a proposal for a software metrics program for your company/project based upon many of our experiences. We suggested that it would lead to both short-term gains at the project level, and measurable trends for your organization in the medium term. Whether your organization produces successful products today or not, such a program is important to the long-term competitiveness of a software-producing company.

We then presented general descriptions of productivity and software metrics. We followed with a description of the general software environment in HP, as well as the methods we used to start our metrics program. Finally we touched upon the engineering and management commitment necessary to sustain such a program. What follows is evidence that such a program is valuable and achievable within a relatively short period of time (you might say, as software programs are measured).

BIBLIOGRAPHY

1. Deardorff, E., Presentation to HP's Third Annual Software Metrics Council Meeting, Palo Alto, Calif. (Nov. 1985).

2. Basili, V., Presentation to IEEE Working Group for Software Productivity Metrics, Nashua, N. H. (Sept. 1984).

3. Peters, T. and R. Waterman, *In Search of Excellence.* New York: Harper & Row 1982, pp. 240, 242.

2

A PROCESS FOCUS

During the late 1970s, it became increasingly clear to many companies in the United States that techniques used in Japanese manufacturing led to significant improvements. In 1978 a group of managers from HP were sent to Japan to visit manufacturing sites and to report on how these techniques could apply to our processes. Actions taken as a result of that first visit caused profound changes in the way we viewed our processes and manufactured our products. In this chapter we examine the lessons we learned and their relevance to our software development processes.

The title of this chapter, "A Process Focus," refers to the focus on the manufacturing process which we believe was the key to many improvements in HP. As we discuss metrics throughout this book, they will fall into two broad categories of product metrics and process metrics. United States manufacturers learned the hard way that lack of product quality meant loss of the competitive edge. We saw this happen in fields such as television sets, hi-fidelity equipment, and automobiles. The software industry is not exempt from the need for product quality, but we have learned from our manufacturing experience that product quality improvements are made by improving the design and building processes, not from simply concentrating on the testing and fixing of problems that already exist.

In this chapter we set the stage for why HP's metrics program strongly emphasizes metrics selected to help understand and improve our processes of developing and producing software. We examine several uses of manufacturing process measurement to illustrate the opportunities which exist for software.

2.1 SEEKING QUALITY

The most significant finding of the group of HP managers was a commitment to high quality in every aspect of every worker's job. At HP we have always produced high-quality products, but our processes were seldom characterized by such an emphasis on quality as the Japanese exhibited. Rather, our objectives for manufacturing were sometimes driven by delivery, cost, or flexibility objectives, as well as quality. It was obvious that Japanese attitudes were a result of both widespread management commitment and steps to reinforce employee attention to quality.

The first step the Japanese used in this reinforcement was a widespread training program in the techniques of statistical methods. Coupled with this program was the establishment of quality circles to take advantage of these techniques. These circles became an important social element among the workers. A sense of belonging and significance of effort helped to make the circles popular, and positive reinforcement guaranteed their success when management took actions based upon circle recommendations. The Deming Award each year gave national recognition to the importance of a person's role in quality circles. It is significant to note that the prize is not necessarily awarded to the company with the highest quality but to the one which performed most effectively in the process of analysis.

This process focus was one of the lessons we learned. Figure 2-1 is an illustration of the steps involved. It shows that the first step to process improvement is to gain an understanding of how things are currently done. With such an understanding, changes often can be made which lead to process improvements and a controlled, repeatable process. Once a process is repeatable, the parts of it most susceptible to automation are easier to define.

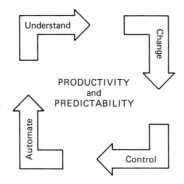

Figure 2-1 Four steps to process improvement.

2.1.1 The Use of Statistical Quality Control Charts

The popularity of quality circles at HP grew quickly in the first years after the visit to Japan. The nature of such circles fit well into the HP culture. As a result, success stories were quickly generated, and our processes improved. What was actually happening was that we were understanding some elements of the manufacturing process for the first time.

The first step to process improvement is better understanding. We used statistical quality control (SQC) charts to help us with this understanding. The basic principle behind the SQC chart is that every process has natural limits, and when these limits are exceeded the process is out of control. (A detailed explanation of quality control charts can be found in the *Guide to Quality Control* by K. Ishikawa [1].) For example, Figure 2-2 shows an SQC chart.

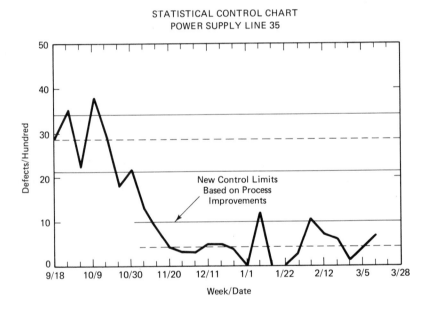

Figure 2-2   A statistical quality control chart.

The horizontal solid lines define the bounds of this particular process when it is in control. In the left part of the chart we can see instances when the process went out of control both above and below the established bounds. By examining what happened at these times, it was possible to learn important facts about the production process. For example, there are two possible explanations for why the number of defects went below the lower control limits. One is that something went wrong with the testing process, and many of the defects normally captured during the process were missed. The second explanation is that one or more of the root causes of defects was found and eliminated. In the right part of the chart, we can see that a fundamental change occurred in the process after the earlier examinations and the changes they initiated. As a result there are two new horizontal lines which define the new bounds for the process. Such impressive changes were not unusual once SQC charts became understood and widely used.

The software opportunity:

Thus we see that understanding led to both immediate change and better control of the process measured. We expect that applying metrics to software processes will produce similar results: Measurements will lead to better understanding and increased predictability of the process. Understanding why different types of defects are present or not in different software projects will lead to the elimination of these types of defects.

2.1.2 The Effect of Rework on Cycle Time

In order to use SQC charts, the overall process has to be defined well enough that repeatable parts of it are identified. The repeatable parts can then be charted, measured, and controlled. The use of SQC charts was just one way of reducing cycle time in the next example. Figure 2-3 represents the entire production process for one of HP's product lines in 1979. The overall production cycle averaged over twenty weeks. When we look at the time relationships among the various elements of a process before and after change, the effect of rework can appear dramatically. Rework includes all efforts over and above those required to produce a defect-free product correctly the first time.

One of the first things that a focus on quality and rework showed was that the loops for rework not only happened once, but frequently occurred many times for one product. To complicate the process even more, when failures during final test occurred, there were often multiple failures in the same unit. This made the job of analyzing the root causes very difficult and caused the troubleshooting process to be quite lengthy.

The solution to the problem was to find and change those parts of the process where problems were introduced. For example, by heat stressing components after incoming inspection or even before incoming inspection at the vendor's plant, one source of failures during final test could be significantly reduced. Through similar steps a major effort was launched to force detection of defects to the earliest cost-effective point in the process. The results were remarkable. Figure 2-4 shows the same production process only two years later. The cycle time was reduced to only two weeks, and the number of units which entered the rework paths were down to the 5 to 20 percent range. The average production cycle was less than three weeks. Of course, the whole story

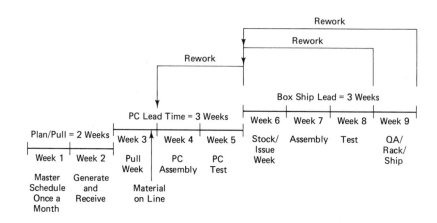

Figure 2-3 Production cycle for a product in 1979.

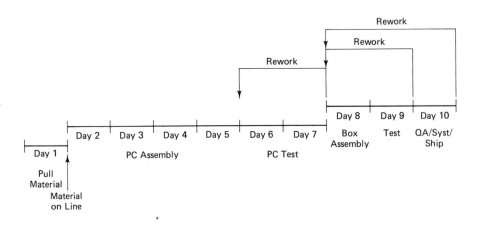

Figure 2-4 Production cycle for the same product in 1981.

of this particular success is much longer and includes discovery of unnecessary process steps and introduction of some additional automation to the process. This story was not unusual, though, once a process focus on quality achieved management-level support at HP.

The software opportunity:

The parallel to software development is interesting. The average cycle time (the calendar time to develop and release a software product) is typically more than a year. Our final test includes multiple rework passes, and fix times can be quite long due to the presence of multiple defects. The opportunity to significantly reduce our cycle times is clear. Identifying defects at an earlier point in the process will lead to increased productivity.

2.2 MEASURING OVERALL EFFECTIVENESS

Although process changes are most easily expressed as success stories, good managers will measure success based on the impact on actual cost savings. When quality circles present proposals for process changes, a part of the presentation always is a return on investment analysis. Similarly, it is necessary for the sum of all of the individual successful proposals to be reflected in some visible way for management. Figure 2-5 shows one such representation at the division where the successes in the previous section occurred.

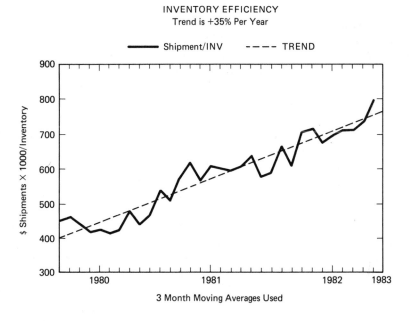

Figure 2-5   Inventory efficiency for a division.

It shows one of four graphs which were plotted on a regular basis as indicators of productivity: direct labor efficiency, total labor efficiency, space efficiency, and inventory efficiency. In all four cases the numerator of the ratio plotted consisted of shipments in terms of dollars. The graph shown in Figure 2-5 had inventory dollars as the denominator. It shows that increasing amounts of shipments were possible with either no change or decreases in inventory levels. The other three graphs also showed steady efficiency gains during the same period, so it was clear that efficiency improvement was broad-based and not localized to one aspect of the process. Finally, a similar graph of quality was tracked to guarantee that productivity was not improved at the expense of quality.

The software opportunity:

We learned from manufacturing that we needed a way to demonstrate process improvements which managers easily interpret. When they see these positive changes, it results in support for additional efforts. The graphs can help management understand software development better, as well as foster enthusiasm on the part of the employees involved.

2.3 CONCLUSION

Our manufacturing experiences gave us confidence that we could significantly improve our R&D processes through process focus and measurements. Prior to establishing a software metrics program at HP, this confidence was reinforced by successes with our hardware R&D development process. Significant improvements were achieved in printed circuit board development by automated checks for quality at several steps in the process, as well as tools to aid in the design process. The cycle time for board turnaround from design to test board was reduced from months to one or two weeks, and the need to repeat the cycle was also dramatically reduced. Even more dramatic improvements were achieved in producing integrated circuit designs.

In 1982 HP's president, John Young, said, "Our aim here is for a major improvement in R&D effectiveness. We are not talking about a 5 or 10 percent scaling. We are talking about a major change in how we do our work; and we are convinced from looking at R&D that it is indeed quite possible" [2]. We have described the successes which led to his belief that software development can also be dramatically improved. The steps begin with measurements. These, in turn, lead to better understanding and control. Finally, when the process is understood and under control, automation can be used to simplify it, reduce the causes of defects, and significantly reduce cycle times.

We learned several important lessons from our manufacturing process improvements. First, widespread involvement of people using meaningful measures is necessary. The people closest to the process are the ones who can most quickly help to bring it under control, and measurements will help them to identify how. Second, long cycle times make it very difficult to understand a process. Focusing on cutting the cycle time by eliminating rework can significantly simplify the problem. Finally, management support is the most significant element of long-term improvements. Providing management with overall measures which are meaningful at their level can result in significant positive reinforcement for the efforts of their people.

BIBLIOGRAPHY

1. Ishikawa, I., *Guide to Quality Control.* Asian Productivity Organization 1976.
2. Young, J., Presentation to HP managers (1982).

3

THE STRATEGY

We have presented the background in our company at the start of our
software metrics program. We felt that this was important, because this book
is specifically about the implementation of software metrics at HP. While
your company may differ from ours, we believe that the steps to implement a
similar program will be basically the same. Before we go any further, we will
summarize these steps so that you have a general picture of the sequence
which follows and its rationale.

In software terms, the strategy which we followed was to produce itera-
tive prototypes of our "product." By defining and implementing metrics to collect in relatively limited sets, we felt that we would get immediate feedback
on their effectiveness which would prevent us from serious misdirection at any
point. This was (and still is) necessary, because software metrics are not
firmly enough established as a science that a specific set of measures are "the
right set." With each new iteration, we learn from the last and refine our
direction to take advantage of what we learned. In this context, we prescribe a
course for you which will yield the benefits that we have experienced, and we
give you our best view of a longer-term strategy.

A warning is necessary, however. *A software metrics program must not
have a strategy unto itself. Collecting software metrics must not be an iso-
lated goal. Software metrics can successfully be only a part of an overall
strategy for software development process improvement.* The steps we
describe will help you to define and implement metrics which will help you to
achieve your process improvement goals.

3.1 STEPS TO SUCCESS

1. Define company/project objectives for program.

   The objectives you define will frame the methods you use, the costs which you are willing to incur, the urgency of the program, and the level of support you have from your managers.

2. Assign responsibility.

   The organizational location of responsibility for software metrics and the specific people whom you recruit to implement your objectives send a signal to the rest of the organization that indicates the importance of the program.

3. Do research.

   We hope that we have simplified this problem for you. This book, the books and articles we include in the bibliography, and a scan of literature which has been published even more recently should be sufficient for you to make your initial decisions concerning which metrics to implement. One month should be enough for this activity.

4. Define initial metrics to collect.

   The starter set of metrics includes ways of measuring size, defects, and effort. You should start with a simple set, such as the one described in Chapter 5.

5. Sell the initial collection of these metrics.

   The success of a metrics program depends upon the accuracy of the data collected, and this accuracy depends upon the commitment of your people to taking the time to collect it. They must be convinced of its importance.

6. Get tools for automatic data collection and analysis.

   Tools help simplify the task of collection, reduce the time expenditure on the part of your people, ensure accuracy and consistency, and reduce psychological barriers to collection.

7. Establish a training class in software metrics.

   Training classes help ensure that the objectives for data collection are framed in the context of the company/project objectives. Training is also necessary to achieve the widespread usage of metrics that is necessary to resolve widespread process problems.

8. Publicize success stories and encourage exchange of ideas.

   Publicity of successes provides feedback to the people taking measurements that their activities are valuable. It also helps to spread these successes to other parts of the organization.

9. Create a metrics database.

    A database for measurements collected is necessary to evaluate overall
    organizational trends and effectiveness. It also provides valuable feed-
    back concerning whether the metric definitions you are using are ade-
    quate, since poor definitions will yield either no data or data which
    varies widely.

10. Establish a mechanism for changing the standard in an orderly way.

    As you understand your development process better, the process and the
    metrics that you collect will evolve and mature. There must be a
    mechanism in place which basically repeats steps 1 thru 9 above.

4

INITIAL DATA AND RESEARCH

Both academia and industry have conducted software metrics research for many years. In preparation for the first meeting of HP's Software Metrics Council, we investigated papers and books describing this research. Recently published experimental results were the most valuable, because they gave us idea for conducting our own experiments and set our expectations for our own results. It was our belief that this investigation (combined with HP's software development experience) would lead us toward a measurement standard. This chapter presents data from the experiments which most influenced the software metrics activities at HP, as well as more recent data which is of interest. This data will help you get started with your own metrics program.

4.1 PRODUCTIVITY

In a speech to HP software engineers in July of 1983, Don McNamara of General Electric stated that the typical U.S. rate of software production is 100–500 lines of source per person per month [1]. In contrast, he stated that in one particular Japanese software factory, their rate for generation of only new code is 500–800, and when reusable code is included the rate increases to 2500–3100. There are several unknown variables in such a statement, such as whether these rates include comments, whether they are based upon the coding phase only, what type of software is being produced, and what type of quality is achieved under these conditions. A key point, though, is that lines of source per person per month is a commonly accepted measure of productivity but is meaningful only if this other information is available. Figure 4-1 shows a graph of productivity at Toshiba over a ten-year period [2]. When productivity data is graphed over time, the absolute definition of productivity doesn't matter a lot, as long as it is applied consistently.

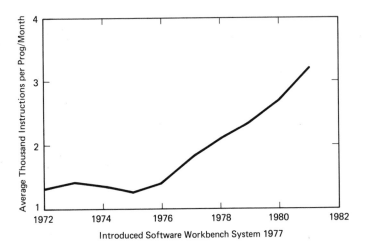

Figure 4-1   Software productivity at Toshiba, © May 1983, IEEE.

Understanding the relationship between the rate of generating lines of source and other objectives of a software project is critical if such rates are to be effectively used to measure productivity. Thirteen years ago, Gerald Weinberg and Edward Schulman performed an experiment where five different programmer teams were asked to write the same software [3]. Each team was given a different objective to optimize. Table 4-1 shows that in each case the teams were successful when evaluated against their major objective. However, the secondary effects and the relative rates of productivity (as measured in source instructions/programmer hour) varied considerably.

A more recent study (published in 1984) of 44 projects in ITT demonstrates that various techniques which have gained popular acceptance among the software engineering community definitely do have a positive impact on productivity [4]. The five "modern programming practices" which had the strongest correlation with productivity were top-down design, modular design, design reviews, code inspections, and quality assurance (QA) programs. Productivity was measured in the study using delivered noncomment source statements per person year, and the degree of modern programming practice was

TABLE 4-1   Weinberg Productivity Experiment*

Group Objective	Ranking					Productivity
	Min. Core	Output Clarity	Prog. Clarity	Min. State.	Min. Hours	
Minimum Core	1	4	4	2	5	0.7
Output Clarity	5	1	1-2	5	2-3	5.5
Program Clarity	3	2	1-2	3	4	2.2
Minimum Statements	2	5	3	1	2-3	1.1
Minimum Hours	4	3	5	4	1	4.5

*From *Human Factors*, 1974, 16(1), pp. 70–77. Copyright 1974 by the Human Factors Society, Inc; reproduced by permission.

derived from a questionnaire filled out by project managers which asked what percentage of the project was developed using each of twelve practices.

With knowledge of some of these productivity variables in mind, we can look at some of the early data collected at HP (Figure 4-2) with the strong caution that there are not enough projects represented to be statistically significant. One possible effect on productivity is the language which is used. The data shown represents historical projects where data was kept representing thousands of lines of noncomment source statements (KNCSS) divided by total project time in engineering months. Each bar represents the average productivity of projects written in that language. The bar labeled "reused" means that at least 75 percent of the code already existed. "Mixture" is used when no one language represented 75 percent or more of the code. In most cases, we have provided tools which scan source code and count the number of lines of source divided into comments and other statement types, so the burden of collecting the data is minimized.

We see a striking difference here between the productivity of those projects which used a large amount of reused software versus those that didn't. The bar chart below shows that new code was produced at a rate of 400–700 lines per engineering month, but projects with reused code were produced at a rate of over 2500 lines per engineering month. These numbers are almost identical to the data presented by Dan McNamara with a new code to reused code ratio of about 5 to 1. Providing a methodology for making reuse of software easy is an important opportunity for productivity improvements. It

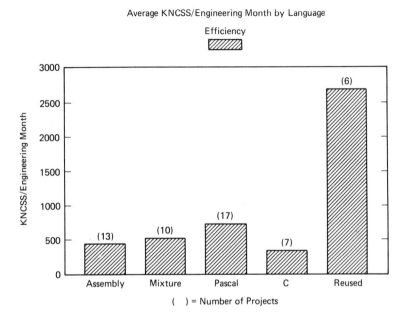

Figure 4-2   How efficient is the process?

represents a tremendous opportunity for software developers which we will see repeated in other views of HP data in later chapters.

4.2 QUALITY

In manufacturing, the Japanese have demonstrated that *productivity gains follow naturally from quality improvements in the process*. It is important to consider quality measurements during the development process as a link to improved productivity. In HP we have kept very detailed records of software defect data after product release for years. Only recently have some divisions started to analyze the causes of defects found prior to release.

Japanese companies are measuring software quality with the same interest that they showed in manufacturing quality. At Hitachi they have plotted what they call "spoilage" since 1976 [5]. This represents the cost to fix postrelease defects. Figure 4-3 shows their success at improving software quality as a ratio of spoilage to total project cost. When a company (or any part of a company) can reduce rework by such a large amount, it frees up substantial engineering resources to produce additional revenue-producing products.

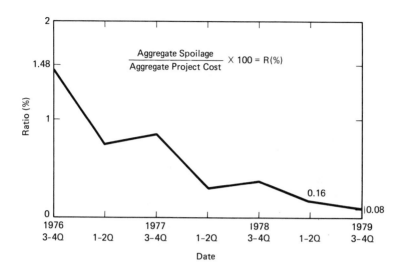

Figure 4-3   Quality improvement results from Hitachi, © May 1981, IEEE.

In another Japanese company the expected number of defects in a given software project is calculated from statistical models which they have derived. From these models, they expect to find a minimum number of defects (this number varies with the amount of reused code, and it peaks at 12.2 defects/1000 lines of source) prior to releasing software to third-party test [6]. The prerelease defect density of HP's first 57 projects (excluding projects using greater than 75 percent reused code) was 8.12. These two sets of data compare very well, although there are probably differences in how data is counted, but the key point is that in both cases an attempt is underway to characterize the process. Once characterized, a process can be analyzed for ways to improve error-prone parts.

Over the past fifteen years, various authors have reported results of defect analyses. Many of them have attempted to normalize defects to lines of code, although at least two authors have persuasively argued that there is a much better correlation of defects to program complexity [7,8]. When we look at results from six different studies [9,10,11,12,13,14]*, we can see a wide variation in results. Figure 4-4 shows a bar chart of defect densities with the year when the data was reported and the total size of each project in "KLOC." We use this term because the different sources reported their results in various ways. Some of the terms included "program steps," "machine language instructions," and "executable lines."

---

*Data for Figure 4-4: Rubey and Endres, copyright © 1975, IEEE; Belford, copyright © 1979, IEEE; Sunazuka, copyright © 1983, IEEE.

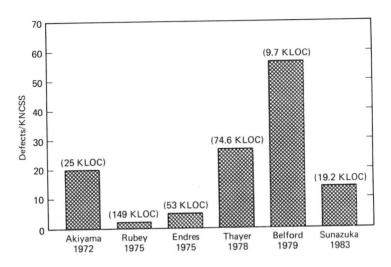

Figure 4-4   Reported defect densities.

We have already discussed the factors which cause KNCSS (or KLOC) to vary a great deal. Since these numbers include KNCSS in the denominator, it is not too surprising that there is such a wide variation among the different studies. In the case of defect density we have the additional variable of how defects themselves are defined and counted. Despite the fact that reported defect densities vary so widely, we strongly believe that consistent definition and measurement of defects is an important cornerstone of any software metrics program.

In an even more recent book by Capers Jones (1986), he lists defect densities for five projects of different types and sizes that range from 49.5 to 94.6 [15]. From these various numbers, we expect that numbers from projects in HP or any company would vary over a wide range.

Another important way of looking at defect data is to focus on percentages of defects by phase of the process. Two studies at IBM and TRW presented by Barry Boehm give us some insight into what to expect [16].* Design seems to be the process area to address first. Indeed, most HP divisions use formal design inspections to reduce the number of defects early in the process. But Figure 4-5 suggests another area of opportunity currently almost ignored: documentation defects. Documentation is frequently treated as a low priority under a great deal of schedule pressure, seldom with real formal review. Yet the figure shows that overall quality of software is very

---

*Barry W. Boehm, *Software Engineering Economics,* © 1981, reprinted by permission of Prentice-Hall, Englewood Cliffs, NJ.

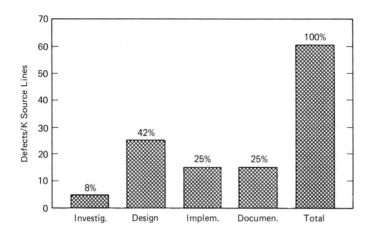

Figure 4-5   Introduction of software defects (from IBM and TRW studies).

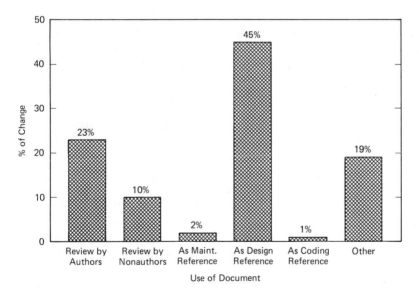

Figure 4-6   Discovery of need for change, © March 1981, IEEE.

much a function of documentation [16]. Boehm's software error introduction/removal model suggests that 25 percent of all software defects are in documentation deliverable to the customer.

A detailed study of defects in a specifications document was done for the Naval Research Laboratory by Victor Basili and David Weiss [17]. They report on various characteristics of 88 defects detected and corrected after formal validation of the specifications document. Figure 4-6 shows one example of how such data can be useful. For that particular document, fewer than 25 percent of the defects reported were discovered by the authors of the document. While this data may not directly apply to other documents like manuals, it illustrates what activities uncovered defects in this case. The data suggests that for this particular application, knowledge which would improve the development of future products could be obtained by studying and analyzing why the defects discovered during use of the document as a design reference were not found in earlier tests or reviews.

The study also classified defects according to the amount of effort necessary for change. The breakdown was 68 percent, less than 1 person-hour; 26 percent, 1 person-hour to 1 person-day; 5 percent, 1 person-day to 1 person-week; one defect took six weeks of effort to fix.

There are uses for defect data, once a division has characterized its average defect rate. The first use is to report more details about the defects in order to direct process improvements to the areas of greatest leverage. The second is to predict and track the prediction of defects during a project as a project planning tool. Figure 4-7 shows an example of tracking predicted versus actual discovered defects as currently used by several divisions [18]. This model will be explained in more detail in Chapter 9.

The motivation to substantially improve our overall quality is clearly understood when we examine how many resources are necessary to support completed projects.

Figures 4-8 and 4-9 show the percentage of time spent in enhancement/maintenance versus development in a study of data processing organizations [19]. As can be seen from the graphs, nearly 50 percent of the total software effort is spent in the maintenance phase, and while data processing organizations may well be different from R&D organizations, the trend toward a large maintenance burden is definitely present in R&D (at HP we generally refer to these activities as CPE, or Current Product Engineering) as well. Maintenance is clearly a part of the process which needs to be better understood. There are at least two approaches to minimizing the cost to fix postrelease defects. First, release a high-quality product. Second, improve the productivity of the maintenance team. It is important to measure both the total resources consumed in the maintenance phase and the productivity over time. Lines of code vs. time is not an appropriate metric for the enhancement/maintenance part of the R&D process, and we do not yet have a metric which is used throughout HP.*

---

*Lientz & Swanson, *Software Maintenance Management* , © 1980, Addison-Wesley Publishing Company, Inc., Reading, Massachusetts, reprinted with permission.

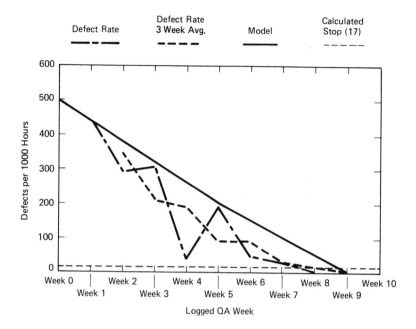

Figure 4-7   Defect discovery model — defect rate and 3 week average.

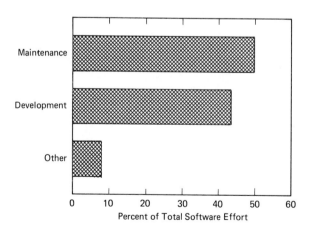

Figure 4-8   Software development and maintenance costs for data processing organizations.

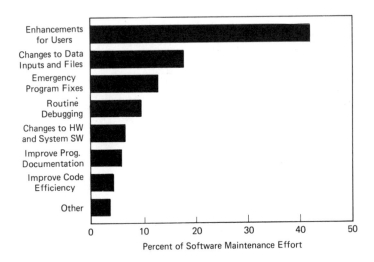

Figure 4-9 Distribution of software maintenance effort for data processing application systems.

4.3 PREDICTABILITY

There are a number of software predictive models used by industry today. Each model uses different but similar measurements, computes "the answer" in a different way, and each model claims that although it works well under certain circumstances it will not predict well in all cases. Inside HP, a program called Softcost contains a model which has gained widespread usage. Other examples of models include: Barry Boehm's COCOMO, Larry Putnam's SLIM, and Purdue University's COPMO. Here is a brief, simplified presentation of each of these models:

I. COCOMO [16]. There are three related COCOMO models: basic, intermediate, and detailed.*

A. BASIC MODEL

Development effort = $a \times \text{SIZE}^b$

or

programming months = $a \times$ (thousand lines of delivered source)^b

The constants a and b vary depending on the difficulty of the project.

---

*Barry W. Boehm, *Software Engineering Economics,* © copyright 1981, reprinted by permission of Prentice-Hall, Englewood Cliffs, New Jersey.

Boehm describes three levels of difficulty for projects:

ORGANIC MODE: 2–50 KDSI (thousand delivered source instructions) for a type of project with
which the project team is familiar

$$a = 2.4 \qquad b = 1.05$$

SEMIDETACHED MODE: 50–300 KDSI for a project staffed with engineers of a medium average experience level

$$a = 3.0 \qquad b = 1.12$$

EMBEDDED MODE: This mode is characterized by severe constraints

$$a = 3.6 \qquad b = 1.20$$

B. INTERMEDIATE COCOMO

Whereas the basic COCOMO model assumes average constraints on the development team, intermediate COCOMO takes into consideration the factors which determine the cost of a software project. These cost drivers are listed below. Each has a numerical scale associated with it. (The average value is always 1.) The user of COCOMO assigns a value to each cost driver. In addition, the constants in the development effort equation change to:

ORGANIC MODE: $a = 3.2 \qquad b = 1.05$
SEMIDETACHED MODE: $a = 3.0 \qquad b = 1.12$
EMBEDDED MODE: $a = 2.8 \qquad b = 1.20$
Programmer months $= a \times \text{KDSI}^b \times c(i)$
where the $c(i)$ are the 15 cost drivers:
    required software reliability
    database size
    product complexity
    execution time constraint
    main storage constraint
    virtual machine volatility
    computer turnaround time
    analyst capability
    applications experience
    programmer capability
    virtual machine experience
    programming language experience

modern programming practices
use of software tools
required development schedule

C. DETAILED COCOMO
The detailed COCOMO model is very similar to the intermediate
COCOMO but is more precise about quantifying certain cost drivers,
such as project personnel attributes. It also requires a more detailed
decomposition of the proposed program and is more accurate on a
phase-by-phase basis.

II.   SLIM (PUTNAM) [20]*

$$S_s = C_k K^{1/3} t_d^{4/3}$$

where S_s = Number of delivered source instructions, K = Life cycle
effort in engineering years, t_d = Development time in years, and C_k = a
"technology constant."

The technology constant depends on the use of modern programming
techniques, project team experience and ability, availability of necessary
capital equipment, and the like. It is determined by fitting a curve using
a database of historical data for projects similar to the projects that will
be predicted by using the model.

III.   COPMO (Purdue University) [21]

Total effort = Programming effort + Coordination effort

Effort = $a + b \times$ KLOC(thousand lines of code)

$+ c \times$ (average number of programmers)^d

The coefficients a, b, c, and d are determined by regression. COPMO
attempts to predict effort independent of software type or development
environment. Attempting to measure and account for the effect of communications directly on schedule makes COPMO different from the other models.

We do not know which model fits HP's software process and corporate
environment the best. In fact, we will never know until we have collected the
numbers that serve as inputs to the various cost predictive models. The point
is this: An imperfect model is still better than many current estimation techniques. Detailed COCOMO, for example, claims an average error margin of
no more than 20 percent in 70 percent of the projects using it [16].

A common basis for all of the predictive models discussed is the same metric, lines of code, discussed earlier under both productivity and quality. When asked when software projects commit to schedules, over three-quarters of HP project managers who were surveyed replied that *commitments are made prior to completion of external design.* This seems to point to a fundamental cause of poor schedule prediction. Even an approximate count of lines of code cannot be known until at least the external design is complete. Figure 4-10 shows an HP software project as originally projected *after completion of external design* along with the actual rate of code generation (not debugged). We can see that both the amount of code and the schedule predictions were quite accurate, and as a result this graph was a useful project management tool. Thus, it certainly is possible to predict lines of code reasonably accurately.

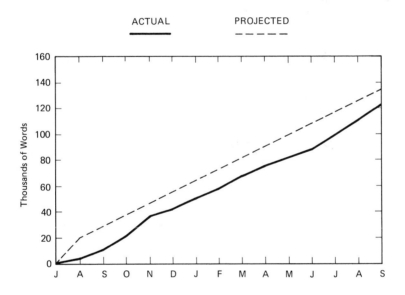

Figure 4-10   Total code generated.

4.3.1 HP's Initial Experience with Tools for Project Estimation

Several years ago one division experimented with a software package which implements one of the accepted estimation models. This model was studied in terms of its accuracy and assumptions concerning the development process. A major problem with it was the ease with which managers could manipulate the inputs to the model to get virtually any answer, realistic or unrealistic.

An estimating tool, Softcost, based on a paper written by Robert Tausworthe of the Jet Propulsion Laboratory [22], was then developed by the division in order to avoid this problem. Softcost's functionality includes [23]:

1. Estimation of project size and difficulty. The Difficulty Factor provided by Softcost is based on various aspects of the project environment, such as product complexity, staff experience, support of the programming environment, and so on.

2. Estimation of development resources. Softcost approximates the total amount of engineering effort, time, and staffing required for development of the project (from internal design through manufacturing release).

3. Acceptance of arbitrary resource budgets and comparison of tradeoffs between time and effort. Softcost allows the user to specify certain budget constraints, and shows what the time/effort/staffing tradeoffs are.

4. Generation of a staffing schedule. For large projects, effort is applied in a predictable way, following what is known as a Rayleigh curve [16].

Softcost's goal is to provide project managers with a comparison between their expectations of a project's behavior and industry-based statistical expectations of that project's behavior. It provides an additional basis for budgeting time and effort to a project based on estimated confidence limits for successful completion. Further, continued use of this estimation tool can aid in developing an information base of productivity factors which are candidates for improvements.

The metrics data collected has shown that for a small number of the division's projects, Softcost predicted the duration within 20 percent and the effort within 30 percent when correction factors were used. These results are shown in Figures 4-11 and 4-12 [24]. The diagonal line in each figure represents instances where an actual project result would be identical to the Softcost estimate. Points above the lines were overestimated, and points below the lines were underestimated.

The use of Softcost has spread. Another division doing firmware development found Softcost's estimates to be far too optimistic. However, it was consistently wrong by the same relative amount, so that modified Softcost estimates were good predictors for them also. (Again, a limited number of projects have been used. For four projects, an offset factor of 2.5 appeared good.) The need to calibrate the model for a specific development environment gives projects an incentive to collect accurate data for local calibration.

PROJECT DURATION

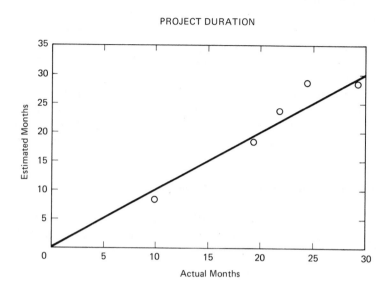

Figure 4-11   Softcost estimate (corrected).

DEVELOPMENT EFFORT

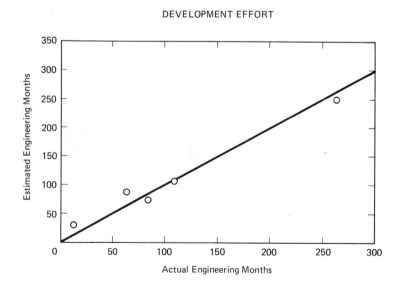

Figure 4-12   Softcost estimate (corrected).

Managers use Softcost outputs as a check against their own best judgment. In some cases, schedules have been revised as a result of the large discrepancy between the managers' initial estimates and the estimates produced by Softcost. Softcost's biggest advantage, however, is reminding the project manager in the investigation phase of most of the factors that affect a project's schedule.

The next step is to study the model itself and try to understand how to make it more responsive to factors which have a big impact on project schedules in the HP environments. As data is collected on projects producing different software types, the model will be calibrated to give more accurate estimates in each software environment.

4.3.2 Effort and Calendar Time Percentages

Several studies of project data have reported percentages of engineering time spent in investigation, design, implementation, and test [16,25,26,27].* Data from these four studies, and the percentages reflected by data from 56 HP projects are shown in Figure 4-13.

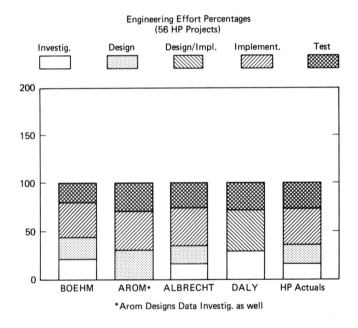

Figure 4-13 Engineering effort percentages (56 HP projects).

---

*Data for Figure 4-13: Barry W. Boehm, *Software Engineering Economics* , © copyright 1981, Prentice-Hall Inc., Englewood Cliffs, New Jersey; Daly, copyright © 1977 IEEE. All references reprinted with permission.

When a project is planned, required calendar time is just as important as total engineering effort. Figure 4-14 illustrates that the percentage of time spent in each of the major phases can be quite different depending upon what type of software is being developed. Of course, the number of data points reflected in Figure 4-14 is still too small to be used too seriously as a guideline, and specific projects can easily vary from the average for any group. The terms *firmware, systems and applications* as applied to HP are defined in more detail later in this chapter.

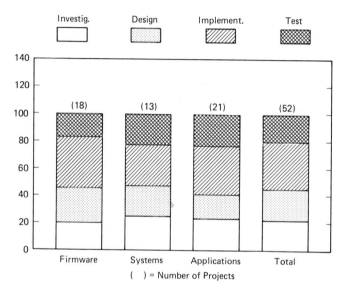

Figure 4-14   Percentage of calendar time in each phase (52 HP projects).

One more aspect of project estimation deserves discussion. When the Software Metrics Council discussed the metric of programmer time, it became clear that there was a common failing in many projects. We frequently complete a project and use fuzzy hindsight to base new estimates on our experiences. The argument goes, "We had six programmers and it took us 12 months, so a comparable task will take six programmer years." What we forget is that the team worked 60 hours a week for three months of the project, so our new schedule has three months of overtime already built in. When such commitments are made by the development team, other associated departments (marketing, support, QA) base their schedules on unrealistic data. Then all members of the team enter a vicious cycle in which time is spent unproductively, delivered materials are not adequate, and everyone is trying to achieve an impossible goal. To try to eliminate this problem and maintain ease of data collection, project managers at HP now record total engineering time as well as percentage of overtime or undertime worked.

4.4 ENVIRONMENTAL FACTORS

We saw in the previous section that most predictive software models attempt to achieve maximum accuracy by including factors which account for differences in people and surroundings. There have been several studies concerning environmental factors which have yielded quantified results which we will discuss in this section. The results from many such environmental studies are not easy to justify due to the difficulty in controlling so many variables and due to the fact that they frequently rely on subjective data from questionnaires.

Let us start the discussion of environmental factors by describing what we mean when we refer to "environmental." Environmental factors include the physical surroundings, the engineer-machine interface, the need for and means for communicating with other humans and machines, the standards for communication of written and diagrammatic material, and the ability to access stored information. Even examining this expanded definition of "environmental" factors, we found few published research results which included measurements. One reason for this, possibly, is that in the field of software production most of these factors have changed so rapidly in recent years, that it hasn't made much sense for anyone to try to scientifically improve any one of them before they were totally replaced. All of these areas represent opportunities for future research.

One view of the engineer's environment which is free from the technological change experienced by all of the above is illustrated by Figure 4-15. In this figure, we have generalized all tasks into project verbal activities, project quiet activities, and non-project activities. Examples of project verbal activities include meetings, reviews, and discussions. These activities can easily occupy over a third of all engineering time, particularly on projects with large teams. A large part of the software project management task, then is to optimize job communication.

An engineering environment which optimizes the efficiency of verbal activities is not necessarily well suited for activities like reading and writing code and documentation, some aspects of design, and written communications. These activities can also account for a third or more of all engineering time, but these activities probably need a much more private, quiet environment than the one which is needed for job communication. A recognition of the need for quiet is illustrated within HP by a strong trend over the past ten years from relatively open-space work areas in R&D to individual cubicles consisting of acoustical partitions. One way to bridge the apparently

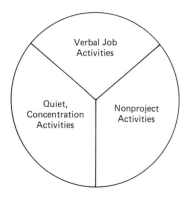

Figure 4-15   Job activities affected by environmental factors.

conflicting environments needed to increase engineering productivity is to provide a quiet office space and fast electronic mail for many of the communications which don't require face-to-face interaction or immediate response.

The final environmental "third" is the time devoted to non-project activities. These include items like training, presentations by personnel, moves,
travel (have you ever kept track of how much time engineers spend walking to
and from printers or copying machines?), and personal activities. It is useful
to separate these non-project activities from those directly related to any
specific project, because they tend to be independent of any development
methodology. Judicious control over these factors can have a significant positive or negative impact on a project team or schedule, and very little research
related to software engineering has provided any positive conclusions or
recommendations.

All of these factors are accounted for by the various estimation models,
since they are based on historical project data which did not separate out the
factors. The third group is controllable by the project manager for short times
during critical parts of a project schedule. The first two groups present a
difficult balancing act, though. We might assume, for example, that during
the specification phase of a project, a very open, interactive work environment
is necessary. During implementation, however, a more closed, quiet work
environment should be provided.

One study performed by Tom DeMarco and Tim Lister focused on
strictly the coding activity [29]. In this study, 166 programmers from 35
different organizations implemented the same well-defined specification. This
study determined that a variation in performance of 5.6 to 1 existed from best
to worst as measured in terms of time to complete the task. But what the
study really tried to determine was the relationships between the work

environment and performance. In this regard there was a high correlation between high performance and positive answers to a set of subjective questions regarding office space, quiet environment, interruptions, and the like. What was missing was the effectiveness of environment on noncoding tasks, which we have already seen represent at least 80 percent of today's software engineering task. Nevertheless, the final conclusions seem valid - that the potential improvement of 5.6 to 1 in coding activities is worth investing in an improved environment.

In another study by Mary Jo Hatch of two companies, the effect of open office space versus private offices was investigated [30]. Participants at the companies kept accurate records of their time for one week. The primary goal of the study was to measure the effects of the physical environment on the amount of time employees spent working in private, versus with others. Contrary to expectations, it was learned that the people who worked in open offices spent significantly more time working alone than those in private offices. A work model was proposed which showed the need for immediate discussion of issues to take precedence over allowing other individuals the luxury of uninterrupted work. This model raises serious concerns about how to address the potential productivity gains demonstrated by the DeMarco/Lister study. Unfortunately, the Hatch study presented no conclusions concerning the effectiveness of the two environments monitored, and so we are left without resolution of what environment is best.

A third study involved the effect of distance on technical communications between individuals. In a decentralized company such as HP, we frequently have groups working on a common project separated by management, divisional, and geographical boundaries. The impact of at least the physical boundaries is illustrated by Figure 4-16. It is taken from a study at MIT on the effects on technical communication between individuals and groups separated by distance [30]. It was measured by analysis of responses by 512 people in seven R&D labs to a weekly questionnaire over periods of three to six months.

It is, therefore, important to consider the drastic reduction in technical communication that takes place due to physical distance when allocating work spaces and partitioning projects.

As we stated at the beginning of this section on environmental factors the published work indicates some interesting directions, but it is less conclusive than the task and product-oriented measures which have been studied. Several divisions at HP are pursuing environmental factors and have experienced some success, but we feel that it is too early to determine whether these results simply represent the Hawthorne effect or not. (The Hawthorne effect is named after a series of productivity studies of production workers in the 1920s. In these studies environmental factors were controlled and changed in an attempt to create improvements. The unexpected results were that the productivity of the workers involved in the study improved just because they were

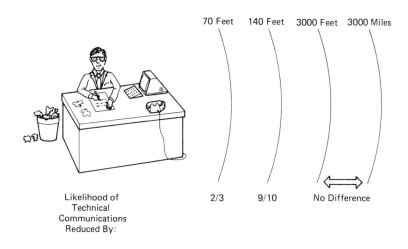

Figure 4-16   Effect of distance on R&D communications.

being studied, or because their work mattered enough to management to warrant change. Such improvements are not long-term or transferable to other groups).

4.5 PRODUCT REQUIREMENTS AND DEVELOPMENT ENVIRON-MENT CHARACTERISTICS

One challenge for any company is to identify the characteristic processes used to develop software and to determine which attributes these processes have in common. Through the use of software metrics we hope to identify development processes which are alike so as to be able to compare data meaningfully among them. For example, the process for developing an operating system is different in many ways from the process for developing a customized application.

Software at HP is created for a wide spectrum of uses and customer types; some of these types of software are probably produced at your company. For the sake of convenience, here is one way they can be categorized: firmware, systems, applications, and custom. Firmware consists of software generally designed to execute from ROM (Read Only Memory) or RAM (Random Access Memory) under control of a microprocessor. Examples of divisions designing firmware are those producing instruments and computer peripherals. Systems software consists of software generally designed to execute from the memory of minicomputers. It functions as the framework for developing and executing other software. Examples of divisions designing systems software include divisions directly involved in producing computers, network software, languages, and databases. Applications consist of software that operates on top of and uses systems software. Applications software also generally solves a generic class of problems for a narrow set of customers and needs. Examples of divisions designing applications software include those dealing with manufacturing, medical, and financial customer solutions. Custom software at HP consists of software which generally does not fit the other three categories. In many cases custom software as defined here operates on top of or, in addition to, applications software, instruments or systems. Examples of custom software include information systems and software done by such groups as Production Engineering, Quality Engineering, and test software done by the lab team. When we refer to information systems in this category, it is important to clarify what we mean. At HP, large information systems are developed for financial, marketing, personnel, and manufacturing systems by centralized corporate groups. These information systems fall into the applications category, such as we have defined here. In addition to these programmers, each division has its own information systems group which customizes these applications to the needs of the division. We consider this software to be custom software.

   Table 4-2 illustrates some characteristics of these four categories of software. Because each of these types has different characteristics, discussions concerning software among the many R&D groups encounter difficulties when people try to compare methods, tools, priorities, and estimates.

TABLE 4-2   HP Software Development Types

Influencing Factors	Firmware	Systems Software	Applications	Custom
Team Size	Small	Large*	Large*	Small
Market Size†	Small→Large	Large	Large	Small
Language	Asmb. Pascal	C/Pascal/SPL	High-level	All
User	Single	Multiple	Multiple, extensive interactions	Single
Critical Communications	Among project members	Project to project	With customers	With customers
Timing	Important, sometimes critical	Critical	Mild importance	Varies in importance
Methodology	Few standards	Control-oriented	Data-oriented	Varies
Cost of Change after Release	Large→Huge	Large	Moderate	Small
Major Application Concern	Timing of ext. processes	Process interaction, peripheral generality, recovery	Data integrity, user interface, portability	Single-problem oriented

* Project sizes not large, but generally aggregates of projects are large.
† As measured in number of customer sites.

4.6 SUMMARY

By examining data external to your company, the opportunity exists to compare results with those of others. In this chapter, we presented an overview of software metrics which influenced the HP metrics program. We also described some HP data and tried to put it into the context of industry data. In subsequent chapters we will see how some of our initial impressions have changed, how our measurements increased in sophistication, but how this initial research set a significant foundation for a long-term program.

The bibliography at the end of this book supplements the data presented in this chapter. In particular, the first part of the bibliography is organized according to different metric categories like size, defects, complexity, and the like to facilitate additional research into topics of interest.

BIBLIOGRAPHY

1. McNamara, D., Presentation to Hewlett-Packard engineers, Cupertino, Calif. (July 1983).
2. Kim, K. H., "A Look at Japan's Development of Software Engineering Technology," *Computer* . (May 1983), p. 33.
3. Weinberg, G. and E. Schulman, "Goals and Performance in Computer Programming," *Human Factors* . Vol. 16, no. 1, (1974), pp. 70-77.
4. Vosburgh, J., et al., "Productivity Factors and Programming Environments," *IEEE 7th International Conference on Software Engineering* (March 1984), pp. 149, 151.
5. Tajima, D. and T. Matsubara, "The Computer Software Industry in Japan," *Computer* (May 1981), pp. 96.
6. Lundberg, D., "A Method of Predicting the Software Release Date Based Upon Source Code Changes," *HP Software Productivity Conference Proceedings.* (April 1984), p. 1-70.
7. Lipow, M., "Number of Faults per Line of Code," *IEEE Transactions on Software Engineering* , Vol. SE-8, no. 4 (July 1982), pp. 437-439.
8. Schneidewind, N. F., and H. M. Hoffmann, "An Experiment in Software Error Data Collection and Analysis, *IEEE Transactions on Software Engineering* , Vol. SE-5, no. 3 (May 1979), pp. 281-283.
9. Akiyama, F., "An Example of Software System Debugging," *Proceedings of the 1971 IFIP Congress* , Amsterdam: North-Holland (1971), p. 355.
10. Rubey, R. J., J. A. Dana, and P. W. Biche, "Quantitative Aspects of Software Validation," *IEEE Transactions on Software Engineering* , Vol. SE-1, no. 2 (June 1975), p. 151.
11. Endres, A., "An Analysis of Errors and Their Causes in System Programs," *IEEE Transactions on Software Engineering* Vol. SE-1, no. 2 (June 1975),p. 144.

12. Thayer, T., M. Lipow, and E. Nelson, *Software Reliability: A Study of Large Project Reality.* Amsterdam: North-Holland, Inc. (1978), p. 128.

13. Belford, P. C., and R. A. Berg, "Central Flow Control Software Development: A Case Study of the Effectiveness of Software Engineering Techniques," *IEEE Proceedings of the Fourth International Conference on Software Engineering*, Munich (September 1979), IEEE CH 1479-5/79.0000-0378, pp. 88-89.

14. Sunazuka, T., M. Azuma, and N. Yamagishi, "Software Quality Assessment Technology," *IEEE Proceedings of the Eighth International Conference on Software Engineering* London (August 1985), IEEE 1985 CH2139-4/85/0000/0142, pp. 143-144.

15. Jones, C., *Programming Productivity.* New York: McGraw-Hill Book Co. 1986, p. 172.

16. Boehm, B. W., *Software Engineering Economics* Englewood Cliffs, N. J.: Prentice-Hall, Inc. 1981, pp. 66, 68, 75, 78, 79, 115-117, 382, 495.

17. Basili, V. R. and D. M. Weiss, "Evaluation of a Software Requirements Document By Analysis of Change Data," *Proceedings of the Fifth International Conference on Software Engineering,* (March 1981), pp. 253-262.

18. Kenyon, D., "Implementing a Software Metrics Program," *HP Software Productivity Conference Proceedings* (April 1985), p. 1-107.

19. Lientz, B. P. and E. B. Swanson, *Software Maintenance Management.* Reading, Mass.: Addison-Wesley 1980, pp. 24, 73.

20. Putnam, L. H., "A General Empirical Solution to the Macro Software Sizing and Estimating Problem," *IEEE Transactions on Software Engineering*, Vol. SE-4, no. 4 (July 1978), p. 345-361.

21. Conte, S. D., H. E. Dunsmore, V. Y. Shen, and S. D. Conte, *Software Engineering Metrics and Models.* Menlo Park, Calif: Benjamin/Cummings 1986, p. 314.

22. Tausworthe, R. C., "Software Specifications Document, DSN Software Cost Model," Jet Propulsion Laboratory, JPL Publication 81-7, Pasadena, Calif., (1981).

23. *SOFTCOST: Software Cost Estimation Tool, User Guide for Version A.00.07* (1984).

24. Lebowitz, L., Presentation to Second Annual HP Software Metrics Conference (August 1984).

25. Aron, J. D., "Estimating Resources for Large Programming Systems," *Software Engineering: Concepts and Techniques, Proceedings of the NATO Conferences* (Ed. by P. Naur, B. Randell, J. Buxton). New York: Petrocelli/Charter, 1976, pp. 207.

26. Albrecht, A. J., "Measuring Application Development Productivity," *Proceedings of the Joint SHARE/GUIDE/IBM Application Development Symposium* (Oct. 1979), p. 90.

27. Daly, E. B., "Management of Software Development," *IEEE Transactions on Software Engineering* (May 1977), p. 232.

28. DeMarco, T. and T. Lister, "Programmer Performance and the Effects of the Workplace," *IEEE Proceedings of the Eighth International Conference on Software Engineering* , London (August 1985), IEEE CH2139-4/85/0000/0268, pp. 268-272.

29. Allen, T. and A. Fusfeld, "Design for Communication in the Research and Development Lab," *Technology Review* (MIT Alumni Association) (May 1976), p. 66.

5

ESTABLISHING STANDARDS

The HP Software Engineering Lab was established in 1983. Its first task was to establish measurement standards across the company as a common vehicle of communication. These could then be used in measuring the effectiveness of increasing software productivity within the company. In this chapter we discuss how we approached the process of defining which data to collect and the forms which are currently used. By understanding these, it is easier for you to formulate an approach for your project or company.

5.1 CREATION OF THE HP SOFTWARE METRICS COUNCIL

For many years, HP has collected and reported detailed information concerning customer-reported defects, using a system called STARS (Software Tracking and Reporting System). Although the consistent reporting of defects and enhancement requests provides HP with a measure of its success and helps to address the most important problems, it falls short of providing a leveraged method for understanding the development process and accurately predicting results. What was needed was common terminology and measures for the process of software development that could be used throughout HP early enough in the development process to effect change. In August of 1983, a group of twenty software managers and developers from thirteen divisions was invited to establish the Software Metrics Council. These representatives were chosen on the basis of software development experience, software management experience, interest, prior work in software measurement, and/or influence within their organizational entities to implement the council's decisions. Personal commitment and enthusiasm were also important. In addition, developers of all the various types of HP software were represented.

5.2 FIRST MEETING OBJECTIVE

The objective of the meeting was:

> To gain agreement on a set of software measurement criteria which managers feel are meaningful, reasonable to collect, and can be used to measure progress and predict results.

To gain agreement . . .
Agreement is necessary if each organization wants to share what it has learned about software development. We needed to invent a common language with which to communicate productivity and quality indicators.

. . . on a set of software measurement criteria . . .
We needed to decide:

1. What attributes of software or the software process we wanted to quantify. For example, SIZE is an attribute of software; COST is an attribute of the software process.
2. A precise definition of the measure to be used to quantify each criterion; for example, "lines of noncomment source," "bytes of object code," and "sectors of disc storage" were all possible metrics for the SIZE attribute.

. . . which managers feel are meaningful, reasonable to collect . . .
Managers must benefit from having the data, or it will not be collected. The time spent gathering data should not be excessive. For example, in considering a metric for COMMUNICATIONS, "amount of time spent on the phone" might be very meaningful. It was not chosen as a company-wide metric, however, because of the excessive overhead incurred in collecting the data.

. . . and can be used to measure progress and predict results.
It has been said that those who do not understand history are doomed to repeat its mistakes. Currently, we rely on the gut feel of experienced managers to predict how long a project will take. In his book, *The Mythical Man-Month,* Fred Brooks says, "It is very difficult to make a vigorous, plausible, and job risking defense of an estimate that is derived by no quantitative method, supported by little data and certified chiefly by the hunches of

managers"[1].* It is not surprising, then, that despite the fact that HP hires top-notch people, we have experienced schedule slips common to the rest of the industry. In order to predict, we must understand quantitatively where we have been and where we are now.

5.3 LITERATURE SURVEY

In preparation for the first Software Metrics Council meeting, many of the popular industry articles on metrics were read. Most companies seemed to have selected criteria to measure which fit a predictive model and then collected the required data just for that model. The council was steered away from this approach for the following reasons:

1. We didn't have a good way of choosing one model over another.
2. Collecting data for only one model eliminated the opportunity of learning from other models.
3. We thought it was possible that HP would need to develop its own models whose inputs would be different from the popular models.

The criteria proposed to the council were the attributes common to most of the models in the literature. Choosing metrics for these common criteria would allow us to experiment with many models and also to form theories of our own. The five criteria proposed were

Size   How big is the software that is produced?

People/Time/Cost   How much does it cost to produce a given piece of software and associated documentation?

Defects   How many errors are in the software?

Difficulty   How complex is the software to be produced and how severe are the constraints on the project?

Communications   How much effort is spent in communicating with other entities?

Data for these criteria can be combined to examine three major software issues to HP: productivity, quality, and predictability.

The meeting was held offsite, away from daily interruptions. The agenda consisted of an industry report (presentation of the literature survey), a guest presentation by Barry Boehm (author of *Software Engineering Economics*),

---

*Frederick P. Brooks, *The Mythical Man-Month* © copyright 1975, Addison-Wesley Publishing Company, Inc., Reading, Massachusetts, reprinted with permission.

and reports from division representatives on what data was currently being collected and analyzed in the divisions. These agenda items were intended to give the council members a common base of understanding concerning state-of-the-art software metrics and HP's progress to date. Workshops were the focus of the meeting.

There were five workshops. Each session consisted of brainstorming possible metrics for the criteria, choosing which metrics we should collect, proposing how the data would be used, and explaining tool requirements for collection and analysis. After proposals from the workshops were discussed, consensus was reached. A company-wide standard was born. Many were surprised that we were able to agree on anything, given our diverse interests. Many people came to the meeting feeling that the situation in their division was unique and would not be addressed by any company standard. Although the chosen metrics addressed newly developed code and not ported or maintained code, most council members felt satisfied with the first try at a standard. This consensus was a key step in establishing a metrics program throughout the company. Without broad acceptance of the basics of such a program, it would have been a long uphill battle.

5.4 EXPLANATION OF THE HP METRICS

Metrics forms were defined for use by project managers in collecting the software metrics on a project. The forms are reviewed and updated at the end of each phase, and the completed forms are sent to the HP Software Engineering Lab upon product release. The data is then added to a database and used to derive some of the graphs shown in this book. Standard metrics are explained below:

Size. The standard metric for size is NCSS (noncomment source statement). This means that the source code, not the object code, is used. Compiler directives, data declarations, and executable lines are counted, but *not* blank lines or lines which consist entirely of comments. In keeping with the "reasonable to collect" objective, it is assumed that an automatic line counter is used. In the absence of such a counter, the size is approximated, and a confidence level is indicated. An educated guess is better than nothing.

People/Time/Cost. The standard metric for cost is the payroll month. It includes time for people doing testing and time that project managers spend doing "engineering work." Not counting vacation or sick days is in line with the "reasonable to collect" objective. Overtime is also measured and reflected as an average for the team over the entire project duration.

Defects. A defect is a problem or an error — anything in the output of the software process which would not exist if the process were perfect.

Defects can occur at any life cycle stage. There is no attempt to distinguish severity in the standard metrics (severity data is encouraged at the local level). All defects are counted equally.

At the first Software Metrics Council meeting, standards were defined for difficulty and communication in addition to the standards for size, people/time/cost, and defects. Collection of data for difficulty and communication during the next year was not done at most entities, though, so these two categories were made optional. The original definitions are included here for completeness.

Difficulty. The standard metric for difficulty is a number between 35 and 165, with 165 as the most difficult. The number is determined by filling in a questionnaire and inputting the responses to Softcost. The questionnaire asks about stability of requirements, experience of personnel on the project, familiarity with the type of software and development environment, access to needed hardware, and many other general project questions. In addition to generating the difficulty factor, the questionnaire helps us qualify productivity numbers that are computed.

Communications. The standard metric is the number of interfaces that a lab project team has. The intent is to quantify constraints on the project team due to dependencies with entities politically and physically distant. If this metric were thought out at the beginning of the project, it:

1. Could influence the partitioning of the task to minimize necessary interfaces.
2. Would raise awareness of who the suppliers and customers are for the project.

Four of the most current forms used are shown in Figures 5-1, 5-2, 5-3, and 5-4. Detailed instructions for their completion are on the reverse sides of the forms. The form originally defined for communications has been eliminated (see Appendix B). The form for difficulty consisted of a series of 45 multiple choice questions used by Softcost, and it is now optional. All of the original forms are shown in Appendix B.

5.5 CREATING YOUR OWN METRIC STANDARDS

We have described HP's approach to defining standard metrics which are now used throughout the company in a consistent way. We included examples of summary collection forms in this chapter to calibrate your expectations for what is possible for you to achieve in a short period of time. *We would like to emphasize the importance of the core metric definitions you select. We feel that one of the successes of our program was the selection of a small set of clearly defined terms, given (in their third revision) on these forms. By the* time you finish this book, we expect that there will be no doubt in your mind that a software metrics program is worthwhile. But if you decide to start, as we have, with these forms, you must understand every part of them well enough to *own* them for yourself. You have to explain to your engineers your reasons for keeping any part of these forms and what your intentions are for the use of the information they are designed to capture. Then you can delete the HP logo and add your own.

Before we leave the forms, we will discuss some of their content (the parts that seem least obvious) with our particular reasons for including it. The database which we reference is discussed in detail in a later chapter.

5.5.1 Cover Form

All of the fields on this form are stored in a database for use as qualifiers for predefined graphs or for the use of project managers as they browse the database, with the exception of prototyping information and number of installations. (It is likely that these will be added to the database, also.) One of the major qualifiers used for many graphs is that of software category. In addition, the following information is requested:

Prototyping information. The use of prototypes at HP has proved very effective for some projects. For project managers interested in metrics data for past projects, it was felt that it was important to know whether prototypes were involved.

Number of installations. The feeling was that specification, design, and testing approaches are quite different if a large number of installations are expected versus a relatively small number.

5.5.2 People/Time/Cost

Accuracy of data. The basis for engineering time is the payroll month. Project managers are encouraged to collect and report data which is more accurate than that which is required by payroll, when possible.

Percentage of overtime (or undertime). This field represents the primary mechanism for capturing the intangibles of "project urgency" or department constraints. It acts as one more qualifier that someone looking at the database can use when comparing their estimates with past projects which are stored.

5.5.3 Size

Line counter (or other technique). We found out very early that it is very important to know how size numbers were derived. If an accurate counting method was not used, the resulting data is sometimes meaningless.

Number of procedures, lines in engineering documentation, and figures in engineering documentation. These are all experiments in measuring complexity. They may be retained if they prove useful.

5.6 HOW THE FORMS ARE USED

First and foremost, these forms define a common terminology which is consistently used. They are filled out once for each project at the end of the project and sent to an organization which takes the data and incorporates it into a database. These forms were not designed for use during a project, so project managers must provide for accurate data collection by using tools such as the ones described in subsequent chapters.

Groups which are most successful at capturing data have assigned some individual who is responsible for sending in the data. Despite the fact that the forms are short and easy to fill in, people forget to take the time to fill them in unless they are reminded. Experience has shown that when someone comes by, sits down, and offers to write down the data, the data gets turned in. Some divisions which are successful have simply added the metrics forms to the checklist required for signoff for product release.

5.7 CONCLUSION

After our first meeting we realized that not everyone in the company would be as enthusiastic as we were about studying software development processes. The council accepted the responsibility to act as sales representatives for metrics. Responsibilities included giving presentations to engineers, project managers, and division management. Council members were to consult with projects who wanted help in collecting and analyzing the data. They were to collect feedback on the meaningfulness and ease of use of the metrics for discussion at a six-month update meeting.

To arm our sales representatives with the appropriate sales tools, SEL prepared an overhead slide presentation; a management summary of the conference was written and distributed to all division, lab, and QA managers, and the paper forms included here were distributed. In addition to the efforts on the metrics council, Bob, the SEL manager, made presentations to many high-level managers. We visited many divisions and gave presentations and answered questions. In summary, a sales campaign had been launched.

In this chapter, we described the process which we followed in establishing our initial standard definitions of HP's software metrics with the belief that many of the steps we followed will be of use to you. We emphasized the importance of keeping your initial set of metrics simple, but meaningful. Experience at several HP divisions showed that more ambitious collection of metrics too early was met by resistance and failure. In the next chapter we will arm you with some of the most persuasive results of metrics data that we have seen.

BIBLIOGRAPHY

1. Brooks, F. P., *The Mythical Man-Month.* Reading, Mass.: Addison-Wesley 1975, p. 21.

 **HEWLETT
PACKARD**

SOFTWARE DEVELOPMENT METRICS FORM

Instructions

Fill out the general information on this page and the detailed information on the following three pages for the project when it achieves initial release. Use the back of this page to provide additional comments. Fold the package together so that the return address is showing and send via internal mail.

General Information

Project Contact : _____   Division : _____

Project Name : _____   Release ID (version) : _____

Manufacturing Release Date : _____

General Category of Software :

_____   Firmware

_____   Systems (including OPSYS, Data Comm, Compilers, etc.)

_____   Applications

_____   Other (specify) _____

Was Prototyping used in developing this project?

_____   not used

_____   evolutionary (Prototype evolves into a product; Prototype code is used in final project)

_____   simulation   (Prototype used for user feedback, feasability, and human factors verification; Prototype code is <u>not</u> used in final product)

Number of installations expected in the first year?

Internal _____   External _____

Release Information

May we publish the **Project Name** in the Software Metrics Data Base?
_____ yes   _____ no

May we publish the name of the *Project Contact* in the Software Metrics Data Base?
_____ yes   _____ no

_____
Project Contact's signature

Revision Date : 2/1/86

 **HEWLETT**
PACKARD

SOFTWARE DEVELOPMENT
METRICS FORM

PEOPLE/TIME/COST

Project Name : _____   Release ID : _____

ACTIVITIES	ENG. PAYROLL MONTHS	CALENDAR MONTHS
Investigate / Spec.		
Design		
Implement		
Test		
TOTALS		

% of overtime (or undertime) = _____ %

Instructions

Fill out the appropriate row for each life cycle activity.

Indicate undertime with a minus sign.

At MR send to :   Metrics Administrator
                         Software Engineering Lab
                         Building 26U
                         3500 Deer Creek Rd.
                         Palo Alto, CA 94304

Revision Date : 2/1/86

People/Time/Cost Definitions

Engineering Payroll Months

The sum of calendar payroll months attributed to each project engineer, including people doing testing, adjusted to exclude extended vacations and extended leaves. This does not include time project managers spend on management tasks.

Overtime (or undertime)

Engineering time over/under the 40 hour engineering week averaged over the duration of a project. % over/under time can be used as a normalization factor for engineering payroll months. Indicate undertime with a minus sign.

Investigate / External Specification

All activities relating to the investigation and external specification of the project. This includes evaluating and reviewing project requirements and writing external specifications (ES).

Design

All activities relating to the high and low level design of the project. This includes development of the design, design reviews, and writing of the internal specifications (IS).

Implement

All activities relating to the implementation of the project. This includes coding, code walk-throughs, unit (informal, private) testing and correcting defects.

Test

All activities relating to system (formal, public) testing. This includes writing test plans, writing test code, system and integration testing, and debugging defects found during test activities.

Calendar Months

Time elapsed in calendar months between specific project checkpoints. The total calendar time must equal the sum of the calendar times for individual activities.

The checkpoint signaling the end of the investigate / external specification phase for calendar months is approval of the ES.

The checkpoint signaling the end of the design phase for calendar months is the approval of the IS.

The checkpoint signaling the end of the implement phase for calendar months is the start of system (formal, public) testing.

The checkpoint signaling the end of the test phase for calendar months is manufacturing release (MR).

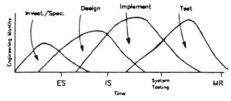

HEWLETT PACKARD

SOFTWARE DEVELOPMENT METRICS FORM

PRE—RELEASE DEFECTS

Project Name : _____   Release ID : _____

⬚⬚⬚ Dotted areas are optional.

ACTIVITIES	DEFECTS INTRODUCED	DEFECTS FOUND	DEFECTS CLOSED
Investigate / Spec.			
Design			
Implement			
Test			
TOTALS			

Instructions

At the end of each activity, fill in defects found and defects closed, and update defects introduced. If defects are not collected during a particular activity, leave it blank rather than enter zero. However, it is strongly recommended that accurate information be kept for all activities.

At MR send to :   Metrics Administrator
Software Engineering Lab
Building 26U
3500 Deer Creek Rd.
Palo Alto, CA 94304

Revision Date : 2/1/86

Defect Definitions

Defect
>   A defect is a deviation from the product specification or an error in
>   the specification if the error could have been detected and would have
>   been corrected. If the error could not possibly have been detected, or
>   it could have been detected and would not have been corrected, then it
>   is an enhancement, not a defect. Defects do not include typographical
>   or grammatical errors in the engineering documentation.

Defects Introduced
>   The number of defects attributed to a flaw in the output of a particular
>   activity which might not be found until a later activity. Do not
>   include duplicates.

Defects Found
>   The number of defects found in a particular activity. Do not include
>   duplicates.

Defects Closed
>   The number of defects corrected in a particular activity (Closed Service
>   Requests, as defined by STARS, or Resolved Defects, as defined by DTS).
>   Do not include duplicates.

Examples

Investigate / External Specification
>   Defects can be found in a formal review of engineering documents
>   produced; e.g. ES, functional models, etc.

Design
>   Defects can be found during design inspections or through modeling.

Implement
>   Defects can be found during code inspections or unit (informal, private)
>   tests.

Test
>   Defects can be found during system (formal, public) or integration
>   testing.

 **HEWLETT**
PACKARD

SOFTWARE DEVELOPMENT
METRICS FORM

DELIVERED SIZE

Project Name : _____   Release ID : _____
Language A   : _____   Language B : _____
Line Counter (or other technique) : _____

▭ Dotted areas are optional.

	LANGUAGE A	LANGUAGE B
NCSS		
Comment Lines		
Blank Lines		
% of Recycled Code		
# of Procedures		
Bytes of Object Code		
# Lines in Engineering Documentation		
# Figures in Eng. Documentation		

Instructions

Use an automatic line counter. If no tool is available, estimate NCSS, comment lines, and blank lines of code (confidence level = _____ %).

At MR send to :   Metrics Administrator
                         Software Engineering Lab
                         Building 26U
                         3500 Deer Creek Rd.
                         Palo Alto, CA 94304

Revision Date : 2/1/86

Delivered Size Definitions

Delivered Size
 Those lines of code which go into the product delivered to the customer.

NCSS
 Non-Comment Source Statements which include compiler directives, data declarations, and executable code. Each physical line of code is counted once. Each include file is counted once. Print statements are lines of code.

Comment Lines
 Lines containing only comments. A commented executable line is counted as executable code, not as a comment. Blank lines are not counted as comment lines.

Engineering Documentation
 Documentation not included in the source code or in end-user documentation, such as user's manuals, administrative guides, or tutorials. Any documentation or messages in files that are not source files or end-user documentation are engineering documentation.

 Examples of lines of engineering documentation are text lines in the ES, IS, test plans, etc. If estimating lines of documentation, use 54 lines per page.

 A figure is a diagram or pictorial illustration of textual matter. Examples are data-flow diagrams, hierarchy charts, etc.

Recycled Code
 Code incorporated into this product that was either used intact or highly leveraged from a different product or another part of this product.

At MR send to: Metrics Administrator
 Software Engineering Lab
 Building 26U
 3500 Deer Creek Road
 Palo Alto, CA 94304

6

THE SELLING OF METRICS

A sales campaign is an activity with which many engineers and managers with an engineering background feel somewhat uncomfortable. Combining this feeling on the part of the council members with the fact that membership in the Software Metrics Council was definitely a secondary priority to normal engineering and management responsibilities, it is easy to see that the launching of a campaign was a very delicate matter. It was critical that the enthusiasm for the results achieved at our first meeting sustain the council at least long enough for them to get others enthusiastic, particularly top-level managers. No matter what metrics you choose to implement, the next challenge you will face is to convince your engineers and managers of the value of metrics and to foster enthusiasm and correct usage.

6.1 IDENTIFICATION OF THE CUSTOMER

The key to any sales campaign is to know the customer well. Although there were several other important classes of customers for software metrics in HP, we (SEL) quickly realized that our most important customer was the Software Metrics Council itself. It was critical for us to provide them the materials and support necessary to maximize their success. We were much like a factory marketing organization, with them as a *field selling force*.

The other three major classes of customers were top management, project managers, and software engineers. Thus we knew that our campaign and the sales material required had to address the needs of four different customers for us to succeed.

6.2 DEVELOPMENT OF A SALES STRATEGY

The first order of business was to quickly follow up the conference with a widely distributed summary of its results to management, and to concurrently provide sales materials (i.e., a set of annotated, professional-looking overheads) to the members of the Software Metrics Council. Our goal for sending a letter to division managers, R&D managers, and QA managers was to generate some hope and enthusiasm on their part for the program and to publicly praise the accomplishments of the council so that its members felt that associated activities were important. This letter played the role of a *management brochure.*

The sales materials planned for the council took the form of well-designed, hardcopy metrics forms (shown in the previous chapter), as well as the overheads necessary to present a consistent, effective message. After distribution of these materials, we followed up by soliciting names of projects committed to collecting metrics from each of the members of the council. From these names, an overhead was made which focused on quantity and divisional representation, and peer pressure rapidly caused the list to grow. After only two months, the list contained over forty projects.

Just like the members of the Software Metrics Council, the project managers of these forty-plus projects needed support and encouragement (development of *key accounts*). To reinforce their efforts, the council members made numerous lab-wide presentations and provided individual encouragement, and we made presentations at company-wide management meetings (division managers, R&D managers, and QA managers) which occurred six to eight months after the program began.

Probably the most critical job necessary to long-term success, though, was the identification and publication of success stories. Individuals from these divisions became *reference accounts*, and short-term benefits became available by wide publication of data within HP.

6.3 SALES PITCH

A description of the selling of software metrics in HP is not complete without a copy of the script sent to all members of the council within one month of our first meeting. What we include here is the natural evolution of the original script to a form which takes advantage of what we learned during the first three years of metrics experiences. Even with the original script, a strong emphasis was placed on how the data could be used, and this script has that emphasis, as well.

When we give presentations, these slides form the backbone of what we currently say. Many of the slides shown here are explained in detail in later sections of this book, so chapter and figure references are provided if you get too impatient for additional details. The presentation is divided into sections which try to specifically address different groups, that is, top management, project managers, and engineers. While all of the material should be of general interest to everyone, we frequently rearrange or add/delete material when dealing with specific audiences.

Our objective in including this chapter is to provide you with a set of overheads which can help you to be immediately effective in gathering support for your own metrics program.

<table>
<tr><td>

S/W PROCESS METRICS
WHAT? WHY?

</td><td>

Purpose of slide.   Title slide. Introduces the questions you propose to answer during your presentation.

Points to emphasize.   The software metrics on which you will focus measure the *software development process*. Many software metrics collected in the past measured *products*.

</td></tr>
<tr><td>

"It is very difficult to make a vigorous, plausible, and job risking defense of an estimate that is derived by no quantitative method, supported by little data, and certified chiefly by the hunches of the managers."

(Mythical Man Month)

</td><td>

Purpose of slide.   To highlight the fact that making project estimates is difficult without access to accurate historical data and a method for analysis [1].*

Points to emphasize. Many of the estimates for project completions still take place under these circumstances.

</td></tr>
</table>

*Frederick P. Brooks, *The Mythical Man-Month* copyright 1975, Addison-Wesley Publishing Company, Inc., Reading, Massachusetts, reprinted with permission.

SOFTWARE METRICS CONFERENCE
MEETING OBJECTIVE

Gain agreement on a set of software process
measurement criteria which managers feel are
meaningful, reasonable to collect and can be used
to measure progress and predict results.

Purpose of slide. Introduce one approach to software metrics and the objectives of the first meeting of HP's Software Metrics Council.

Points to emphasize. The criteria on which the participants of the meeting were seeking agreement needed to be fundamental to the development process and relatively easy to collect.

Chapter reference. 5

SOFTWARE PROCESS MEASUREMENT
CRITERIA TO CONSIDER

– Size
– Defects
– People/Time/Cost
– Difficulty
– Communication

Purpose of slide. Display five criteria which are important to consider.

Points to emphasize. These are major metric categories for which studies have already been performed in industry and academia. Whichever ones you start with, the "units of measure" for each criteria have to be developed.

Chapter reference. 5

```
                                              Purpose of slide.    To get
                                              management thinking about
                                              why it is useful to collect
                                              software metrics data.

        HOW CAN S/W METRICS                   Points to emphasize.   With
        HELP TOP MANAGEMENT                   this slide and the slides that
        MANAGE THE PROCESS?                   follow, you are going to
                                              show that software metrics
                                              can help top management
                                              measure and better under-
                                              stand the software develop-
                                              ment process.
```

Purpose of slide. Shows that software productivity is a major national issue.

```
    RATES OF GENERATING
   COMPLETELY DEBUGGED CODE
  (LINES OF SOURCE/PERSON/MONTH)

Typical U.S. average          100–500

In a Japanese software factory
   New code only              500–800
   Including reused code      2500–3100
```

Points to emphasize. This measure of productivity uses two of the principle metrics - size and time. There are problems with measuring lines of code. Do these numbers include comments? What type of software and quality is assumed? Are they based on the coding phase only? They do show that there is significant leverage in reuse of code [2].

Chapter reference. 4

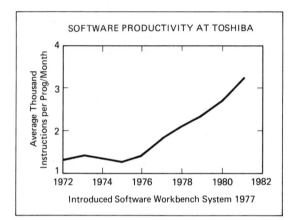

SOFTWARE PRODUCTIVITY AT TOSHIBA

Introduced Software Workbench System 1977

Purpose of slide. Gives an example of metrics which measure the efficiency of the development process.

Points to emphasize. Without such a high-level measure, it is impossible to set realistic goals and to achieve them. It is frightening to think that some companies have had effective measures in place for over ten years. It is also frightening that it took Toshiba four years after establishing their measures before significant improvements were measured [3].

Figure reference. 4-1

SOFTWARE DEFECT RATES		
	U.S. Commercial Software	Japanese Commercial Software
Potential Defects per KLOC	50	40
Pre-delivery Removal Efficiency	90%	95%
Delivered Defects per KLOC	5	2

Purpose of slide. Shows that software quality is also a major national issue [4].

Points to emphasize. As a country, the United States has lost significant shares of entire markets due to unacceptable levels of quality. Quality must be designed in, measured, and verified for any software company to competitively succeed in the future. Potential for defects relates to development techniques, skill factors, and types of applications. Removal efficiencies relate to the number of tests and their effectiveness [5].

Chapter reference.   4

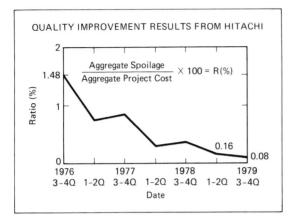

Purpose of slide. Gives an example which shows how metrics are used to measure software quality.

Points to emphasize. Just as with the productivity example, this graph illustrates how one company is able to set significant improvement goals and accomplish them. Again, a long-term program of metrics is illustrated [6].

Figure reference. 4-4

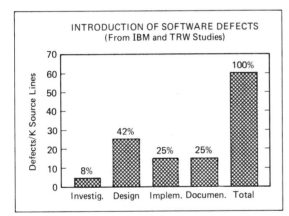

Purpose of slide. Present one example of defect categorization.

Points to emphasize. That software design represents the strongest opportunity for improving software quality [7]. We must find ways to make the design process more effective and to eliminate the causes of design defects. In the interim, we must pursue methods to uncover design defects earlier.

Second, what is the source of so many documentation defects, and what steps can be pursued to detect and eliminate them?

Figure reference. 4-6*

---

*Barry W. Boehm, *Software Engineering Economics* copyright 1981, reprinted by permission of Prentice-Hall, Englewood Cliffs, New Jersey.

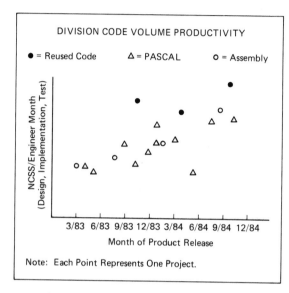

DIVISION CODE VOLUME PRODUCTIVITY

● = Reused Code   △ = PASCAL   ○ = Assembly

NCSS/Engineer Month
(Design, Implementation, Test)

3/83 6/83 9/83 12/83 3/84 6/84 9/84 12/84

Month of Product Release

Note: Each Point Represents One Project.

Purpose of slide. Shows the first of three HP graphs which represent productivity and quality for an entity. You need similar graphs to track progress at a high level.

Points to emphasize. NCSS stands for noncomment source statements, and it represents a count of all source lines excluding comments and blank lines. NCSS was the metric that HP agreed to use for the measurement of size. Design, implementation, and test times are all included in order to emphasize improvement for more than just the coding process. There is provision for isolating separate languages and particularly for emphasizing reused code.

Figure reference. 12-1

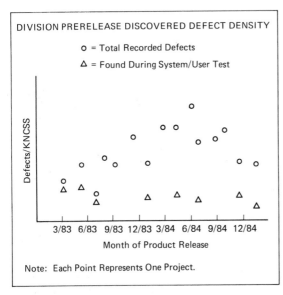

DIVISION PRERELEASE DISCOVERED DEFECT DENSITY

o = Total Recorded Defects

Δ = Found During System/User Test

Defects/KNCSS

3/83 6/83 9/83 12/83 3/84 6/84 9/84 12/84

Month of Product Release

Note: Each Point Represents One Project.

Purpose of slide. Shows the second of three HP graphs which represent productivity and quality for an entity.

Points to emphasize. Provides an aggregate view of quality during the development process over time. Defects reported during formal test will show the greatest consistency. This graph provides a long-term check against the productivity graph. Both must improve.

Figure reference. 12-2

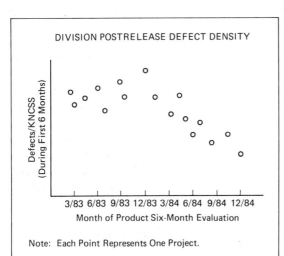

DIVISION POSTRELEASE DEFECT DENSITY

Defects/KNCSS (During First 6 Months)

3/83 6/83 9/83 12/83 3/84 6/84 9/84 12/84

Month of Product Six-Month Evaluation

Note: Each Point Represents One Project.

Purpose of slide. Shows the third of three HP graphs which represent productivity and quality for an entity.

Points to emphasize. Quality after release is the final measure of customer satisfaction. This graph provides a long-term check against the prerelease discovered defect density graph. Both must improve.

The combination of these three graphs can provide a useful summary of software development for any division or company.

Figure reference. 12-3

HOW CAN S/W METRICS
HELP PROJECT MANAGEMENT
MANAGE THE PROCESS?

Purpose of slide. To get project managers thinking about why it is useful to collect software metrics data.

Points to emphasize. With this slide and the slides that follow, you are going to show that software metrics can help project managers monitor and predict project completion and software quality.

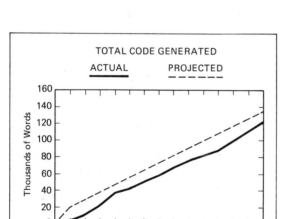

TOTAL CODE GENERATED

ACTUAL   PROJECTED

Purpose of slide. Gives an example which shows how metrics can help to track project completion.

Points to emphasize. This particular project did not estimate the projected code until a substantial level of design was complete. It is useful to track different levels of code completion as well, like code unit tested or integrated.

Figure references. 4-10, 7-1

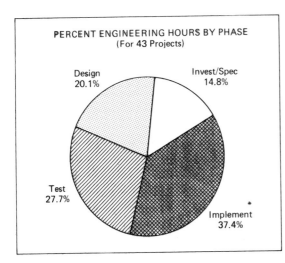

PERCENT ENGINEERING HOURS BY PHASE
(For 43 Projects)

Design 20.1%
Invest/Spec 14.8%
Test 27.7%
Implement 37.4%

Purpose of slide. Gives an example showing how metrics could be used as a predictive tool for future products.

Points to emphasize. This pie chart represents a simplistic breakdown of data into four software project phases: investigation/specification, design, implementation, and test. Once a project has completed investigation and/or design, these percentages provide a reality check for the project manager's staffing plans. Similar percentages can be used to check schedules.

Figure references. 8-8, 4-15

Chapter reference. 11

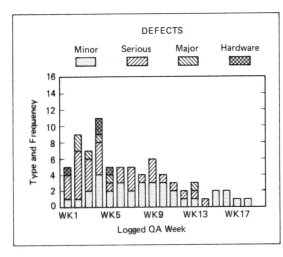

DEFECTS

Minor   Serious   Major   Hardware

Type and Frequency
Logged QA Week

Purpose of slide. Gives an example which shows how software quality can be tracked [8].

Points to emphasize. This type of graph not only shows a trend toward zero defects remaining, but also reassures a project manager that the most serious defects are being addressed first.

Figure reference. 9-10

DEFECT DISCOVERY SCHEDULE

25% of defects are found & fixed
    in 2 hours/defect (rate of .50 defect/hour)
50% of defects are found & fixed
    in 5 hours/defect (rate of .20 defect/hour)
20% of defects are found & fixed
    in 10 hours/defect (rate of .10 defect/hour)
4% of defects are found & fixed
    in 20 hours/defect (rate of .05 defect/hour)
1% of defects are found & fixed
    in 50 hours/defect (rate of .02 defect/hour)

Purpose of slide. Presents a model which can be used to predict the cost of obtaining a given level of quality.

Points to emphasize. This model is based upon data gathered for one particular entity, but seems to work well for others. It requires that you know the code size (which you do at test time), and that you know the average defect density for similar software [9].

Figure reference. 9-8

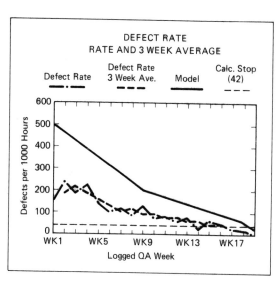

DEFECT RATE
RATE AND 3 WEEK AVERAGE

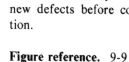

Logged QA Week

Purpose of slide. Illustrates the use of the defect discovery model [8].

Points to emphasize. Objectively predicting and verifying when an acceptable level of quality is achieved is important to balance against normal project schedule pressures. The model provides a visual indication of the approach to completion and includes a predetermined number of hours of new test creation without discovery of any new defects before completion.

Figure reference. 9-9

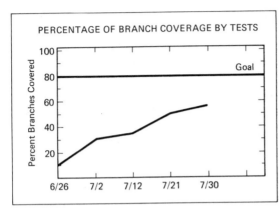

PERCENTAGE OF BRANCH COVERAGE BY TESTS

Purpose of slide. Illustrates another useful metric for achieving high product quality.

Points to emphasize. Measuring the coverage of test cases is an important complement to the defect discovery model and other test creation strategies. Goals for high coverage have been most effective at HP for unit-level testing.

Figure reference. 17-8

HOW CAN S/W METRICS
HELP THE S/W ENGINEER?

* Help identify areas where tools are needed

* Help identify complex program modules

* Help keep schedules realistic

Purpose of slide. To get software engineers thinking about why it is useful to collect software metrics data.

Points to emphasize. Process-oriented metrics will help to identify areas where tools are needed, as well as the effectiveness of tools when the process is changed. Tools which analyze designs and code can provide useful feedback to software engineers. Accurate tracking of projects will aid in more accurate estimating and more acceptable schedules.

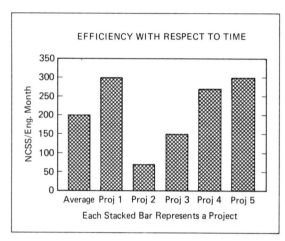

EFFICIENCY WITH RESPECT TO TIME

NCSS/Eng. Month

Average Proj 1 Proj 2 Proj 3 Proj 4 Proj 5

Each Stacked Bar Represents a Project

Purpose of slide. This slide and the next demonstrate how metrics can help identify the effectiveness of certain tools [8].

Points to emphasize. One of five firmware projects used different development tools. It demonstrated one-third the productivity and seven times the number of defects that the other projects did. It is critical that the management approach to interpretation of metrics data be nonthreatening. After demonstrating this data, it was easier to justify the expense of better tools.

Figure reference. 7-2

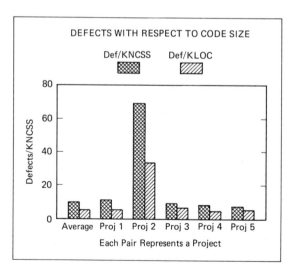

DEFECTS WITH RESPECT TO CODE SIZE

Def/KNCSS   Def/KLOC

Defects/KNCSS

Average Proj 1 Proj 2 Proj 3 Proj 4 Proj 5

Each Pair Represents a Project

Points to emphasize. see above.

Figure reference. 7-3

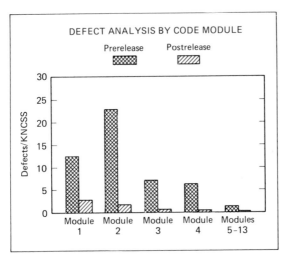

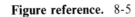

Purpose of slide. To discuss the advantages of identifying the most complex software modules.

Points to emphasize. This analysis was done too late in the development process. Even the prerelease defects were not known until testing was under way. Tools to identify which modules are most error-prone are needed when designs are created.

In this case 24 percent of the code was responsible for 76 percent of the defects, and the same three modules had the most defects pre- and postrelease.

Figure reference. 8-5

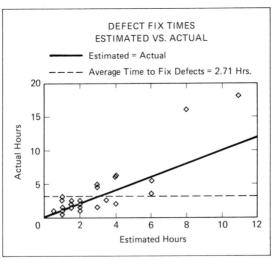

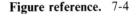

Purpose of slide. Illustrate how keeping accurate track of time spent can lead to better scheduling.

Points to emphasize. Everyone is asked to estimate times. This is an example of the records one engineer kept of how long it took to fix defects. These records helped establish expectations for the entire CPE (Current Product Engineering) group.

Figure reference. 7-4

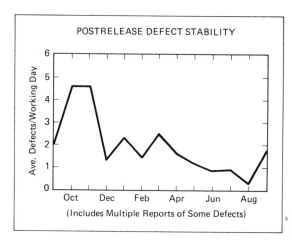

POSTRELEASE DEFECT STABILITY

Ave. Defects/Working Day

(Includes Multiple Reports of Some Defects)

Purpose of slide. We have looked at rates for fixing defects; we need to characterize rates of defect arrival as well.

Points to emphasize. When a product or update is released, the incoming rate of defects increases for a period until a known backlog of the most frequently encountered defects is established. It then stabilizes at some lower rate. The metrics council jokingly named this pattern "the hump phenomenon."

Figure reference. 8-14

WHAT IS THE MINIMUM
SET OF SOFTWARE METRICS
TO COLLECT?

Purpose of slide. Introduction to slides which define metrics of effort, time, size and defects. Substitute your own definitions in these next few slides if they are different from those presented here.

Points to emphasize. These *process* metrics are most effectively utilized at the project level.

KEY EFFORT DEFINITION

Engineering Payroll Month

* Includes project engineering times and times of people doing testing.

* Does not include clerical help.

Purpose of slide. Gives the definition which HP uses for Engineering Payroll Month, a metric for the people/time/cost criteria.

Points to emphasize. For small projects, Engineer Month includes time project managers spend working on software development. Even though the effort definition is given in terms of payroll months, project managers are encouraged to keep more accurate weekly records. It is only by doing this that they will understand all of the factors which consume time, some of which are caused by inefficiencies under their control.

Chapter reference. 5

KEY CALENDAR TIME DEFINITIONS

Investigation/Specification
– Ends when ERS (external reference specification) approved

Design
– Ends when coding starts for final product

Implementation
– Ends when system test starts

Test
– Ends at MR

Purpose of slide. Delineates four project phases which all software projects can be broken into. Even though it is possible to subdivide these times even further, the end points of additional subdivisions are not as clearly recognized as for these.

Points to emphasize. One of the significant results of your program is an agreement on some basic definitions to be used when collecting and discussing software metrics.

Chapter reference. 5

KEY SIZE DEFINITION

NCSS (noncomment source statements)

* Defined as the number of source statements in a program minus comments and blank lines.

Purpose of slide. Shows what NCSS stands for.

Points to emphasize. NCSS is the primary metric for the size criteria. It will appear in the numerator and denominator of a number of important quality and productivity ratios (e.g., defects per KNCSS). Tools are available which automate collection of NCSS and other counts.

Chapter reference. 5

DEFECT DEFINITION

* A defect is any flaw in the specification, design, or implementation of a product.

Purpose of slide. Define what is considered to be a defect.

Points to emphasize. If a flaw could not possibly have been detected, or if it could have been detected and would not have been corrected, then it is an enhancement. Defects do not include typographical or grammatical errors in engineering documentation.

Chapter reference. 5

PROCESS MEASUREMENT
RESPONSIBILITIES

* Project team will participate in data collection
  — keep data accurate

* Project managers will collect and analyze data

* Metrics council will propagate understanding and consistent usage of metrics

* SEL will facilitate data sharing

* SEL will develop data presentation tools as necessary

Purpose of slide. A summary of who has responsibility for process measurement tasks which must be completed in the future. You must substitute your equivalents of a metrics council and SEL.

Points to emphasize. Everyone must follow through with the metrics collection program in order for the results to be beneficial and meaningful.

```
┌─────────────────────────────────────────┐
│            JOHN YOUNG'S 1986              │
│        HP SOFTWARE QUALITY GOALS:         │
│                                           │
│     Achieve a tenfold improvement in two key  │
│   software quality measures in the next five years:  │
│                                           │
│          Postrelease defect density       │
│                                           │
│          Open critical and serious KPRs    │
│                                           │
│    The first is aimed at our design process; the  │
│   second, at our ability to solve problems once  │
│        customers have our products in place.   │
└─────────────────────────────────────────┘
```

Purpose of slide. Introduction to concluding slide; emphasis on how serious HP is about software metrics and their role in business strategy.

Points to emphasize. Both of these goals address long-term customer satisfaction issues, as well as our belief that software quality will be the key survival factor for many of our businesses in the 1990s. Neither of these goals will be achieved without fundamental understanding of our development processes via accurate measurements.

Postrelease defect density (presented earlier) is a long-term measure of fewer defects getting through the process at all, and open critical and serious KPRs (a Known Problem Report is the term used in HP for a defect which has been reported and recognized as a defect after release of a product) are the key measure of our responsiveness to reported defects [10].

Chapter reference. 9

```
ACTIONS NEEDED:

* Set breakthrough expectations.

* Request objective data to understand your
  process.

* Establish a focal point for process
  measurement and improvement.

* Modify and standarize the software process
  to bring it under control.

* Invest in/use tools to automate the process.
```

Purpose of slide. Concluding slide to leave the final thought that *the audience must take action.*

Points to emphasize. You must set high expectations for quality, productivity, and predictability. Assign someone to be the focal point in your organization to understand and improve the development process. Be certain that improvements are substantiated by measured results. We hope that you are convinced that individuals at all levels of the *organization can effectively utilize software metrics to improve their understanding of their own jobs.

6.4 CONCLUSION

In this chapter we have described how the decisions of the first Software Metrics Council meeting were presented to HP entities. In retrospect, the process was clearly beyond the scope of a normal HP council or task force and only worked because HP SEL committed sufficient concentrated resources up front and enough dedicated people were part of the original council to nurture the ideas. It is this commitment which must be created as part of any metrics collection effort, whether it is for just a project or for an entire company.

We presented a "sales pitch" in such a way that with some adjustments, it is useful within any organization. This message must be repeated innumerable times to capture and maintain momentum in a software metrics program.

BIBLIOGRAPHY

1. Brooks, F. P., *The Mythical Man-Month.* Reading, Mass.: Addison-Wesley, 1975, p. 21.

2. McNamara, D., Presentation to HP engineers, Cupertino, Calif., (July 1983).

3. Kim, K. H., "A Look at Japan's Development of Software Engineering Technology," *Computer* (May 1983), p. 33.

4. Jones, T. C., letter (July 25 1986).

5. Jones, T. C., *Programming Productivity* New York: McGraw-Hill Book Co., 1986, pp. 170-173.

6. Tajima, D. and T. Matsubara, "The Computer Software Industry in Japan," *Computer* (May 1981), p. 96.

7. Boehm, B. W., *Software Engineering Economics* Englewood Cliffs, N. J.: Prentice-Hall, Inc. (1981), p. 382.

8. Kenyon, D., Presentation to Second Annual HP Software Metrics Conference (August 1984).

9. Kohoutek, H., "A Practical Approach to Software Reliability Management," 29th EOQC Conference on Quality and Development, Estoril, Portugal (June 1985).

10. Young, J., letter to all general managers, management council, and QA managers (April 1986).

7

THE HUMAN ELEMENT

About two years after HP's software metrics program was initiated, we met with several managers from a major Japanese manufacturer to discuss software development. Their new product development included a large and ever-increasing software content, and they were on a fact-finding tour to determine what steps they should take to improve productivity. While discussing software metrics, they wanted to know how we at HP dealt with the strong reluctance of engineers to be measured. They went on to say that they already knew that measurement of the software development process was a critical element of their success, but that they hadn't determined how to deal with the human element yet.

One of the most frequently voiced concerns for metrics collection is that engineers don't like to be measured. This is a very real concern, and all managers involved in a metrics program should be aware of the underlying basis for the concern so that they can work with their people to maximize their cooperation and willingness to collect good, meaningful, nonthreatening data. The issues involved are complex, psychological ones, and we won't pretend that we are experts in the field of psychology. What we can do is present a variety of positive and negative experiences with collecting software metrics, both from inside HP and outside, to illustrate some of the concerns that people have and how to deal with them by anticipating or avoiding certain situations.

7.1 WANTING TO MEASURE PEOPLE

At our third annual Software Metrics Council meeting we had several brain-storming sessions, as we usually do. One of them addressed "how to reassure people that data will not be used against them." In the session, members were asked to present horror stories, success stories, what project managers should do to be successful, and what the council itself should do to facilitate success. To prime the pump the following true "horror" story was presented.

At one division a functional manager (a functional manager is one who oversees an entire division, or the lab, marketing, manufacturing, or quality department within a division) approached a software project manager and a lab engineer and wanted to discuss how metrics data could be used in performance evaluation. What followed was a rather heated discussion, with the project manager on one side staunchly arguing that such a use would be totally contrary to the objectives of collecting metrics to improve the process of software development. On the other side the functional manager played devil's advocate by asking why, since we would have data pertinent to individual performance, shouldn't we also use it to evaluate people? Through all of this, the engineer sat somewhat dumbfounded, probably thinking about how, personally, they were going to start reporting their data just a little differently. The story ends, fortunately, with the project manager victorious in the argument, and with the functional manager later going off and success-fully battling with others of the functional staff over the same issue.

What is really astonishing about this story is not that it happened, but that two different members of the metrics council thought we were talking about their divisions. Each expressed surprise (and some concern) that we had heard about it, since each had tried to minimize widespread discussion of the incident. There was a fear that the whole story would not be heard and that the metrics program would suffer as a result. We responded that the story we presented didn't describe either of their divisions, but yet a third division.

Why is it that management has this urge to use software metrics to evaluate people, and what primal fears does this desire stir? It is ironic that the power of computers today has helped all management to be at home with complex accounting reports and charts to help them to manage an organization. It is the pervasiveness of this type of data which suggests that everything can be reduced to numbers. In Chapter 4, we described an experiment which Gerald Weinberg ran some years ago where five teams wrote the same software while focusing on different objectives. The results of the experiment showed that software engineers can and will successfully work to maximize whatever elements you choose to give priority to. *The fear is, though, that either you will pick the wrong thing to measure or that whatever you pick can't be measured consistently or accurately.*

The siren song of many metrics studies is that clearly there are substantial differences among individual performers. It is the lure of this knowledge which leads many to believe that you can achieve substantial productivity gains by determining who the top performers are and weeding out or reassigning others. Ideally, they are right. Some day it will be reasonable to do so, but our experience tells us that it is still a very emotional issue at HP, and that it is inappropriate to apply metrics in this way yet.

It is inappropriate because:

- We have not measured long enough to be certain of the accuracy of our measurements.
- We don't know yet *which of the measures* or what combination of metrics correlate best with the behavior we want to encourage.
- We feel that such a use would lead to distortion of the data, and we depend on the measurements to give us insight into the entire development process.

One particular company we talked with recently did use metrics as a tool for judging performance. They determined that the average number of compiles run prior to program completion for one group was eleven. One individual who averaged 27 was fired. This extreme example points out one of the fears of measurement. What factors affected the person fired? Were they personal, health, background, expertise, surroundings, or was the person really a dud? Even more significant, how important really is the number of compiles in the performance of that person in that specific job?

HP offers a class internally which trains engineers and managers in the use of software metrics (see Chapter 13). The trainer says that over the course of running this class over the past year, he has frequently heard the following two concerns strongly voiced about metrics:

"I don't know if my engineers will be willing to do this."

"I don't know if my manager will be willing to do this."

It is really fascinating that both "sides" of the measurement process consistently feel that the other side might be unwilling to measure. At HP we have a very people-trusting orientation. Other companies with whom we have talked more typically say:

"I'm afraid top management will misinterpret the data."

"I don't think the engineers will report data honestly."

No matter which way the statements are expressed, they voice the same basic concern. Engineers and their immediate managers who are close enough to development to understand it are equally concerned over the potential misuse of metrics data.

7.2 METRICS IN A UNIFYING ROLE

Let us look at the use of metrics in a case which had a visible positive impact on a project team. This project team was responsible for porting a software product from one environment to another. Before committing to a schedule, they decided to do the complete translation of a couple out of some fifty or so modules to gain an accurate basis for their estimates. After completing these modules, they prepared a graph to track their week-to-week actual results against their estimates and posted it in a prominent public place. Figure 7-1 shows that they did quite well compared to their estimates [1].

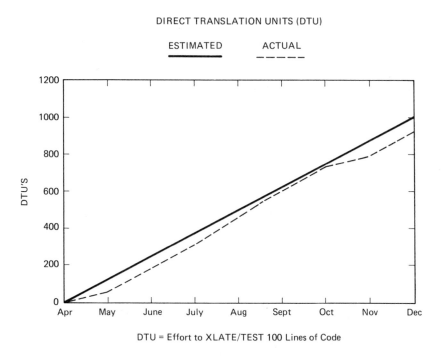

DIRECT TRANSLATION UNITS (DTU)

ESTIMATED   ACTUAL

DTU = Effort to XLATE/TEST 100 Lines of Code

Figure 7-1   Current project status.

This example demonstrates several interesting factors which can contribute toward the success of metrics collection.

1. The means of measurement and level of effort it took were well understood and minimal.

2. The team was measured and plotted, not the individuals.

3 The team agreed up front that the measurements were meaningful.

4 By going through the process before committing to a schedule, the team approved of showing the data publicly.

The result was that the team felt in control. At times they would slip behind the estimated schedule, but the feedback provided by the graph allowed them to focus their energies to get back on track. This type of positive, unifying result is not an unusual case.

The next case illustrates how the data collected by another project team highlighted a problem. In this case, similar firmware products were produced by small teams of developers within the same division. After a number of projects accurately tracked size, time, and defect metrics through project completion, a consistent pattern developed, with one exception. One particular project demonstrated a productivity rate which was about one-half the overall average. In addition, their prerelease defect density was *seven times as high as the others*. This data is shown in Figures 7-2 and 7-3 [2].

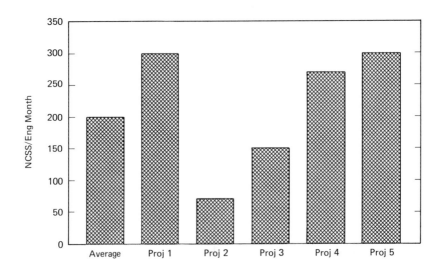

Figure 7-2 Efficiency with respect to time.

This type of data can be extremely threatening. Looking at this data, one might wonder what was wrong with development team number 2? Was there a problem with the project manager? What was unusual about this

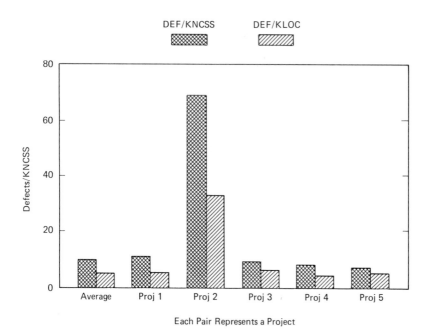

Each Pair Represents a Project

Figure 7-3   Defects with respect to code size.

product? Fortunately, there was one obvious difference between the development environment used by this team and that used by the others. This team used a different set of development and testing tools than the other teams. The result of this discovery was that it was much easier for developers to justify additional, necessary equipment to do their jobs. Subsequent data from additional projects (some including this "different" project team) supported the conclusion that the environment was the key difference.

It is difficult to say what the results of this experience would have been had the cause of the problem not been so obvious. What seems to be the key is that *the management approach to interpretation of metrics data must be nonthreatening.* Data should not be used to distort reality or to (consciously or unconsciously) push a private agenda.

7.3 METRICS AT AN INDIVIDUAL LEVEL

So far we have given examples of some of the human reactions to software metrics at the project group and management level. Let's now look at several cases at the individual level. The first case involves a software engineer who was assigned the responsibility for resolving a large backlog of defects against

a newly released product. Since the engineer did not work on the product originally, the task of estimating how long it would take the engineer to get familiar with the design and code, and then fix the most critical defects was
difficult. The project manager approached the engineer and asked him if he
would be willing to keep accurate records of his time so that, together, they
could understand the overall time necessary to do the job. There was no baseline for "average time to fix a defect," so there was no implied threat to the
request. Furthermore, by establishing such a baseline for himself, the engineer
felt that he had control over his job and could set targets for himself. Figure
7-4 shows a scattergram of estimated hours versus actual hours for 24 defects.
The average time to fix a defect was 2.71 hours, and the time the project
team currently schedules for defect fixes is an average of four hours. This
time takes into account overhead activities so that scheduled release dates can
be accurately predicted. It also produced an initial positive motivator to the
engineer collecting the data. When the project manager learned that the
engineer was investing significant hours in training other new engineers and in
other important activities, both the scope and complexity of his job were
better appreciated, and priorities were set to help him.

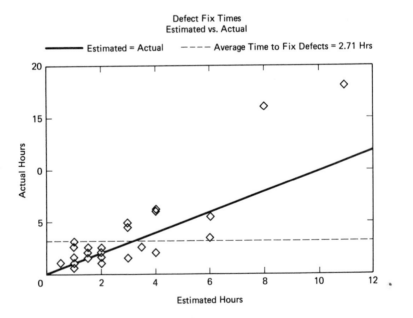

Figure 7-4   Defect resolution rate for one engineer.

This process worked well for them, and it became predictable within a
month. By understanding how long the defect resolution process would take,
the project manager was able to plan the other appropriate resources to insure

that testing and documentation support were available in a timely fashion. Note that there are several significant things the project manager did not do, which helped to make this a positive experience. The project manager did not use the data to make value judgments about the engineer's performance, did not suggest that anyone else's performance should be better or worse than what this data suggested (although the data does help one to understand the ramp-up time for learning and average time for fixing defects for products of similar size and complexity), and did not challenge the accuracy of the data kept, since consistency was the primary concern.

A second case has a more unfortunate ending. A project team of four engineers and a project manager decided to collect some data. They were creating a new software application which they did not totally understand, so they decided to use a prototyping approach. One of the engineers proposed some metrics which could be automatically collected and implemented some utilities to aid in the collection process. The rest of the team basically accepted these measures and went on with business as usual, glad not to be bothered with having to spend any extra time collecting data themselves.

After these utilities had been in place for some time, the engineer who wrote them started bragging about how much more productive he was than the others on the team and referred to the data to prove it. This started relatively quietly and proceeded to the point where the engineer was making it quite clear to other members of the team that they were lacking.

The unfortunate end to this story is that the engineer created so much disharmony that he was encouraged to take a different job. This, in turn, caused great disruption to the project. Nobody ended up as a winner in this situation. In the early seventies Gerald Weinberg coined the term "egoless programming" [3] to describe an approach to preventing the problem created by this type of individual, and it is unfortunate in this case that metrics served as the catalyst for the problem. Whether the individual was "right" or not about his productivity was irrelevant under the team circumstances dictated by the project. Productivity cannot be a contest among members of the same team working toward a common goal. Different members will always have different strengths which cannot be measured equally, and it is the balance of these strengths which the project manager strives to combine to optimize the entire team's performance. When individuals focus on their own performance instead of their contribution to the team as a whole, the project is threatened. It is clear, then, that metrics can be misused not just by managers, but by engineers as well.

The problem described in this next case is even more difficult for managers to deal with. In this case the metrics program under way at a division was widespread, received management encouragement, and was generally successful in most of the positive senses we have discussed. Part of the success was the assurance that the data collected would remain anonymous. One of the metrics carefully tracked was engineering hours. After data had been collected for some time, it became clear that one of the engineers was not reporting, or working, a 40-hour week. The quandary we present to you is, what would you do with the information? The question at this entity was resolved with a rather heated discussion between the lab manager and the section manager who reported to the lab manager. The section manager basically refused to divulge the name of the offender, on the grounds that their accurate data would dry up if the confidentiality was violated. What would you do?

7.4 BRING ON THE LAWYERS

Another case illustrates how complex business can get when trust completely breaks down. A legal case was brought against a major company in Italy, where a statute exists which restricts two aspects of monitoring individuals. While the article seems to discuss data entry personnel rather than programmers, the types of automated measurements feared in this case are just like those which are desirable for software metrics collection.

> The statute is composed of two parts, the first of which sets a ban on "the use of audiovisual equipment and other machinery that aims at the remote control of the workers' activity." The second part governs cases where remote monitoring is not the primary objective of a particular machine or tool, but is a by-product, resulting from "organizational and productive requirements or from guaranteeing the security of the work "[4].*

An initial agreement between the company and a union provided for use of two commercial software packages to monitor usage and remote access of computers. This agreement finally broke down though, because the union representatives expressed distrust of the ultimate use of the data:

> Behind the label of "confidentiality and security," the unions say they see a hierarchical control of access to sensitive information. Behind the label of "performance evaluation," they see an insidious monitoring of the quantity and quality of individual workers' performance [4].*

Once this level of mistrust exists, it is extremely difficult to convince people that they have any control over measurements or the interpretation of them. Yet it is crucial to measure quantity and quality in order to improve them. This case summarizes the extremes of human concern over measurement better than any other we have come across.

7.5 CHANGE AND TRANSITION

We have discussed numerous real examples of experiences with software metrics, some of which were clear successes, and others of which would be considered failures. Now we are going to shift the focus and talk more generally about reactions of people to major change. The first concepts discussed deal with more extreme situations than the cases presented already, but the basic principles are still relevant. We follow this discussion by examining human reactions to measurement, also from a more theoretical standpoint. The concepts presented are primarily derived from two papers which deal with change, transition, and dealing with people's fears. They help to explain some of the underlying reasons why people initially react the way they do to suddenly being measured. We try to summarize the concepts which best apply, but we encourage you to read the entire articles, since the points are so important.

The first of these papers is by William Bridges and is titled "Managing Organizational Transitions." The first key distinction that he makes is that of the difference between change and transition. Change is structural, and the daily routine is different as a result. In our context, change occurs when, at some level, someone decides and announces that software metrics will be collected. Transition is the psychological response to the change. All changes require individuals to adapt to new circumstances. It is a grave mistake to assume that any announcement, no matter how insignificant, is the end of the process. All transitions begin with an ending.

Transition is a three-phase process in which individuals:

1. Let go of an old situation and the old self-images that were appropriate to it.
2. Go through a difficult "wilderness" time in the gap between the old reality and the new one.
3. Then (and only then) emerge with new energy, purpose, and sense of self to make a new beginning [5].

Now these definitions seem rather extreme to a simple case like measuring one or two elements of the software development process, but it is only a matter of degree. When we started our software metrics program, we faced a decision whether we should recommend a program which could grow from the grassroots, or whether we should recommend to top management a set of standards which would be required of everyone. Either approach (or some variation in between) could be made to work. The decision we made to work from the grassroots was better suited to HP's culture: one which strives for consensus. Once the metrics council achieved consensus, it was much easier for people to accept the standards which insured company-wide consistency. For us, this was a way of gradually dealing with the "wilderness time." For companies which more normally deal in top-down decisions, it would be better to apply the appropriate research to defining a good standard, to announce the standard with the rationale behind it, and then to help people to deal with the transition.

Understanding the ways that changes are threatening and the typical reactions of people can go a long way toward choosing the most effective ways to introduce change. It is the job of managers to gracefully deal with the "wilderness" time, and to work with the individuals involved to resolve concerns.

Bridges describes another effect of change which can explain why transitions are a difficult time for people. One of the effects of change is that it threatens individual identity. There are four ways that it does this:

1. Meaning.   What is the personal significance of a change?
2. Mastery.   How can an individual regain control of a situation?
3. Merit.   What is a person worth under the new situation?
4. Morale.   What difference does it make whether a person tries or not?

It is only natural that unconscious reactions begin when such threats to personal identity occur. Applying this theory to a metrics program, we can expect people to react as follows:

1. Meaning.   They will resist the added duties and time required to collect the metrics. They will question how their performance will be judged by the availability of the data.
2. Mastery.   They may resent collection of metrics if they don't feel they have any control of the results. They will strive to make the data reflect their efforts positively. They will also strive to make the data prove their own points of concern regarding organization or work environment.
3. Merit.   They will support metrics which reflect areas of their performance of which they are proud and attempt to make those metrics most important. For example, they may be meticulous at ensuring that their code is defect-free. If so, they will want attention focused more on defect densities than on productivity.
4. Morale.   No one wants to collect data if it is going to show only how poorly he or she did. Unless the ground rules for interpretation of data are spelled out ahead of time, morale can drop.

A second paper by Thomas C. Tuttle and D. Scott Sink introduces the concept of "force-field analysis." The principal use of such an analysis is as an aid in defining a strategy which increases the balance of positive forces versus negative forces in a particular situation. In this way the process of transition can be more effectively managed. We can reflect on our software metrics "sales pitch" as an attempt to provide material to both reinforce forces for positive change, and lessen the forces against the change. Figure 7-5 shows a diagram of the forces for and against productivity measurement [7].

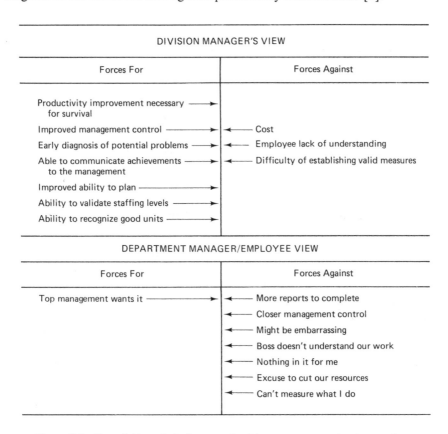

DIVISION MANAGER'S VIEW

Forces For	Forces Against
Productivity improvement necessary ──► for survival	
Improved management control ──►	◄── Cost
Early diagnosis of potential problems ──►	◄── Employee lack of understanding
Able to communicate achievements ──► to the management	◄── Difficulty of establishing valid measures
Improved ability to plan ──►	
Ability to validate staffing levels ──►	
Ability to recognize good units ──►	

DEPARTMENT MANAGER/EMPLOYEE VIEW

Forces For	Forces Against
Top management wants it ──►	◄── More reports to complete
	◄── Closer management control
	◄── Might be embarrassing
	◄── Boss doesn't understand our work
	◄── Nothing in it for me
	◄── Excuse to cut our resources
	◄── Can't measure what I do

Figure 7-5 Force-field analysis for a productivity measurement implementation. Copyright Executive Enterprises, Inc.

If we look at the history of HP's software metrics program, our initial thrust emphasized :

Early diagnosis of potential problems
Improved ability to plan
Ability to recognize good units

These were all positive forces, not just from top management's viewpoint, but also from the department/project management viewpoint. At the same time we took steps to minimize:

Cost
More reports to complete
Closer management control
Might be embarrassing

We tried to minimize these "forces against" by keeping the metrics forms simple, by providing tools to aid in collection of data, and by encouraging trend monitoring as opposed to absolute value judgments.

Our second metrics thrust focused more on top management with a set of graphs (see Chapter 12). This had the effect of emphasizing:

Productivity improvement necessary for survival
Improved management control
Able to communicate achievements to management

There is one additional "force for" which is not shown on the force-field analysis in Figure 7-5. Many engineers are encouraged by increased management involvement through productivity and quality measurements. This is because engineers want managers who don't have a software background and experience to understand and sympathize with the problems that the engineers face. They see such measurements as a possible vehicle for better understanding.

7.6 SUMMARY

In this chapter we have tried to illustrate some of the complex human factors which arise in collecting software metrics. We have discussed how every change initiates a transition to an unknown, new state of equilibrium, and that such transitions must be carefully managed. In particular the measurement of the process of software development represents a threatening change to both developers and their managers, because the process itself is ill-defined and constantly changing.

On the other hand, we have also seen that software metrics can play a significant role in unifying a team around a limited set of measurable objectives, or focusing on one narrow aspect of the development process which can be improved. It is vital to understand that in these cases the measurement process is an agreed-upon partnership between engineers and management, with common goals and objectives.

Finally, we have discussed cases where managers attempted to use software metrics to evaluate engineers. It is clear that the motivation to do so is reasonable and that some day building software will be as well-defined and consistent as building a tract house. At that time some subset of software metrics (which might be very different from what is collected today) will be added to the accounting system, and fair, consistent measurements will be possible. We cannot emphasize too strongly, however, that *software metrics today are not consistently enough defined and understood that anyone should consider using them to measure and evaluate people. Furthermore, premature usage of metrics data for such purposes will only cause future data to be distorted and useless.* There are great potential benefits to be realized by using metrics to more sharply define and understand the software development process and its weakest areas. This use of metrics must be the one on which we concentrate our efforts for the nearterm.

BIBLIOGRAPHY

1. Finch, B., Presentation to Second Annual HP Software Metrics Conference (August 1984).
2. Kenyon, D., Presentation to Second Annual HP Software Metrics Conference (August 1984).
3. Weinberg, G., *Psychology of Computer Programming.* New York: Van Nostrand Reinhold Co., 1971, p. 56.
4. Merlini, M., "Is Big Blue Big Brother?," *Datamation* (March 1984), pp. 52.
5. Bridges, W., "Managing Organizational Transitions," paper presented at Pajaro Dunes, Calif. (Feb. 1985), pp. 4,6,9,10.
6. Tuttle, T. and D. Sink, "Taking the Threat Out of Productivity Measurement," *National Productivity Review* (Winter 1984-85), p. 27.

8

THE NEED FOR TOOLS

For a program of software process measurement to be widely successful, tools must be available to insure consistent measurements as well as to minimize interference with the existing processes of software development. This chapter starts with the original software metrics defined by the HP Software Metrics Council. It then presents the initial set of measurement tools needed and made available to encourage collection of metrics. Finally, it discusses additional needs which appeared as soon as widespread collection began.

8.1 METRICS WORTH COLLECTING

All project managers are acutely aware of schedules. This is, of course, because accurately predicting schedules is a very difficult task, so as many intermediate schedule points as possible are defined, scheduled, and tracked. Most project managers also define and track functional modules or programs at some convenient size through the various intermediate schedule points. Finally, most project managers track defects during at least the testing, integration, and postrelease parts of a product's development. This data is shown in the context of the four major development phases used for the HP standard metrics in Table 8-1. Table 8-1 also shows some additional tools which are used by some project managers to capture the rest of the metrics defined in the categories of size, people/time/cost, and defects. In this context, tools include techniques such as paper forms which help to focus and simplify the collection process. We have indicated information which most project managers already collect by an asterisk and have approximated the incremental additional time for the remainder. The totals represent an estimate of the upper and lower limits of time necessary to collect this set of data during any given phase of software development.

TABLE 8-1   Existing Tools for Software Metrics Collection

Development Phase	Metric Primitive	What Mngrs. Collect Already	Tools	Estimated Additional Time/Week (Minutes)	
				Engineer	Manager
Investigation	Time — calendar	✓		*	*
	— progrmr		Time matrix	1	5
	Defects		Defect log	--	--
Design	Time — calendar	✓		*	*
	— progrmr		Time matrix	1	5
	Defects		Defect log	10	10
Coding	Time — calendar	✓		*	*
	— progrmr		Time matrix	1	5
	NCSS		Code count	3	--
	Code status	✓	Code summ.	*	*
	Defects		Defect log	3	5
Test	Time — calendar	✓		*	*
	— progrmr		Time matrix	1	5
	Code status	✓	Code summ.	*	*
	Defects	✓	Defect log	*	*
Postrelease	Time — calendar	✓		*	*
	— progrmr		Time matrix	1	5
	Defects	✓	Defect log	*	*
* It is assumed that these times are already spent as part of job.			Total	1 TO 11	5 TO 15

8.1.1 The Key to Measuring Is Time Investment

The reason project managers collect data is that it is impossible to make responsible, informed decisions without it. However, there is a cost to data collection. It is an investment whose return depends on the implementation of the data collection and analysis process.

The first cost is time spent before data collection actually starts; time is required to decide which data to collect, to decide which tools will help, and to train project team members on how to use the tools and their outputs. Ideally, this should be done before a new project starts; however, a project already in progress is well advised to invest this time. If the project is going well, numerical snapshots of the project should be taken which can serve as a good example of data for a project under control for future comparison. If the graphs suddenly show unexplained behavior (data which is unexpectedly counter to current trends), you know immediately that something is wrong and can investigate and start corrective action.

The manager of a project which is behind schedule is likely to resist spending the necessary time to start collecting data. Data collection will probably not tell how to make up time in the schedule, but will only confirm that the project is in trouble. However, once data is collected, the use of "management by data" helps detect problems as they occur rather than waiting until the next milestone. The early detection and resolution of problems can avoid many small schedule slips in favor of more accurate, long-range estimates. Whether a project is going well or not, the investment in time to begin collecting metrics at any point in the process is well worthwhile.

The second element of time investment is the ongoing project investment in collecting the actual data. This time is of definite concern to the project manager, since it represents a continuous overhead factor for the duration of the project. It is this area where effective tools are necessary to aid in the collection process.

8.1.2 The Simple Toolset for Metrics Collection

One of the simplest, most useful data elements to collect is programmer time. There is historic resistance on the part of both project managers and engineers to collecting this data. This resistance derives from a concern over how such data is to be used. Interpretation of all metrics can be distorted when used out of context. Fortunately, the software field is more mature today, and it is recognized that many factors besides the oft-reported LOC (Lines Of Code)/programmer month must be examined in parallel in order to understand programmer performance (type of application, design complexity, clarity of documentation, stability of specifications, defect density, and size and organization of project team, to mention just a few).

The burden to software engineers to track their time is quite minimal when a simple form such as the one shown in Figure 8-1 is used. This particular example shows what one software engineer might fill out in pencil for one week. It also raises some important questions regarding what is collected. Should you collect very accurate actuals? (The example numbers are unlikely to be accurate, since they seem so evenly split into days and half-days.) Must the actuals reflect accounting hours - that is, should they reflect undertime to account for personal activities or meetings or overtime to reflect extra time? What about *effective time* - that is, should you count time as design or coding when you were interrupted five times during an hour?

Weekly Time Summary

Phase Project	Investigate/ Specify	Design	Implement	Maintain/ Test	Enhance	Support	Manual	Total
DTS-UNIX				28	4			
DTS-3000		8						
P-PODS								
HP-MAGIC								
PERSEUS								
PM2L								
Total								

Figure 8-1 Simple paper collection tool for engineering time.

The HP Software Metrics Council has struggled a great deal over these questions. In Chapter 5 we saw that the times reported on the current forms reflect payroll hours plus an adjustment factor for over/under time. This form is the result of a conscious tradeoff of accuracy versus our desire to get a large number of projects to collect data.

We feel strongly that it is a benefit to a project to collect more accurate data than is generally reported to accounting. One of the authors has personally used the form illustrated in Figure 8-1 to help manage a 25,000 engineer-hour project with engineers reporting "real" hours to half-hour accuracies. They were willing to provide this accuracy, but they were not asked to adjust for interruptions, and personal activities and meetings not related to the project were simply not counted.

The Figure 8-1 example is oriented toward a small lab, but some project managers prefer more detail shown for their own projects. In either case, the time investment in collecting the data is insignificant, and valuable information is captured.

Some project managers collect code status in a form similar to Figure 8-2. This form is easy to maintain either on paper or online and requires only addition to get NCSS (noncomment source statements) totals.

Code Status				
Responsible Engineer	Module Name	Function Name	NCSS	Status
Smith	Initial	Globals	220	C
		Equivlnt	80	C, W, D
Jones	Scanner	Parser	400	R
		asc_bin	125	C, D

C = coded
W = walked through
D = debugged
R = reused

Figure 8-2   Simple code status table.

Collection of accurate size metrics can be reasonably accomplished only by using automatic counters. These counters need not be run frequently during the project in order for a project manager to track status consistently. By using a simple approximation for NCSS such as source page count * 50 * 2/3 (assume 1/3 to 1/2 comments and blank lines depending on team standards and style) and then running automated counters once a month on all sources, minimum time is invested. Figure 8-3 shows common languages used at HP and automated counters which are available to HP developers. Some

Matrix of Line Counters

Language	Computer								
	64000	150	1000	3000	UNIX Series 500/200	PASCAL WKSTN Series 200	VAX	Spectrum UX	Spectrum MPE
SPLII	X	X	X		X	X	X	X	X
SPL	X	X	X	plines	X	X	X	X	X
PASCAL	sourcecent			pasmet analyze pmetric plines	pasmet pmetric	sourcecent	pmetric	(assume SEL port)	
FORTRAN	X	X				X			
C					ccount cmetric BFA Anac		cmetric	assume SEL port)	
Modcal		X		pmet pasmet plines	pasmet		X		
Assembly	sourcecent (68000 asmb)					sourcecent (68000 asmb)			
sh-scripts			X		X	X			
BASIC	X			analyze		sourcecent PRO-BASIC			
COBOL	X	X	X	knt	X	X	X	X	X
Transact	X	X	X	knt	X	X	X	X	X

Figure 8-3

101

counters with similar functionality are commercially available. These counters fill the needs of about 85 percent of software developers at HP. A blank box indicates that no counter currently exists, and an "X" in a box indicates a machine that does not support the corresponding language.

Time investment can become an issue even when automated counters are "available." One project team reported that at their division the line counters were located several machines away via nontransparent point-to-point network links. They didn't have the time to move all of their sources or to move the counters over to the machine they were on. Unless there is some individual or group in the lab to provide available tools and basic training for the tools where they are needed, when they are needed, the tools will not be used. This then leads to either inaccurate collection and later inaccurate estimations based on previous data, or to no collection at all, which leads to later estimations based on fuzzy recollections. HP has created the job function of "productivity manager" to deal with the issue of tool availability, among other things. These individuals are in the labs of each division, and they provide a strong force for communication among divisions concerning best practices and tools, and they help to propagate usage of new technology more rapidly throughout the company.

The last of the fundamental metrics collection tools is the defect logging form. This is another simple form which minimizes the pain of collecting information, but assures consistency and some reliability of status. An example is shown in Figures 8-4 and 8-5.

There are three separate views of a defect which are taken between the time it is initially found and the time it is ultimately fixed. The first view is the customer view. Figure 8-4 deals with the necessary data concerning who the customer is, the symptoms seen by the customer (internal software developers and users, in this case), and the severity from their point of view. (When one is dealing with external customers additional information is necessary for efficient tracking purposes.) The second view is illustrated by the top part of Figure 8-5. This view is taken by the product support staff after a product is released, or by the project manager prior to product release. This view is one which is global to all reported defects. It weighs relative importance of different defects and availability of staff to address them. The third view is illustrated by the bottom part of Figure 8-5. This view is always taken by the project manager responsible for the product. The project manager tries to capture enough information to characterize the root causes for defects, the overall health of the components of the product, and the effectiveness of the organization in dealing with problems. *It is the fact that there are three distinct viewpoints for every defect which causes frequent confusion in attempts to simply describe them.*

Defect Tracking System Classification Worksheet

Defect number: _____   Date defect found: _____
Submitter: _____   Phone number: _____
Impacted project/lab: _____   Computer name: _____
Defective software: _____   Version Number: _____

Please indicate how serious the problem is. Use the following severity codes:

_____ 0 = User misunderstanding
_____ 1 = Cosmetic defect: can still get job done
_____ 2 =
_____ 3 = Implementing workaround is simple
_____ 4 =
_____ 5 = Workaround is difficult
_____ 6 =
_____ 7 = Incorrect results are produced
_____ 8 =
_____ 9 = Major feature is not working, system crashes, loss of data

Does problem keep project from meeting a critical checkpoint?   Y   N

Any attached documents to help clarify problem?   Y   N
Description of defect: _____
_____
_____
_____

Found any workaround for problem?   Y   N
If answer is yes, describe workaround: _____
_____
_____

How was problem found?
_____ regular use
_____ gestalt (flash of inspiration to try something)
_____ team/group review
_____ reported from an external source
_____ other: _____

What were the symptoms of the problem:
__ system crash   __ data lost   __ enhancement request
__ deadlock/hang   __ unfriendly behavior__ interface to software
__ inconsistent behavior   __ incorrect behavior __ message unclear or wrong
__ infinite loop   __ unexpected abort   __ documentation missing
__ interface to operating system   __ file lost   __ documentation wrong
__ other: _____

Date fix required by: _____

Figure 8-4

Defect Tracking System Resolution Worksheet

Information Provided by Responsible Lab

Defect fix priority

_____ 9 = Defect will be resolved immediately (HOT!).
_____ 8 =
_____ 7 = Defect will get high attention.
_____ 6 =
_____ 5 = Defect will be looked at in normal queue.
_____ 4 =
_____ 3 = Lower priority: use workaround or fix in the interim.
_____ 2 =
_____ 1 = Lowest priority: will be fixed as the last thing.
_____ 0 = Defect will not be fixed.

Impacted functional component: _____

Responsible project manager/engineer: _____

Estimated fix date: _____

Information Provided by Defect Fixer

Date fixed: _____ Engineering hours to fix: _____

Defect resolution

What were the symptoms of the problem?
__ Code change   __ Specification change
__ Design change   __ User error
__ Change deferred   __ Duplicate fix
__ Not reproducible   __ No change (explain below)
__ Duplicate defect report   __ Other (explain below)
__ Documentation changed to disallow action __ Documentation changed to support action

Engineer who fixed module: _____

Phase introduced: __ Invest/Spec   __ Design   __ Implementation   __ Integ/Test
Phase found: __ Invest/Spec   __ Design   __ Implementation   __ Integ/Test
Phase fixed: __ Invest/Spec   __ Design   __ Implementation   __ Integ/Test

Additional related information: _____
_____
_____
_____

Figure 8-5

8.2 SECONDARY METRIC NEEDS

The metrics shown in Table 8-1 and described in the previous section were the result of the Council's top-level definition of HP's basic software measurement needs. These can be referred to as primary metrics. The primary metrics are good for comparing projects at a very high level. They form a vocabulary which is common to all HP divisions for the purposes of sharing information. Also, the primary metrics are good for tracking a project over time. For example, in the implementation phase, tracking total code size weekly versus the estimated schedule can give a good indication of whether or not a schedule is being met. Tracking the number of unresolved defects can indicate whether the test phase is progressing as expected. Having a historical database of these basic metrics can help to establish the schedule for other projects based on data instead of intuition alone.

The primary metrics have advantages for tracking and estimating, although they are not adequate for process analysis and improvement. They can hint at what might improve a process, but more details are needed to identify what improvements can be made. Each project uses a slightly different development process. Understanding a process involves defining what the process is and deciding what metrics make sense to collect. We will call these more detailed metrics secondary metrics, not because they are less important, but because the need for them was recognized only after a basic understanding of the primary metrics was reached at a given division. Table 8-2 shows some secondary metrics which appeared very early in HP's metrics programs at several divisions. We will discuss these additional metrics and the information they were designed to determine.

8.2.1 Understanding Where Effort is Spent

Several aspects of effort expenditure go beyond simply keeping track of engineering hours by development phase. One division is addressing the fundamental question of engineering efficiency by recording half-hours of uninterrupted time. The premise under investigation is that interruptions break the thinking process and result in large inefficiencies [1].

Another division uses a tool to keep detailed records of time invested in design and code walkthroughs. By keeping such detailed records they hope to discover which defects to expect in future projects, what the cost of finding them is, and how they can best organize the reviews to maximize success.

In SEL, among others, the time to fix defects is under scrutiny. By keeping accurate records via DTS (Defect Tracking System) [2], it is possible to characterize the average times to find and fix different categories of defects. It is also possible to characterize the incoming defect rate. Once done, these facilitate prediction of how long it will take to prepare an updated product release which fixes a given set of problems.

TABLE 8-2 Metrics which Managers Found Useful to Characterize the Development Process

Primary Metric	Secondary Metric	Collection Tool	Form of Presentation
People/Time/Cost	Noninterrupted time	Time log	Report
	Design review time	INSPECT/LOG	Report
	Defect fix time	DTS	PM2L graph
Size	Halstead volume predictor	PASMET	Report
	NCSS (more consistent)	"Pretty printers"	Changed SOURCE file
	Code maintainability	PMETRIC/CMETRIC	Report
	NCLS	BFA	Report
Defects	Percentage introduced per phase	DTS	In database
	Frequency by category	DTS	Report/bar chart W/HP draw
	Severity	DTS/STARS	Report/PM2L

DTS is a UNIX-based tracking system which was designed to operate in a distributed development environment for HP developers. It consists of a set of routines which:

1. Facilitate the reporting of defects.
2. Provide for automatic routing of defect information to the responsible individual on the appropriate machine in a timely manner via electronic mail.
3. Provide for defect status tracking, reporting, and automatic notification upon resolution.
4. Report on defect status via summaries tailored for several different levels of users.

The forms in Figures 8-4 and 8-5 gave a preview of DTS, because they were specifically designed for one set of users who did not have convenient access to UNIX machines. They illustrate the information normally entered via a set of screens when a problem is encountered, received (responsibility is accepted), and fixed.

Figure 8-6 shows an example of a report that engineers can get in order to keep track of the status of their responsibilities [3]. A similar report is available for project managers which combines the reports of groups of engineers. Figure 8-7 illustrates a more global summary report which is used to track overall project progress [3]. Several of the charts shown later in this chapter were produced for projects from this type of DTS summary report.

Engineer Summary of Defect Information for Lynn Smith

Total Showstopper Defects	1
Total Open Defects	2
Total Resolved Defects	1
Total Defects	3

Engineer Defect Information:

Lynn Smith

DSDaa00013 Submit Num: 00011CLLaa OPEN S:4 P:1   Recvd: 840630
Dsc: 'cat "any plain file" > >/dev/null' gets file listed to terminal

DSDaa00022 Submit Num: 00015FSDac RESOL S:8 P:9 URGENT
                                                    Recvd: 840702
Dsc: System will not boot after FSCK.

DSDaa00034 Submit Num: 00017FSDDac OPEN S:1 P:2 Recvd: 840730
Dsc: Manual is incorrect on page 10. Unsolid should be Unresolved.

Figure 8-6   DTS engineer defect summary report.

General Defect Report Summary for: DLC					
Project Name	Unrec	Open	Reslv	Total	Unrec/Open Showstopper	Resolved Showstopper
Commands	9	34	102	145	1	4
Kernel	3	17	89	109		5
Total	12	51	191	254	1	9

Total Unreceived and Open defects by Severity										
Project Name	0	1	2	3	4	5	6	7	8	9
Commands	1	4	2	8			9	3	9	7
Kernel	2	1	1	2	5		5	1	2	1
Total	3	5	3	10	5	0	14	4	11	8

Total Resolved Defects by Severity										
Project Name	0	1	2	3	4	5	6	7	8	9
Commands	9	9	13		5	49	10			7
Kernel	5	6	10	14	15	10	10	9	5	5
Total	14	15	23	14	20	59	20	9	5	12

Figure 8-7   DTS general defect summary report.

8.2.2 LOC Is Only a Gross Measure

There are many cost-estimating programs described in the literature. Two of these are used in HP today: Softcost [4] and COCOMO [5]. The problem with these models (and most others) is that code size is the biggest cost driver. How do we know during project definition how large the final code will be? In order to make better predictions eventually, some divisions are experimenting with early code size prediction models such as the Halstead volume predictor [6] and DeMarco "Bang" [1].

One problem with accurately measuring size is defining precisely the unit of measure. This is true of function points [6], DeMarco's token count [1], as well as lines of code. Different counters use slightly different counting rules. Another problem with the lines-of-code metric is that programmer style can greatly affect the size measurement. "Pretty printer" programs help to remove some of these differences. Style analyzers such as PMETRIC and CMETRIC are used to review elements of style which make code difficult to read and maintain. These two give scores for coding elements such as mix of comments, average variable name lengths, use of indentation, and use of goto's. Use of predefined style standards can eliminate variability in physical source line counts. An attempt at eliminating both problems is to count NCLS (noncomment logical statements) rather than physical lines of code. The definition of a logical statement depends on the computer language. In general, it includes "actions of evaluation, assignment, and control of evaluation order" [7],* and in some languages declarations are considered statements. Counting logical lines of PASCAL, for example, is more like counting semicolons than counting carriage returns (although it is not as trivial as counting semicolons). Counting NCLS requires a smarter analyzer but eliminates the differences in size based on coding style. It is also more intellectually satisfying because what is counted is closer to functionality — assuming that each statement adds a single function to the software.

8.2.3 Getting at the Causes of Defects

In order to eliminate the introduction of defects into a software product, the causes of the defects must first be found. By making the process of recording defects, their causes, severity levels, and priorities to fix as simple as possible, the data will be available to analyze patterns both in the defects themselves and in the fixing process.

Categorization of defects is used to identify the most frequently occurring types of defects. The impact of each category can be analyzed by using Pareto charts; the Pareto principle states that 80 percent of the problems can be fixed with 20 percent of the effort. (There is a fascinating discussion of the derivation of the name "Pareto principle" in the *Quality Control Handbook* by Juran et al. It is named after the Italian economist Vilfredo Pareto, who apparently never stated the principle in its current form. Juran did. Pareto also apparently never used the bar charts which we refer to as Pareto charts. M. O. Lorenz did [8].) For example, analysis of defects reported against one product for the first few months after initial release showed that a few modules were much more error-prone than the rest (refer to Figure 8-8). In fact, 24 percent of the code was responsible for 76 percent of the defects reported. This analysis led initially to heavy testing of those modules, and long-term plans to totally rewrite the error-prone modules. Notice also that the three modules out of thirteen having the highest defect densities prerelease also had the highest defect densities postrelease.

Categorization of defects is also useful as a breakdown by process phase. One division determined that design defects represented close to half of their total. By focusing their attention on the source of these defects, they learned

---

* Aho & Ullman, *Principles of Compiler Design* © copyright 1977, Addison-Wesley Publishing Company, Inc., Reading, Massachusetts, reprinted with permission.

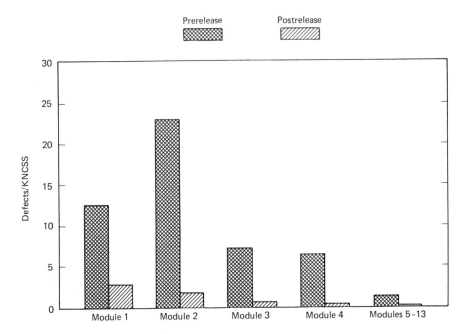

Figure 8-8   Defect analysis by code module.

that over half of the design defects actually occurred during redesigns. This analysis led to introduction of review mechanisms whenever redesign occurs.

Defects at HP are typically further broken down into severity levels of low, medium, serious, and critical. Severity levels are a measure of customer dissatisfaction, and quantities are tracked to measure responsiveness. One of the graphs produced monthly from the STARS postrelease defect data for each division shows the trend of serious and critical defects by product line. Severity data weighs heavily in the establishment of priorities. Setting priorities must take into account the number of problems to be solved, the number of modules to be affected, and the estimated time it will take to fix the problems. As a result, defects of low and medium severity are sometimes fixed at the same time as critical or serious defects, because the same code is affected.

8.3 HELP WITH PRESENTATION AND ANALYSIS

Once methods were established to collect data, the need for simple, consistent analysis tools became apparent. Data produced in a variety of locations and forms needed to be presented in a form which would allow appropriate analysis and decision making.

Tabular reports were easily produced, but a graphic representation was clearly more useful in efficient analysis. While tools existed which produced graphic output, the task of taking data from various sources and then creating graphs from scratch required more effort than most project managers could afford. A tool was developed to produce useful graphs from a minimal, standard set of data. This tool, PM2L (Project Management Metrics Tool), was an interface template to a commercially available spreadsheet. Data is usually entered into PM2L and graphed weekly. A second tool was created to facilitate analysis of project completion metrics. This tool, SMDB (Software Metrics Database), is discussed in detail in Chapter 10.

8.3.1 Graphs Which Help Prior to Implementation

We have stated that code size is the biggest cost driver in most estimating models. This implies that early in the life of a project, detailed analysis must occur which allows accurate prediction of code size. Once this prediction is made, the project schedule can be evaluated against the average code volume productivities shown in Figure 8-9, which are taken from the HP Software Metrics Database. (A more detailed discussion of historical data is presented in Chapter 10.) Note that projects in the database reported as "reused" consisted of greater than 75 percent reused code.

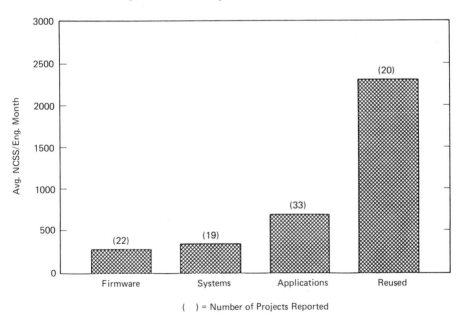

Figure 8-9   HP code volume by application class.

Historical defect density data can also help in estimating the number and type of defects to expect. This knowledge leads to better test planning and effort allocation to the testing process.

The graph illustrated in Figure 8-10 from the HP Software Metrics Database shows defect densities reported for different development software types.

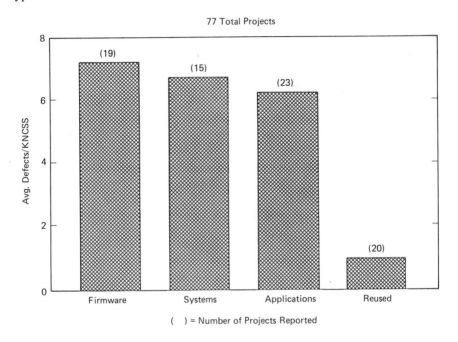

Figure 8-10 HP prerelease discovered defect density by application class.

Finally, the average times in engineering hours for the major development phases can be examined at each checkpoint during a project as a general comparison to estimates. These are shown in Figure 8-11.

8.3.2 Graphs Which Help During Implementation

Just as there are three graphs of immediate value prior to implementation which correspond to the three categories of primary metrics, there are three graphs produced by PM2L which help project managers to monitor the same categories of code, defects, and engineering time. With or without this tool, it is easy to plot these graphs weekly, and they provide a great deal of information. Examples are shown in Figures 8-12, 8-13, and 8-14. Figures 8-12 and 8-14 contain sample data, while Figure 8-13 is from an actual project.

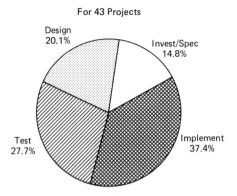

Figure 8-11   Percentage of engineering hours by phase.

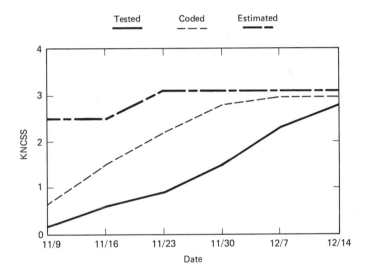

Figure 8-12   Project code status.

Of course, there are other ways of looking at this information, and the advantage of having data in a general-purpose spread sheet is that it can easily be manipulated and viewed in different ways. PM2L has 22 predefined graphs separated into categories of code, defect status, administrative, quality investment, and project closure statistics.

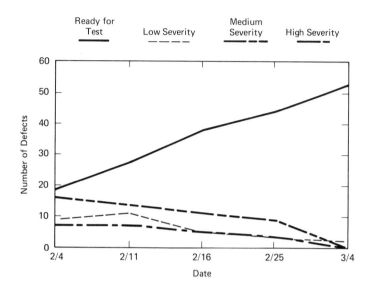

Figure 8-13   Prerelease defect resolution.

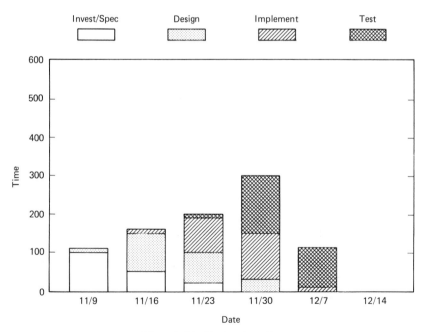

Figure 8-14   Engineering effort.

8.3.3 Graphs Which Help after Release

The third general category for graphic presentation of data is that of postrelease project data. Many of the same graphs which are useful to project managers prerelease are also useful postrelease. Several which are of particular interest in characterizing the finding and fixing aspects of the maintenance and enhancement process include resolution of defects by week, time to fix defects, and reported average defects per day of a product. Examples of these are shown in Figures 8-15, 8-16, and 8-17. They are all data from an actual project.

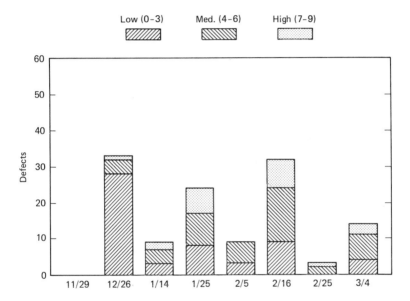

Figure 8-15   Resolution of defects (since previous report).

At the lab level, the first thing done with each weekly report was to compare the current data with that of the previous week. Were we resolving the most important (to our customers) defects? Figure 8-15 is a graphic representation of one project's defect resolution data. It shows that when the data was first examined (in December), a large number of defects were resolved. The problem was that the vast majority of the defects were considered to be of low severity by the customer base. After this trend was pointed out to the project team, you can see that the balance quickly shifted to resolving the defects considered highest severity. This data, along with the data illustrated in Figure 8-13, presents a very powerful picture of what is happening.

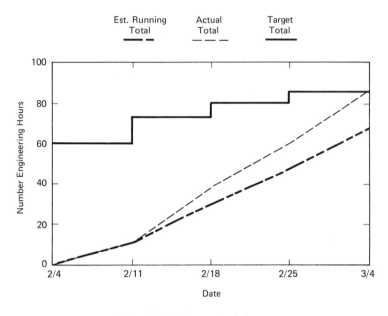

Figure 8-16   Time to fix defects.

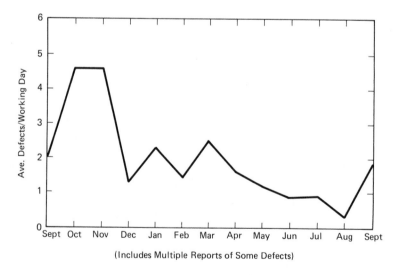

Figure 8-17   Postrelease defect stability.

How well could we predict when we would be finished with the next release? Figure 8-16 shows one technique for tracking and revising estimates that the project team used. The target total represents the estimated total investment in engineering hours, revised each week as the amount of time to fix defects became more accurately known. The estimated running total was the original estimate only. The key to using this technique successfully was that the engineers chose to keep very accurate records of their time to reflect how much real time was available for actually fixing defects each week. How stable was the product, and how many more defects could we expect before we completed the current release? Figure 8-17 illustrates the pattern of defects after release. After initial product usage began, defect reports increased for a period of time until a known backlog of the most frequently encountered defects was established. Defect reports then decreased and stabilized (more or less) to a constant rate until a new product release occurred. The Software Metrics Council jokingly named this pattern "the hump phenomenon" because of the initial hump shape. Many council members have observed this pattern of reported defects after release of a product.

8.4 CONCLUSION

Successful integration of collection and use of software metrics into the software development process is our main objective. When the tools which provide for automatic collection of some data, simplified manual collection of other data, and flexible analysis of all data are available, that objective can be met. A common complaint is that the whole collection process should be automated, leaving only the results to be analyzed. However, there is a positive aspect in doing manual data collecting. It gives the manager a detailed awareness of the data and its significance. Forms and questionnaires expedite the manual processes. Also, automation too early may "freeze" useless measures into the project process. Some experimentation is always needed at first.

Now we are entering our second generation of software metrics with a better understanding of the tools necessary to support managers and engineers who need the data. In this chapter we have discussed these tools and examples of the data collected and presented. Our measurements have shown us where to make positive changes to our development processes. The time factor in learning these new methods has been the primary obstacle in the way of their implementation. What is to be measured? How is it to be measured? And how much time is needed weekly to do the data collection? The answers to these questions are critical for managers and engineers. As long as there are tools and training which minimize the time it takes, more groups will continue to measure, and through measurements, manage projects more effectively.

BIBLIOGRAPHY

1. DeMarco, T., *Controlling Software Projects.* New York: Yourdon Press, 1982, pp. 90, 144. Reprinted by permission of Prentice-Hall, Inc., Englewood Cliffs, New Jersey.

2. Blair, S., "A Defect Tracking System for the UNIX Environment," *HP Journal,* Vol. 37, no. 3 (March 1986).

3. *Defect Tracking System Users Manual,* Hewlett-Packard (Feb. 1986).

4. Tausworthe, R., "Software Specifications Document, DSN Software Cost Model," Jet Propulsion Laboratory, Pasadena, Calif., 1981.

5. Boehm, B., *Software Engineering Economics.* Englewood Cliffs, N. J.: Prentice-Hall, Inc., 1981.

6. Albrecht A. and J. Gaffney, "Software Function, Source Lines of Code, and Development Effort Prediction: A Software Science Validation," *IEEE Transactions on Software Engineering,* Vol. SE-9, no. 6, (Nov. 1983).

7. Aho, A. and J. Ullman, *Principles of Compiler Design.* Reading, Mass.: Addison Wesley, 1977, p. 53.

8. Juran, J., F. Gryna Jr., and R. Bingham Jr., *Quality Control Handbook, 3rd ed.* New York:McGraw Hill, 1974, pp. 2-16 - 2-19.

9

SOME EARLY SUCCESSES

We have discussed many of the elements which contribute to the framework of a software metrics program. In the last chapter, we briefly touched upon various measurements and methods to apply them to managing projects. In this chapter we describe ambitious efforts at three different divisions to categorize defects and eliminate the underlying causes of the defects from the development process. All three of these results were accomplished within a year after HP's original metrics were defined, and they established the foundation for similar efforts in other divisions.

9.1 DEFECTS AFTER PRODUCT RELEASE

The final test of a product's worth is measured by customer satisfaction. This can be characterized in a number of ways, but one early method, which was established at HP in 1979, was to methodically record and analyze reports of defects and enhancement requests from customers. A customer with a software problem contacts the field service organization, which verifies that the problem is indeed a defect. The field submits a service request to the factory via a system called STARS (Software Tracking And Reporting System). The service request includes an indication of the severity of the problem from the customer's point of view.

In the factory, the marketing organization assigns a priority to fixing it.

Next, the lab diagnoses the problem. Diagnosing and fixing the problem are two distinct steps which might be separated in time. After a fix is produced, it must be integrated into a product update and tested before it is released to customers.

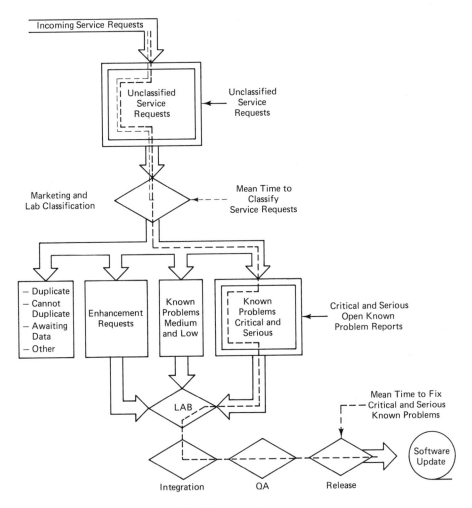

Figure 9-1   Software maintenance process.

Each month, a support division publishes graphs by product line, showing the number of defects reported but not diagnosed, the average amount of time a defect waits to be diagnosed, the number of unresolved defects of critical and serious severity, and the mean time to fix a critical or serious defect (Figure 9-1). The monthly reports give a written analysis of trends indicated by the graphs. Their intent is to raise awareness of the

amount of time it takes to get a software problem resolved from the customer's point of view. They also attempt to give information about the responsiveness of the factory maintenance teams.

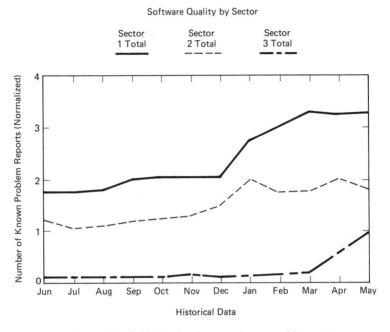

Figure 9-2   Critical and serious open known problem reports.

Figures 9-2 and 9-3 illustrate two examples of monthly graphs for three
of HP's business sectors. A business sector is a set of product divisions
grouped on a convenient basis around divisions dealing with a common market
and related technical product solutions.

Because postrelease data is so sensitive to potential misinterpretation,
these graphs have been normalized so that the actual number of problem
reports and days to fix critical and serious defects are not shown, and the
graphs selected are also not the most recent HP trends. From these kinds of
graphs, though, we can gain some valuable insights into how graphs are used
to manage software quality at a high level.

Historically, the critical and serious open known problems have tended
to continually increase *even though the quality of our products has been
improving.* This is because HP's growth in both the businesses directly related
to software production and in its percentage of product which is software-
related have continuously increased at a high rate for the past ten years or
more. Our emphasis on the importance of controlling this key measure of customer satisfaction is an important element of our long-term success.

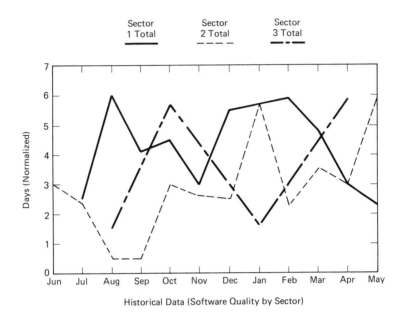

Historical Data (Software Quality by Sector)

Figure 9-3   Mean time to fix critical and serious known problems.

Figure 9-3 illustrates that the mean time to fix critical and serious known problems fluctuates a great deal more than the rate of incoming reports. This fluctuation is largely caused by the gathering of groups of defects into consolidated major updates of a product for distribution to a large customer base. It is not practical to update major products more frequently. Instead, temporary workarounds to critical defects are achieved by the field organization working with customers. (This responsiveness is also tracked as a company-wide metric.)

These graphs have been very successful at focusing top management's attention on the customer satisfaction issue. Since managers know that every month the whole company will know their maintenance status, they make an effort to bring their defect backlog under control.

9.2 PROCESS IMPROVEMENTS

One of the most important results of the use of standard software metrics was that many divisions initiated more detailed analysis of metrics which looked significant. The results of these more detailed studies provided leverage to other groups to extend them in ways appropriate to their own development needs. The remainder of this chapter reviews some of these studies, including how they have led to better understanding of the tasks being done and how long the tasks should take.

9.2.1 An Example of Statistical Quality Control

One experiment, which actually began before the definition of the standard HP metrics, applied the techniques of statistical quality control (SQC) which HP has used effectively for several years in manufacturing areas. This entity believed that by focusing on defect analysis, the causes of the defects could be discovered and permanently removed.

The software studied in this case was a series of applications packages designed for internal company use in support of purchasing and vendor analysis. These types of packages are ultimately implemented in over fifty divisions which operate in a relatively consistent fashion, so development of such systems is typically done in partnership with several divisions. A prototyping approach was chosen to maximize the feedback from the customer divisions and to avoid past problems in achieving agreement on specifications. It was also believed that analysis of defects which appeared in each prototype could lead to elimination of those defects in subsequent prototypes.

The first step was to prepare a list of defects which represented the actual defects that they had encountered in the past. Figure 9-4 shows that they grouped defects into three principal categories [1]. It is important to note that these definitions and categories are relatively unique to this particular type of application and development environment.

A Pareto analysis was then done to identify the most frequently occurring defects. In this case over one-third of the defects corresponded to categories A7, A2, and A1 from Figure 9-4. A complete defect distribution is shown in Figure 9-5. The probable causes of these defects were then determined by using SQC, and changes were instituted into the development process.

A second series of software was completed by using the modified prototyping development process. As was desired, the results showed that instead of these major defect categories appearing after release to the internal customers, they now appeared much earlier in the process during the several prototyping stages. In fact, categories A2 and A7 accounted for over fifty percent of the prerelease defects recorded.

The final measure of success at reducing the number of A-category defects was that during postrelease, A-category defects accounted for only 40 percent of the defects, as opposed to 65 percent during the first software series.

Categories of Software Defects
A.   User Interface/Interaction
1. User needs additional data fields
2. Existing data needs to be organized/presented differently
3. Edits on data values are too restrictive
4. Edits on data values are too loose
5. Inadequate system controls or audit trails
6. Unclear instructions or responses
7. New function or different processing required
B.   Programming Defect
1. Data incorrectly or inconsistently defined
2. Initialization problems
3. Database processing incorrect
4. Screen processing incorrect
5. Incorrect language instruction
6. Incorrect parameter passing
7. Unanticipated error condition
8. Operating system file handling incorrect
9. Incorrect program control flow
10. Incorrect processing logic or algorithm
11. Processing requirement overlooked or not defined
12. Changes required to conform to standards
C.   Operating Environment
1. Terminal differences
2. Printer differences
3. Different versions of systems software
4. Incorrect JCL
5. Incorrect account structure or capabilities
6. Unforeseen local system requirements
7. Prototyping language problem

Figure 9-4 Categories of software defects.

9.2.2 Unraveling Development Process Problems

Another division produces systems software used to develop firmware applications. They have a large team of software developers with projects of varying size which primarily fall into operating system and compiler software, but also include firmware and applications. Their measured productivity for nine projects was 1612 NCSS/Engineering Month, which they felt was quite respectable, but they felt that their ability to predict project completions was poor and that they really didn't have good understanding or control over defects in their process. Their prerelease defect densities had varied from 0.4 to 6 defects/1000 NCSS. (Note that any defect rate is entirely dependent upon how a given organization defines defects. Our early experience shows

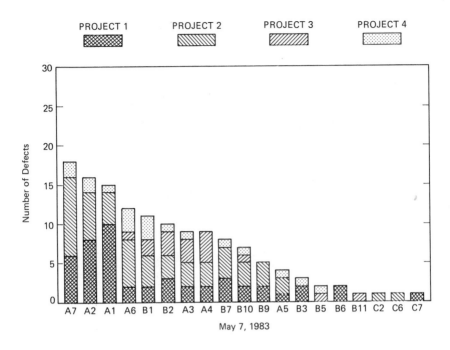

Figure 9-5   Pareto analysis of software defects.

variation of up to a factor of 45 in defect density among different entities, depending upon how defects are defined and recorded.)

Early in the software metrics program, their metrics council representative plotted the ratio of actual development effort versus predicted effort. It showed that, despite their high productivity, their ability to accurately estimate project completion was consistently off by a factor of around two. This simple analysis showed that their process was actually more predictable than they had realized, so they decided to focus on understanding the sources of defects they were experiencing better.

As emphasized earlier, the first step in process improvement is understanding. By focusing heavily on defect analysis, they felt they had the best chance of understanding and improving their process. They used techniques similar to those described for the previous division. Figure 9-6 shows categorization of defects for one of their development areas — a group which developed compilers [2]. Unlike the applications environment discussed earlier where the primary source of defects was in the user interface specifications, we see that this group found its major source of defects was the design process. Figure 9-7 shows a further breakdown of just the category of detailed design defects [2]. Since this category represented almost half of the total defects recorded, they felt that it was worthwhile taking the effort to trace the root causes of these defects.

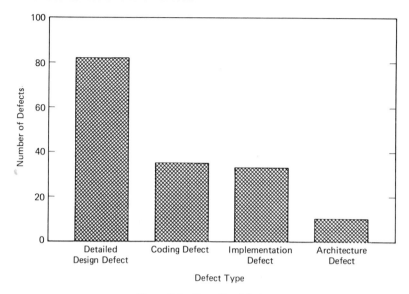

Figure 9-6   Compiler defects.

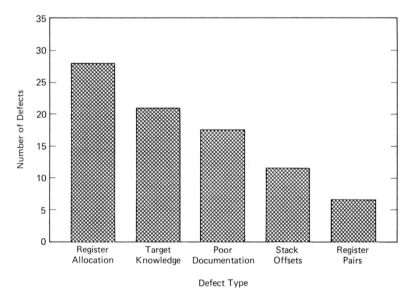

Figure 9-7   Compiler design defects.

An additional tool which was used to identify problem causes was the Ishikawa or "fishbone" diagram [3]. An analysis of the largest design defect category (seen in Figure 9-7), register allocation defects, is illustrated in Figure 9-8 [2]. These diagrams are helpful in brainstorming problems. The primary horizontal line represents the quality factor under examination. The "ribs of the fish" are diagonal lines pointing to the primary line, which are typically broken into materials, workers, tools, and inspection. If any of these major categories contribute to the effect labeled on the primary horizontal line, additional ribs are added to describe the causes. In the example of Figure 9-8 there are two primary causes — side effects of register usage and incorrect register usage. Ultimately both are caused by incomplete knowledge of the operation of the registers. Knowing this incomplete knowledge to be the cause of so many defects allowed this division to take aggressive steps to provide proper training and documentation regarding registers and processors prior to subsequent projects.

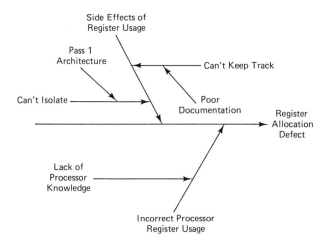

Figure 9-8   Cause/effect diagram.

One of the most interesting results discovered while measuring defects in this project, as well as several others, was that *over half of the reported errors occurred during redesigns*. During redesigns they typically did not have formal review mechanisms in place to ensure quality. These measurements, of course, led to the introduction of reviews.

9.2.3 Predicting the Testing Process

A third division develops firmware used in communications applications. Their projects are typically short (less than six months), but the type of application and the number of installations is such that the final quality of their product is very critical. Because their products are quite similar to one another and their development cycle short, they were able to characterize parts of their process in less than a year. They determined that their average coding rate was 670 NCSS/programmer month and that their average prerelease defect density was 9.6 defects/1000 NCSS. Using these averages, they were able to make their process more predictable.

They focused their attention particularly on the testing cycle. Using the model defined in Figure 9-9 by Henry Kohoutek of HP [4], they started predicting how long the testing phase should take as well as recording and categorizing defects in detail. This model was established with actual data from a similar product line.

Defect Discovery Schedule
25% of defects are found & fixed in 2 hours/defect (rate of .50 defect/hour)
50% of defects are found & fixed in 5 hours/defect (rate of .20 defect/hour)
20% of defects are found & fixed in 10 hours/defect (rate of .10 defect/hour)
4% of defects are found & fixed in 20 hours/defect (rate of .05 defect/hour)
1% of defects are found & fixed in 50 hours/defect (rate of .02 defect/hour)

Figure 9-9 Defect discovery schedule.

In order to use the model, the project team took the total code size (which was accurately known when the test phase was entered) and multiplied it times the expected defect density. This yielded the total defects expected. Using the model, the team calculated directly the total time necessary to discover *all* of the defects. The available staffing was then applied to the total time to predict the schedule.

Figure 9-10 shows the predictive model of a particular project and the actual rate of defect discovery and resolution [5]. In this example, the amount of testing required to achieve a desired level of quality was predicted reasonably well. They used the concept of a "calculated stop point" to estimate when testing could be expected to be complete. The actual decision of when to stop testing was based on testing for a predefined number of hours without discovering any defects, as well as spending a minimum of two weeks below the calculated stop point.

The calculated stop point is a defect rate below which the project is willing to stop testing. Determining this rate involves considering the cost to find and fix a defect prerelease versus postrelease. Notice that the concept of a

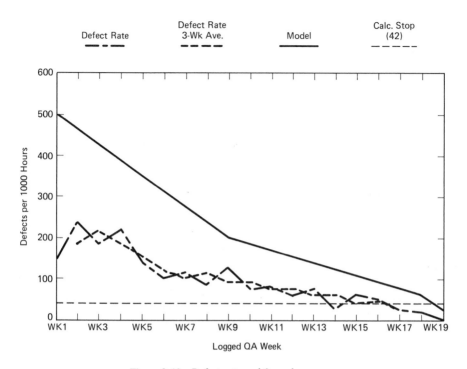

Figure 9-10   Defect rate and 3–week average.

stop point is used to determine the most cost effective amount of testing; it does not aim at zero defects in all cases. In the example shown, the calculated stop point of 42 represents the reciprocal of the number of hours of defect-free testing that has been spent *after the "last" defect has been found* (that is, in addition to the hours defined in the model in Figure 9-9) [6].

In addition to predicting and monitoring defects during the testing process, this division also made an effort to categorize the defects by severity to use as an aid in project tracking. They used three categories of software defect severity: minor, serious, and major. They also had a category for hardware defects. Displaying discovered defects in the form of a stacked bar chart (Figure 9-11 shows defects for the same project displayed by Figure 9-10) on a weekly basis then shows not only the downward trend of defects toward project completion, but also flags the presence of a major problem which occurred in week 13 [5].

Figures 9-12 and 9-13 show a breakdown of defects by project phase and classification for the first dozen projects reported by this division [6]. Again, we see that the predominant causes of defects are different from the two environments discussed earlier. This division found that their major source of defects was in the primary category of implementation, and that

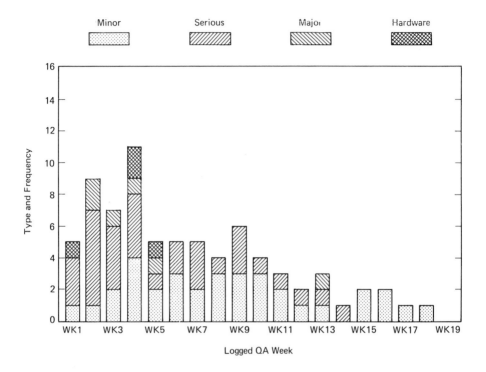

Figure 9-11   Defects.

within that category, over forty percent of the defects were in the implementation of algorithms. These measurements and analyses have not only made their process more predictable, but they have pointed out the primary areas where effort can be focused to improve the process.

As was pointed out earlier, it can be seen from all three examples that the detailed definition of defects was not consistent from division to division, yet in each case significant understanding and progress was made in eliminating the causes of defects from the development process.

Using the Kohoutek model to predict testing time and effort necessary, this division is routinely predicting the testing phase within ten percent of the actual times. For three products which have been released long enough for conclusions to be accurately drawn, they have seen a total of only one defect after this testing process has been completed.

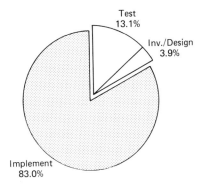

Defects by Project Phase

Figure 9-12   Software defect summary.

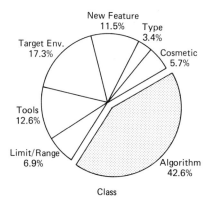

Class

Figure 9-13   Classes of defects in implementation.

9.3 CONCLUSION

We have seen that for three different software development environments, the
primary defect categories were significantly different. The techniques for identifying defects involved discipline in recording defects during the software
development process. Once the primary defect categories were identified, procedures were established to discover many of these defects much earlier in the
development process.

We presented several tools used to evaluate and analyze defects during
the development process. The use of Pareto analysis was valuable for priori-
tizing problem solving. Ishikawa diagrams were useful in brainstorming the

causes of problems. Finally, the Kohoutek defect discovery model has proved promising in predicting how long the testing process should take and in helping to determine when it is complete.

All three of these cases occurred during the first year after the formation of HP's Software Metrics Council. They all sought and achieved fundamental changes which improved their software development processes. The techniques they used were powerful, but not excessively time-consuming, and sharing these successes with other divisions early in our metrics program inspired other groups to make similar measurements of their own.

BIBLIOGRAPHY

1. Sieloff, C., "Software TQC: Improving the Software Development Process Through Statistical Quality Control," *Software Productivity Conference Proceedings* (April 1984), pp. 2-56–2-57.

2. Hamilton, G., Presentation to Second Annual HP Software Metrics Conference (August 1984).

3. Ishikawa, K., *Guide to Quality Control*. Tokyo: Asian Productivity Organization, 1976, pp. 18–28.

4. Kohoutek, H., "A Practical Approach to Software Reliability Management," 29th EOQC Conference on Quality and Development, Estoril, Portugal (June 1985), p. 216.

5. Kenyon, D., Presentation to Second Annual HP Software Metrics Conference (August 1984).

6. Kenyon, D., "Implementing a Software Metrics Program," *HP Software Productivity Conference Proceedings* (April 1985), pp. 1-110, 1-112–1-113.

10

A COMPANY-WIDE DATABASE

From the very beginning of the software metrics program, it was clear that data analysis would occur at two levels. At the project management level, data is useful for tracking and controlling software development. Beyond the project level, data provides useful feedback for entire labs, as well as providing valuable benchmarks from similar developments. A company-wide database of the metrics data to facilitate these two levels of analysis was identified as a necessity at the first metrics meeting. In this section, we will discuss two approaches to such a database which were tried, and we will examine some of the early data to understand its usefulness.

10.1 AN INITIAL SOFTWARE METRICS DATABASE

Our first attempt at a company-wide metrics database used a network database manager on a multiuser system. This had the advantage of needing only one copy and the potential of allowing project managers to dial up this central database for inspection. Data entry forms were created which looked very much like the paper forms designed by the metrics council. The biggest problem with this approach was the inflexibility inherent in a network database. First, we knew that the metrics were likely to change, which meant that every time they changed we would need to create a new schema and reorganize the database. This is much more easily accomplished by using a relational database. Also, we needed the flexibility to create relations from any set of data items. We were not able to predict well enough which relationships existed so as to be able to encode them into the schema of a network database.

10.1.1 Priming the Pump

The first data sent to us for inclusion in the database was historical data collected after product release based on whatever records were kept and the project manager's memory of what happened. Gathering the data in this way tested out the standard definitions to see if they were understandable and feasible. With this first set of relatively inaccurate data we were also able to test out the first version of the database schema.

At first we used one data item for size for each language. For example, there was space allocated for Assembly NCSS, Pascal NCSS, C NCSS, SPL NCSS, COBOL NCSS, and Other. Since one project might have components written in different languages, we needed space to record the size of each component and its language. The problems we encountered with this schema were as follows:

1. The data was sparse, so space was wasted.
2. There were several other languages being used (for example, SALT, Fortran, Transact). Putting data in the "Other" column lost the language name, which defeated the purpose of naming the data by language.

10.2 THE NEXT ATTEMPT

A second approach used a commercial spreadsheet for storing the data. Several different software packages were evaluated before the most suitable one was selected. The advantages of using the spreadsheet we chose were

1. The worksheet schema was easy to modify.
2. Totals were automatically generated.
3. Graphics were created easily and produced quickly.
4. The spreadsheet software was readily available to us and the project managers around the company.
5. It was easy to use.

The disadvantages included:

1. There would be difficulty in integrating with metrics collection tools — no programmatic interface.

2. It ran on single-user personal computers, and it was difficult to update and distribute copies of the data other than by manual means.
3. The amount of data that it could record was limited by the memory capacity of the machines on which it ran.

Even so, it satisfied our growing need for relatively convenient dissemination of data much better than the initial database. Since most project managers had some knowledge of spreadsheets, it required minimal training. This product, the Software Metrics Database (SMDB), is the basis for the remainder of the discussion in this chapter.

Each column of the spreadsheet corresponds to a data item required on the HP software metrics forms. Each row represents data from one project. Figure 10-1 shows the basic spreadsheet organization. Many of the columns shown actually represent multiple columns in the real spreadsheet. For example, there are four columns under cost in months which correspond to investigation/ specification, design, implementation, and test.

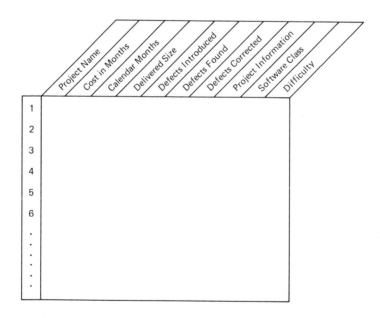

Figure 10-1   Organization of the spreadsheet of company-wide data.

We changed the schema so that there was just one column for delivered size (NCSS) and one column for language name (contained in project information). This worked fine for single-language projects. For multilanguage projects we decided to report the language which composed more than 75 percent of the NCSS or the word "mixture" if no one language dominated. We discovered that not much information is lost this way, because defects and effort are not reported per language. Therefore, you cannot conclude anything about each language in a multilanguage project anyway.

After the first wave of historical data was submitted, the project managers who had sent historical data began collecting data on their current projects and proceeded to send this data to us at release. Within a year, many projects all over the company were collecting data. This led to further enhancements to the database and wider distribution and use.

10.2.1 Distribution Issues

One of the first issues that arose when we were deciding to widely distribute the raw data was, what level of anonymity is necessary so that project members feel comfortable having the data distributed company-wide? Must project names and manager names be erased from the distributed version? Removing the project manager name eliminates an important potential use of the database, which is the ability to call the owner of the data directly with questions. The potential use for putting people with common projects in touch with each other would be lost. However, leaving the names in might discourage sending data in by those who fear negative judgment from the rest of the users. With the names in the database it is very easy to forget that we are evaluating process, not people. We decided to let each submitter indicate whether or not their name or the project name should be distributed. The result is that 95 percent of the project names and 80 percent of the project manager names are currently in the database.

A related issue was security. How do we keep this data internal to HP? We weren't concerned about the anonymous data such as the graphs in this book. The problem was if defect densities are matched to project names, it could be misinterpreted or used out of context by other companies. We decided that it was still desirable to keep the project names. First, we felt that we couldn't become too paranoid over the use of the database, or we would defeat the primary purpose of it, namely, to internally share information. Second, most project names are unrelated to product names, which insures some security. Finally, we felt that the feedback which project teams got in seeing their own project in the database outweighed the minimal risks involved.

Another major distribution issue was the medium of transmission. We found that by uploading the spreadsheet from HP's personal computer to HP's minicomputer, we could send it anywhere in the company via our electronic mail network. The mail packet contained instructions on how to download the spreadsheet to the personal computer at the receiving site. Two interesting problems occurred with this approach. The database is large enough that the first time we did a mass electronic distribution, we virtually choked the company electronic mail system. We now limit the number of copies we ship during any interval of time. Second, project managers seem to strongly prefer to receive a physical copy of the database instead of an electronic one. They get around to using it more quickly, and given the choice of ordering one or the other, they have responded more favorably to the physical copy (a floppy disk).

The last major distribution issue was to whom should we send the database and how often should they be updated? In order to encourage the continued reporting of project data, the following decisions were reached. Each submitter can expect to receive an updated spreadsheet with their new data included within one week of the time we receive the data. The Software Metrics Council and the divisional productivity managers receive quarterly distributions. We ask others who want a copy of the database to tell us what project they are working on and tell us the date when they will send us the data from the completed project. All users receive updates on a three-month release cycle.

10.3 USING THE DATABASE AT THE PROJECT LEVEL

10.3.1 Providing Historical Checks

Many of the graphs commonly used for prediction are built into the HP-wide database. Using the database for prediction involves examining data from similar projects to the one being started or to one which is in progress. For example, suppose that you are interested in all the information that you can find about applications projects. There are several graphs which provide an overview of data for each software type. Figure 10-2 shows productivity of all the applications projects sorted by month of completion, and Figure 10-3 shows the defect density of the same projects during testing.

Notice that there are fewer projects represented with defect data than with productivity data. We have generally included projects in the database, even when some of the data was missing or suspicious. There are two reasons for this. First, we can see from Figures 10-2 and 10-3 that with eighteen projects of programmer output data, we can feel relatively comfortable with project estimates corresponding to 400–600 NCSS/engineering month even though we cannot feel comfortable with any such generalization for defect density.

Second, data was frequently missing from the projects initially reported to the database when the metrics program began. In the particular case of defect density, it has been reported for the last 30 projects submitted. There are still occasional fields which are not reported, but such cases primarily occur when projects or divisions first get involved in collecting data. We generally try to include the data in order to encourage people to continue collecting on subsequent projects. Incomplete projects are excluded when calculating averages and trends for graphs in cases where distortion would occur.

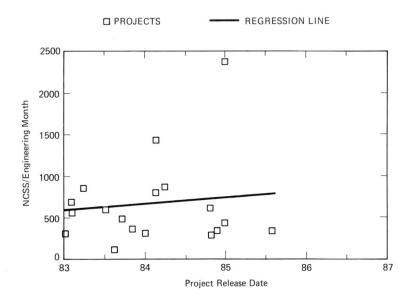

Figure 10-2   Programmer output for applications.

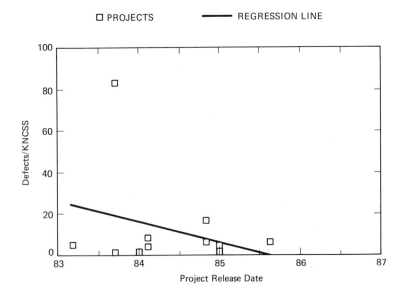

Figure 10-3   Defect densities for applications.

There are two other graphs for each software class which show programmer output and defect densities sorted by increasing programmer productivity. These are illustrated in Figures 10-4 and 10-5 for the software class of firmware. Each point in Figure 10-5 corresponds to the one above in Figure 10-4. The one project which shows very high productivity compared to the others involved greater than 75 percent reused code.

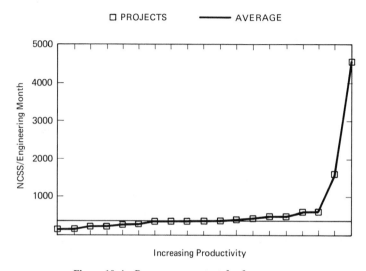

Figure 10-4   Programmer output for firmware.

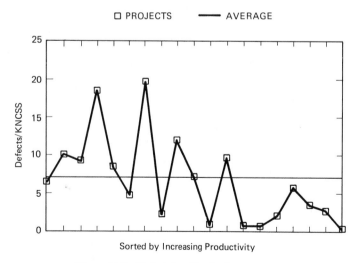

Figure 10-5   Defect densities for firmware.

These two graphs aren't as directly useful as the previous two, but they do show two facts of continuing interest. First, projects of highest productivity are among those with the lowest defect densities. In the examples shown, the seven most productive projects have defect densities below the average, and seven of the ten least productive projects have defect densities above the average. Second, these graphs give the average productivity and average defect density for the particular class of interest. These numbers are very useful for project managers who wish to compare their project estimates to gross averages of other projects of a similar type.

10.3.2 Using the Database to Double Check an Estimate

Having presented an overview of the data contained in the HP-wide database, it might be useful to see how this data can be applied to a specific project. Let us state right up front that *it is not our intention that SMDB be used in HP as the primary source of project estimates for software projects.* We do expect it to be useful as a check upon estimates derived by other means, and the data that it contains is extremely useful for calibrating estimating models against HP project types.

All commercial estimating models are based upon historical data. The trouble for any company is that most of them are not calibrated to their particular environment. In the following example, we show how access to detailed project histories provides an important check against estimates produced by automated models or seat-of-the-pants guesses.

Let us take an example of a firmware project, say an instrument which is a microprocessor-driven version of an older model. Suppose that we have seen similar instruments at other divisions take 30 KNCSS of assembly code and that we have 3½ trained engineers available to implement the firmware. What can we say about such a project? From Figure 10-4, the average productivity of firmware projects is around 400 NCSS/engineering month, and Figure 10-5 says that the average defect density is around 6.5 defects/KNCSS. From one other graph readily produced from the HP-wide database, we know the average time in the various project phases for firmware. With only this data, we can make the first approximations shown in Figure 10-6.

That is all fairly useful information with very little effort. In order to get more accurate estimates, it is possible to examine the data in the HP-wide database in more detail to find projects of similar types, sizes, and languages. It is important to keep in mind, though, that most commercial estimation models are driven from many factors besides the few presented here. Barry Boehm's Cocomo model (refer to Chapter 4), for example, has fourteen primary "cost drivers" like execution time constraints, storage constraints, team experience, and other factors which are not apparent in the HP-wide

A Project Estimate	
1. Engineering months = 75	(30 KNCSS/400 NCSS/EM)
Investigation = 11	(15% of 75)
Design = 17.5	(23.1% of 75)
Coding = 29	(38.8% of 75)
Test = 17.5	(23.1% of 75)
2. Calendar months = 21.4	(75 EM/3.5 E)
3. Total defects in test = 195	(6.5 Def/KNCSS * 30 KNCSS)

Figure 10-6   A project estimate.

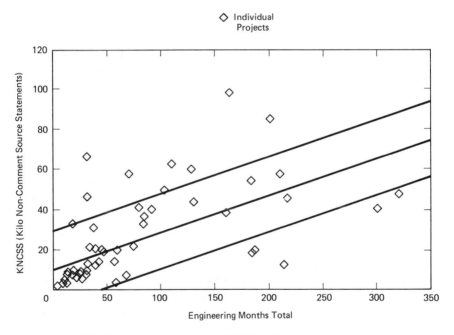

Figure 10-7   Engineering months vs. KNCSS (50 projects, excluding reused software).

database. Even when these models are used, it is useful to double-check results against similar projects catalogued in the HP-wide database. Figures 10-7 and 10-8 show scattergram representations for NCSS versus engineering months (excluding reused software projects) and defect density for all HP data. The scattergram form demonstrates the variations you would expect due to the various cost drivers. The three lines shown in Figure 10-7 represent a linear regression (best fit) for the set of points and the standard deviation. (68 percent of the points fall within the range of the standard deviation.)

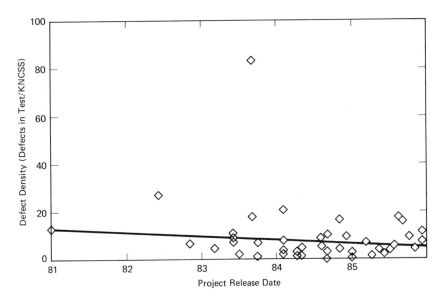

Figure 10-8   Release date vs. defect density (42 projects).

Seeing this kind of distribution, we should be somewhat nervous about the estimate derived above. Is there any way to make it more accurate? Just as the calculations derived above are more accurate by basing them on HP firmware projects only than by basing them on all of the HP data, it should also be possible to examine the database even more closely to find other sources of potential inaccuracies for the case at hand. Figure 10-9 shows the results of a database query for firmware projects with nonzero data for engineering months, calendar months, NCSS, and defect density. The data is sorted by language first and by increasing size second to facilitate looking at projects written in the language of the desired size. At this stage, we are still assuming that the project must be written in assembly language.

Looking at all projects, we first see that the average productivity rate is strongly influenced by one recycled software project. In fact, without it the programmer output average drops to around 400 NCSS/engineering month, which was the estimate we used earlier. The average for just the assembly language projects is slightly higher, but again this average is strongly driven by one project, which reported 1560 NCSS/Engineering Month. On the other hand, these averages assume that each project is the same size. When the NCSS figures for the assembly projects are added together and divided by the engineering month total for assembly, the average output drops to 300

A Database Query for Firmware						
Project Name	EM Total	CM Total	NCSS	Primary Lang	Def Den	Prog Output
PROJ #1	8	5	3000	ASB	0.67	375.0
PROJ #2	57	24	3200	ASB	6.25	56.1
PROJ #3	68	54	7000	ASB	8.57	102.9
PROJ #4	24	24	8818	ASB	10.32	375.2
PROJ #5	38	15.75	11900	ASB	12.77	313.2
PROJ #6	38	7	20000	ASB	0.45	526.3
PROJ #7	300	51	40000	ASB	17.50	133.3
PROJ #8	30	9	46800	ASB	3.76	1560.0
PROJ #9	110	28	63000	ASB	6.14	572.7
PROJ #10	26	18	4955	MAC	8.27	190.6
PROJ #11	12	10	6888	MIX	4.65	574.0
PROJ #12	30	18	9347	MIX	2.25	311.6
PROJ #13	18	16	9414	MIX	2.55	537.9
PROJ #14	11	14	3011	PAS	4.65	286.8
PROJ #15	26	10	8251	PAS	7.15	317.3
PROJ #16	213	87	12121	PAS	10.31	56.9
PROJ #17	79	38	40911	PAS	0.61	517.9
PROJ #18	183	52	54150	PAS	20.22	295.9
PROJ #19	12	12	55000	RCY	0.09	4583.3
Totals	1282	492	407766		127	11687
Avg totals	67	26	21461		7	615
Asmb avgs	75	24	22635		7	446

Figure 10-9   A database query for firmware.

NCSS/ engineering month. It is probably wise to drop our assumed productivity down to this figure.

The defect densities of the projects seem to fit the 6.5 defects/KNCSS we assumed earlier, although we should be careful during the project to monitor their incoming rate carefully, since half of the assembly language projects exceeded 6.5 by a significant amount.

With a little more effort, then, we have the revised estimate shown in Figure 10-10. The fact that its results are so different from the first estimate illustrates that very little about a project is known at the early stages, and it is important to reestimate several times during all projects as more information is available. Having numbers in front of us helps to flag potential problem areas, like the potential for high variation in defect density. A phone call or two to the project managers of projects listed in the database might lead to helpful suggestions to avoid problems. Another potential problem we can see after these latest calculations is that our estimated calendar time of 28.6 months is substantially less than similar projects in the database. We want to emphasize that these estimates are also heavily dependent upon the initial code size estimate. Estimates of code size before design is complete are frequently highly inaccurate.

A Revised Project Estimate	
1. Engineering months = 100	(30 KNCSS/300 NCSS/EM)
Investigation = 15	(15% of 100)
Design = 23.1	(23.1% of 100)
Coding = 38.8	(38.8% of 100)
Test = 23.1	(23.1% of 100)
2. Calendar months = 28.6	(100 EM/3.5 E)
3. Total defects in test = 195	(6.5Def/KNCSS * 30 KNCSS)

Figure 10-10 A revised project estimate.

10.4 USING KNOWN DATA TO CHECK (AND POSSIBLY HELP DETERMINE) PROJECT ESTIMATES

We have stated that it is important to reestimate a project as it proceeds. If the data from the database is to be useful, the natural points to reestimate the calculations illustrated in Figure 10-10 are at the end of investigation/specification, at the end of design, and at the end of implementation. At these times, increasingly accurate estimates are possible, because we know more about the project.

It is interesting that all of the popular estimating models with which we are familiar continue to base estimates on size and fail to take advantage of two pieces of data which are always known at the end of each phase, namely, the elapsed engineering months invested and the elapsed calendar months. Let us explore this data without regard to NCSS to get a feel for how useful they are.

In Figure 10-11, we show the results of another database query which displays the engineering months for thirteen systems projects. For each of these projects we have determined the average engineering months spent in each of the phases and then calculated estimates as if the invested engineering months at the end of each phase were the only thing known. For example, take the engineering month total (1310) and divide it by the engineering month total for investigation/specification (218). Multiply this result (6.01)

Proj Name	EM Inv/ Spec	EM Design	EM Impl	EM Test	EM Total	Est 1	Est2	Est3	Abs Err1	Abs Err2	Abs Err3	EQF	Prog Output	Def Den
Proj #1	4	5	5	32	46	24	25	21	48	46	55	2	418.1	15.44
Proj #2	2	3	31	20	56	12	14	53	79	75	5	2	255.4	26.57
Proj #3	50	30	50	30	160	301	220	192	88	38	20	2	237.5	2.63
Proj #4	3	4	4	2	13	18	19	16	39	48	25	3	3461.5	0.44
Proj #5	0.5	2	6	1	9.5	3	7	13	68	28	32	3	3524.2	0.90
Proj #6	32	96	47	145	320	192	352	259	40	10	19	4	206.9	7.73
Proj #7	15.3	9.8	30.5	5.5	61	92	69	82	50	13	35	4	426.2	21.38
Proj #8	30	18	67	85	200	180	132	170	10	34	15	5	427.0	8.41
Proj #9	4.5	0	4.5	7	16	27	12	13	69	23	17	5	669.5	3.64
Proj #10	2	3	5	7	17	12	14	15	29	19	13	5	1941.2	2.03
Proj #11	20	32	53	23	128	120	143	155	6	12	21	8	472.8	8.71
Proj #12	13	22	14.25	25.25	74.5	78	96	73	5	29	2	11	292.2	6.38
Proj #13	42	34	93	40	209	252	209	250	21	0	20	11	276.7	3.49
Totals	218	259	410	423	1310	1312	1312	1313	551	374	279	65	12609	108
Avg totals	17	20	32	33	101	101	101	101	42	29	21	5	970	8

Figure 10-11 A database query and project estimates for systems software.

145

times the actual engineering months in investigation/specification for any given systems project to derive the first estimate (EST 1). Similarly, multipliers of 2.75 and 1.48 are determined by using design and implementation times for the second and third estimates (EST 2 and EST 3, respectively).

In addition to the estimates, Figure 10-11 shows the absolute errors for each of the three estimates. One of the criteria that experts agree is a good measure of estimating accuracy is if a model can accurately predict within 25 percent of the actual around 75 percent of the time [1,2].

The three estimates shown in Figure 10-11 perform surprisingly well, considering on what seemingly little data they are based. Estimate 1 occurs after investigation/specification is complete, or after 15 percent of the engineering investment for the average HP project. For the data in Figure 10-11, this estimate is within 25 percent of the actual 31 percent of the time. (It is interesting to note that the estimates for this category of systems are significantly lower than the overall average for the HP-wide database. The number of estimate 1's within 25 percent of the project actuals for the entire database were 18 out of 42, or 43 percent. It is quite likely that the lower average for Figure 10-11 is at least partly due to the limited number of data points available.)

As we progress to the third estimate, we see a steady improvement until the third estimate is within 25 percent of the actual almost 80 percent of the time (again, the entire database accuracy is 83 percent), and only three estimates are as much as 30 percent off.

Figure 10-12 illustrates a definition which Tom DeMarco has given for the overall accuracy of estimating [2]. He assumes that each project is estimated several times. The estimating quality factor (EQF) then is the ratio of the area in Figure 10-12 under the dotted line divided by the shaded area (thus, the higher the EQF the better, with ∞ being the best). This figure illustrates EQF for Project 6 of the thirteen projects from Figure 10-11. It had a short implementation phase relative to the other phases and an EQF of 4. The results for all thirteen are given in Figure 10-11. It is interesting to note that the average EQF is 5. DeMarco indicates that the average EQF for projects in one study he performed was 3.8. One HP division calculated project completions for eight projects at their division using the simple method described here and achieved an EQF of 10.39 [3].

It seems clear that the simple measurement of engineering time captures important information about a project. At HP, the project teams for most projects experience little turnover throughout a project. We can speculate that the reason these numbers seem somewhat useful is that they accurately capture data from at least several of the cost drivers of other models. Such variables as product complexity, team experience and capability, and required schedule all impact schedules relatively equally throughout development.

The significance of estimates 1 and 2 is that they are based on available information which is very easy to obtain, and that they provide

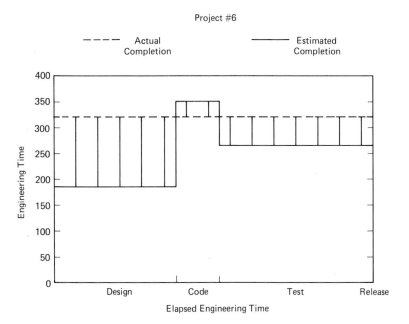

Figure 10-12   Estimating quality factor (EQF).

reasonable checks against size-driven estimation model results. Suppose, for example, that we complete the investigation/specification phase of our earlier firmware example and it took 19 engineering months instead of 15. By using the multiplier for firmware of 6.44, a new estimate of 122 engineering months is found. This, in turn, might imply that 36.6 KNCSS will be required instead of the original 30 KNCSS estimate, or it might imply a less than average team productivity. One possible use for this new information would be to take this new value for code and use it as an input to a size-driven estimation model. However it is used, keep in mind that, at this stage in a project, the standard deviation for estimates is quite high.

10.5 DATABASE USE AT THE DIVISION LEVEL

Hewlett-Packard reviews the progress of each of its divisions once a year in a formal process called a "division review." In the past, graphs were presented which showed the progress of the divisions in hardware R&D. Here are some examples of graphs which can be used to evaluate the progress of software R&D within a division. (See Chapter 12 for a more complete explanation of these graphs.) Since the definitions of two of these standard graphs are built into the spreadsheet, a software lab manager or a division manager can retrieve these graphs automatically.

In the other graphs shown in this chapter, data points from across the company were used. Figures 10-13 and 10-14 show actual data for just one division as it might be displayed for a division review. Both regression lines demonstrate the large influence of four projects which took advantage of reused code (labeled RCY). In the productivity graph we see that the regression slope is positive, although there is a second pattern present. Among the Pascal and C projects, the trend is flat and consists of much lower productivity than for the reused code projects. In the defect density graph, the corresponding defect densities for the reused code projects are quite low, while those for the Pascal and C projects demonstrate wide variation. Such graphs facilitate discussions concerning the software development process, and can be used to measure certain kinds of progress over time.

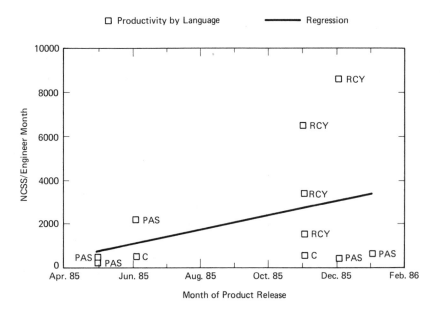

Figure 10-13   Division code volume productivity.

The real measure of success of a division's products is customer satisfaction. One index of satisfaction is the number of defects discovered by customers. We currently have no postrelease data in the database, although this data is available. Our hope is that by looking at prerelease and postrelease quality graphs side by side it will help to answer the following questions:

1. Do prerelease defects predict postrelease defects (in other words, the more defects found prerelease, the more defects one can expect to find postrelease relative to other projects)?

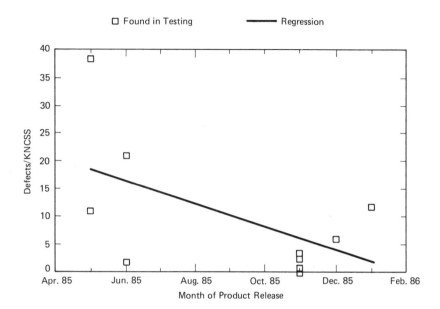

Figure 10-14   Division prerelease discovered defect density.

2. As more defects are found and fixed prerelease, are there fewer defects in the released product for the customer to find?

3. Will using state-of-the-art methods and controls during development to improve postrelease quality simultaneously also improve lab productivity? The answer to this question requires the productivity graph of Figure 10-13, as well.

10.6 INITIAL VIEWS OF THE DATABASE

Preliminary surveys show that the database is being used by the Software Metrics Council, QA managers, software engineers, productivity managers, and some project managers. Most are curious about how their data compares with the data from the rest of the company. Some are using the data to determine a realistic goal for improvement, and some are using it to help estimate new schedules. Having seen the model, some divisions are already adapting the model to local data to achieve most accurate results and explore areas not yet addressed by the Software Metrics Council. Some of the most exciting results which we have seen since the formation of the council have come from such experiments.

10.7 CONCLUSION

The HP-wide metrics spreadsheet serves as a template for keeping local historical data and provides company-wide historical data on software projects. The data allows analytical estimates and evaluations, and the spreadsheet format provides the very fast graphics support necessary for data analysis.

In this chapter we presented a variety of the graphs and data which are available for use by HP project managers. Some results shown are available in graphical form to provide immediate insights. In others, we showed how the HP-wide database is useful for preparing and verifying estimates.

Finally, we introduced the concept that estimating models should take advantage of the known data summarizing engineering months and calendar months, and demonstrated that this data has strong potential for improving current estimates.

We are currently investigating the next generation of SMDB, which plans to use a relational database with a programmatic interface for tool integration. In addition, as projects choose more detailed metrics to collect for their local use and we develop tools to support data collection, our "reasonable to collect" criterion changes. The standard metrics definitions may be refined to be more precise, and the database will need a new schema.

After some experience with cataloguing data, it is clear that there is a great deal to be learned about the processes of software development with the aid of a good, accessible database. It provides a valuable set of reference points for the project manager to track and control projects. For more general users, it helps the understanding of progress for a division in their software R&D activities. Finally, it helps to keep awareness levels high throughout the company regarding progress by many entities. It is this kind of collection and representation of data which the entire software development industry would like to have.

BIBLIOGRAPHY

1. Conte, S., H. Dunsmore, and V. Shen, *Software Engineering Metrics and Models.* Menlo Park, Calif.: Benjamin/Cummings Publishing Co., Inc., 1986, p. 173.
2. DeMarco, T., *Controlling Software Projects.* New York: Yourdon Press, 1982. pp. 157-158.
3. Balza, J., "Improving the Methods of Software Project Estimation at CNO," *HP Software Productivity Conference Proceedings* (April 1986), p. 1-12.

11

REFLECTIONS ON THE
MEANINGFULNESS OF DATA

It was exciting to see how other projects and groups learned and progressed using software metrics and to know that we now had our own database of metrics information to help guide us. But guide us where? And how good a guide is it, really?

When we started, our objective was "to gain agreement on a set of software measurement criteria which managers feel are *meaningful*, reasonable to collect, and can be used to measure progress and predict results." In this chapter we will explore several aspects of how data is meaningful, and try to discover how project managers can, and must, react to metrics data to optimize their use.

Data is meaningful when it is relevant and significant. Therefore, accuracy and applicability of both the data and the model must be better than one's intuition.

11.1 VALIDITY OF DATA

Data validation is usually a two-step process at HP. Chances are good that if data is being collected, it is also being used locally. It is in the project's best interest to base decisions on accurate data. Therefore, the project team validates their own data. When we receive the data, we also inspect it before adding it to the database. The following illustrates what we look for.

There is an apocryphal story which people on expense accounts pass on to new people in the organization. It illustrates the simplest principles of validating numbers. Whenever you fill out an expense report for a trip, you must be careful to follow several cardinal rules. First of all, you never report expenses with even dollar amounts unless you have a receipt. Accounting will think that you didn't really keep track of the actual expenses. Next, you never report too small an amount of expenses, whether you only spent a small amount or not, because the controller will then hold you up as an example to your peers of how they must control expenses. Finally, you never report too large an amount of expenses, because not only will you get chewed out, but your actions might initiate a department-wide campaign to reduce expenses.

This story is only partly tongue in cheek, but it does describe the basics of our first attempts at data validation. Just as with the IRS, certain numbers flag an audit. We look for numbers that are too round, especially for size data. For round numbers we contact the submitter and request information concerning how the round number was determined as well as the confidence level of its accuracy. Another type of flag is raised when data is submitted which includes high or low numbers relative to the numbers in the database. For example, one division sent us data that showed productivity many times higher than the average of the rest of the database. For us, this was very exciting because we believed that from such success stories we would be able to share techniques of development with other divisions to achieve short-term process improvements. Unfortunately, we learned upon investigation that they were not counting engineering months according to the standard definition. Such data must be adjusted before it can be included in the company-wide database.

The emphasis of the software metrics program has been for projects to gain an understanding of their own processes. The data collected first must satisfy the project team's needs and second must satisfy the rest of the company's need for information. The company-wide standard metrics definitions were not suited for detailed process analysis in some cases. For example, by HP's definition, engineering months are counted in whole-month increments. Effort data, by this definition, can be off by as much as one-half month. In fact, many projects report data with fractional values, and we are glad to record these presumably more precise measurements. Projects need to collect effort data in more detail. This is analogous to increasing the sampling rate to better approximate the actual results (like increasing the number of Nielson TV watchers to better represent the entire viewing public's tastes). Some projects have chosen to track actual weeks, actual hours, or in one case uninterrupted half-hours. In these cases, each project invented a mapping between what they were counting and the standard definition. The bottom line is that everyone is better off for having a more precise definition, but the data is no longer being collected in a standard way.

Another example is the NCSS standard for counting lines of code. Some projects have found NCLS (noncomment lines of source) to be more meaningful to them and so have chosen not to follow the standard. They report logical lines to the database, while other projects report physical lines. These two examples have in common the fact that the standards (engineering month and NCSS) were chosen on the basis of the "reasonable to collect" criterion at a time when few projects were tracking actual effort or had a logical line counting tool available. As the need for process analysis has grown, so has the availability of tools. To encourage more consistent use of the standard, we must now modify the standard to match what most projects are collecting and agree upon standard mappings for those projects counting something different. In general, such modifications will lead to better precision than the initial definitions.

11.2 STATISTICAL SIGNIFICANCE

Within the first six months after the HP metrics program was started, we received data from a dozen or so projects. Many were projects which actually collected data before we established our standard. During these initial stages we frequently made presentations describing the agreed-upon metrics and discussing how we expected them to be used. We also presented what we discovered about other companies' use of software metrics and discussed what little data we had thus far. The reaction from the audience became quite predictable. As soon as they heard productivity and quality data from large U.S. software-producing companies or Japanese companies, they immediately wanted to know how we compared. It didn't seem to matter when we cautioned them that we didn't really have enough data yet to draw realistic conclusions. They still wanted to know!

A good example of how such eagerness can be misleading is the data shown in Figure 11-1 and discussed in an early HP paper [1, 2, 3, 4]. From twelve projects-worth of data, it implied that we spent less time in design and had to make up for it by spending a greater percentage of time in test. As much more data came in, the amounts of time spent in the various phases changed to much more closely reflect other companies' data. Figure 11-2 shows a revised version of Figure 11-1 with numbers now based upon 43 projects instead of twelve [5 ,6]. The difference is that we now have data for enough projects, so it is more statistically meaningful. Even now, we must be careful in interpreting trends based on data in the database. Some subsets of data are still not yet represented by enough data points to be statistically significant.

What, then, is "statistical significance?" It represents the point when enough data has been collected to clearly establish both an average behavior and standard deviations from that behavior. What is meant is that when enough measurements are taken, the result is typically a Gaussian or bell-shaped curve (refer to *Software Engineering Metrics and Models* by Conte,

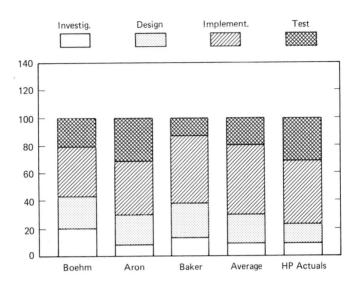

Figure 11-1 Published process percentages.*

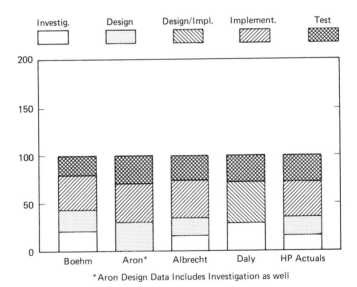

*Aron Design Data Includes Investigation as well

Figure 11-2 Engineering effort percentages (56 HP projects).*

Dunsmore, and Shen [7] for an excellent discussion of statistical distribution, the significant terms, and their meanings).

Before that, you can imagine various distorted versions of the final curve with the center of greatest probability generally around the final center. What is least known is the probability of variation from the center point. If we look at the productivity data in HP's database when we had 75 data points, we see a curve which has not achieved a clear shape yet (Figure 11-3). It appears to be a skewed distribution, probably because of the presence of varying amounts of reused code.

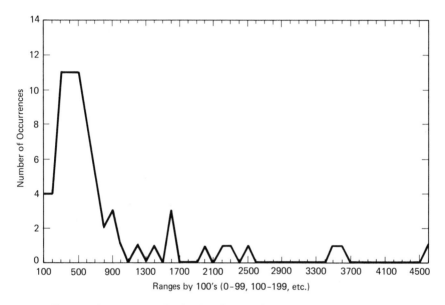

Figure 11-3   Frequency distribution of HP productivity data (75 data points).

Another important way of looking at the data at this stage is from a probabilistic standpoint. The probability of producing a product at a productivity rate between 300 and 500 is 22 out of 75, or 30 percent. Between 250 and 600 it is 55 percent. At least we can caution project managers that few projects have achieved greater than 900, so estimating higher than that number would have little justification unless there is a large reused amount of code expected.

A final statistical concern is bias on the data. Bias is introduced when samples are taken from an atypical cross section of the data population. For example, we have some bias built into our data, which we have recognized is caused by the different types of software developers (firmware, systems, applications, custom). When all of the data is examined together, it is likely that the averages will not be as meaningful to any particular software developer as they will if only the most appropriate category is examined. Another type of bias which could be present is that people who are most likely to collect data might develop software differently from those who don't.

Ultimately, the statistical significance of most of our data will remain low for some time until much more data exists. If the limitations of both the accuracy of the data and its statistical significance are recognized, though, decisions of software engineers can be positively influenced. The next section describes one such case.

11.2.1 When Statistical Significance Doesn't Matter

Starting with no data at all, we needed to convince ourselves that our productivity rates, defect densities, and percentages of time spent on various activities were in the same ranges as published industry numbers. After receiving ten projects from different divisions we felt more comfortable that we were in the industry ballpark and that, on the average, we could expect to produce between 200 and 700 lines of code for each engineering month spent on the project.

Notice, however, that ten projects is not statistically significant, the data was not validated, and no fancy statistical analysis was done to arrive at our conclusion. Yet, as in the following example, knowing the 200–700 lines per month ballpark has had a sobering effect on scheduling new projects.

One of the first opportunities we had to take advantage of the data which we collected for our database occurred when we were approached to do a joint project with two other divisions. This particular project was really time-critical, but neither of the other two divisions had the resources to accomplish the job in the short time frame they desired, so they asked us whether our lab would help. Together, project managers from the three labs had specified the project well enough that they thought that it could certainly be done in three months' time. When we met, we asked the usual uncomfortable question, "How much code will there be?" After some discussion among them, we suggested approaching the answer indirectly. Given three months and one engineer from each lab, and given that the rate of code generation we had seen so far reported to the database was running under 500 NCSS/engineering month (including all phases), it seemed that if they were to finish in three months, the system was likely to be no more than around four KNCSS of code (including test cases).

There was skepticism that the desired functionality would be possible with that amount of code, so we discussed how functionality could be initially limited and how the schedule could be stretched. We also agreed that if we couldn't settle the design and know in much better detail how much code would be produced within three to four weeks' time, then the project would probably not be feasible in the time limit we had. The fact that we had at least some historical data to back up our calculations had helped us to make some very important decisions early enough in the project to be effective.

A postscript to this story is that after the first month had passed, the team thought that about eight KNCSS would be needed. In fact, it turned out to be just over that amount, and first installations occurred about five months after the project started.

11.3 MANAGING FROM THE RIGHT DATA

This book has described many metrics and how we have used them. There are many other useful metrics not described here. The question is, "For my project, which data are the most important for the success of the project?" On what should the project manager focus attention? Here are two ways to determine what is important. Both ways use problem solving and decision analysis techniques.

As a major project at one division recently approached the end of the specifications phase, the project team used a quality circle to brainstorm which metrics they would collect during the remainder of their project. They approached the problem by asking the following questions:

1. Why do we want to collect metrics?
2. What data should be collected?
3. How will they be collected?
4. Who should collect the data?
5. How should data be presented?
6. What decisions should be made based on metrics?

Notice that these questions are similar to the ones used by the original Software Metrics Council. The difference is that they were asked with one specific project in mind. From the answers to these questions they derived a list of 21 metrics which were desirable to collect, and then they brainstormed which ones they actually would collect based upon their best estimates of the time investment required. Figure 11-4 shows one example of their proposed metrics. Importance and feasibility were assigned values from 1 to 5, with 5 meaning most important or most feasible. The numbers were chosen based on group consensus. Note that the precise definition of terms like "importance" are determined by the project team on the basis of specific details of the project. These precise definitions are irrelevant to this discussion because, they are not broadly applicable. Managing from the right data means data which is most useful for your specific project.

A second method of customizing project metrics is to pick and choose from published lists of metrics and to define each term specifically for your

Time Required to Fix Defects for Each Type of Transaction	
Importance	4
Feasibility	4
Used to analyze	Quality of code (code maintainability)
Collection method	SR tracking form (see project standards) (Consider defect complexity factor)
Collection person	Defect fixer
Data presentation	Consolidated module worksheets Reports:scattergram of fix times
Decisions affected	Evaluate technology -avg fix time against other technologies Determine learning curve Evaluate coding standards Evaluate scheduling techniques Determine effectiveness of fix process

Figure 11-4   How to make a metric meaningful.

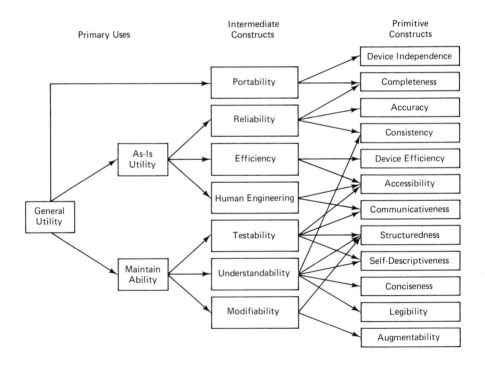

Figure 11-5   Software quality characteristics tree, © October 1976, IEEE.

project. McCall and Walters [8] and Boehm, Brown, and Lipow [9] have described categories of quality attributes and suggested ways of measuring the degree to which software possesses each quality attribute. Figure 11-5 shows the quality attributes from Boehm et al.

A similar breakdown is supplied by an HP model called FURPS. FURPS is an acronym for Functionality, Usability, Reliability, Performance, and Supportability. Figure 11-6 shows the components of FURPS [10].

Functionality	Feature set Capablilities Generality Security
Usability	Human factors Aesthetics Consistency Documentation
Reliability	Frequency/severity of failure Recoverability Predictability Accuracy Mean time to failure
Performance	Speed Efficiency Resource consumption Thruput Response time
Supportability	Testability Extensibility Adaptability Maintainability Compatibility Configurability Serviceablility Installability Localizability

Figure 11-6   Components of FURPS.

One reason the acronym FURPS is effective is that it is a silly mnemonic which is easy to remember. Using the FURPS model involves two steps: establishing priorities and making quality attributes measurable. Establishing priorities is important because of the tradeoffs involved between quality attributes. For example, adding a new function might improve functionality but decrease performance, usability, and/or reliability. Since each project has different priorities, it is necessary to make an early decision of what kind of quality is most important.

Once priorities for quality attributes have been selected, it is necessary to choose measurable goals for each attribute. These goals guide your data collection and analysis. Of all the data you might be collecting, these goals focus attention on what is most important.

Figure 11-7 gives some examples of how each quality attribute can be measured and thus evaluated in each of the major life cycle phases. It is beyond the scope of this discussion to explain all of these in detail. Rather than attempt this, we will describe the specific measures selected for one particular HP project and how they were used. In this discussion we will see that, unlike the standard HP metrics described earlier, these measures are project-specific and may mean different things to different projects.

The specific project we will consider is a printed-circuit board product designed to allow operation of a data acquisition system remotely from a computer. When we examine the FURPS quality attributes established during investigation, we see that some of the qualities were easier to quantify than others:

- Usability: no changes to user application programs should be necessary.
- Performance: the throughput must be at least ten times existing solutions for remote operation.
- Functionality: all functions of the data acquisition system must operate the same as they do locally.
- Reliability: the MTBF of the hardware must be at least five times better than the data acquisition system.
- Supportability: the boards must be capable of a thorough stand-alone self-test, as well as a computer-initiated self-test

They are listed in order of project priority. The quality attributes ultimately tested for this product were not limited to these five; rather, these were the ones selected as most important for product success.

One thing which we see from this example is that the FURPS attributes are not limited to software. Both the reliability and supportability aspects are heavily influenced by hardware design decisions. We will limit our discussion of this example to describing the steps taken to ensure that the functionality, usability, and performance goals were met.

The earliest time when these three objectives were tested was on a breadboard implementation during the design phase. At that time, the relatively straightforward feasibility of the functionality and usability attributes was proven with two different computers and various different configurations of the data acquisition system. As with many data communication applications, the primary concern which remained for the duration of the project was the possibility of communications deadlock (a state in which each of the two ends of the system are hung, waiting for the other end to acknowledge a message).

	Investigation/ Specifications	Design	Implementation	Testing	Support
F	# target users to review spec or prototype % grade on report card from user % features competitive with other products # interfaces with existing products	% spec included in design # changes to spec due to design requirement % users to review change if needed	% designs included in code # code changes due to omissions discovered % features removed (reviewed by original target user)	% features tested at alpha sites % user documentation tested against product # target alpha customers	# Known Problem Reports sales act. reports (esp. lost sales) user surveys internal HP user surveys
U	# target users to review spec or prototype % grade on documentation plan by target user % grade on usability of prototype	% grade of design as compared to objectives # changes to prototype manuals after review	% grade by other lab user % grade by product marketing, documentation % original users to to review any change	# changes to product after alpha test % grade from usability lab testing % grade by test sites	# User misunderstandings
R	# omissions noted in reviews of objectives (reliability goals) # changes to project plan, test plan after review	# changes to design after review due to error % grade of design as compared to objectives	% code changed due to reliability errors discovered in reviews % code covered by test cases # defects/KNCSS during module testing	MTTF (MTBF) % hrs reliability testing # defects/1K hrs # defects total defect rate before release ckpoints	# Known Problem Reports # defects/KNCSS
P	# changes to objectives after review % grade on objectives by target user % grade on objective by product managers	% product to be modeled defined modeled environment	performance tests achieve % of modeled expectations % of code tested with targeted performance suite (module)	achieve performance goal with regard to environment(s) tested (system)	
S	# changes to support objectives after review by field & CPE	# design changes by CPE & field # diagnostic/recovery changes by CPE & field input	MTTR objective (time) ⟶ MTTC objective (time) ⟶ time to train tester, use of documentation		same

Figure 11-7 Examples of setting measurable objectives using FURPS for each life cycle phase.

161

The early performance measurement presented more of a problem. While all of the components which were selected operated at high speed, the initial end-to-end throughput was only slightly higher than existing products. Because it was measured so early in the project, though, there was ample opportunity to adjust the design in order to meet the required goal.

The second test of the objectives occurred during the implementation phase. By this time, the hardware design had stabilized and the results depended entirely on the firmware. A relatively large number of boards were produced in order to perform extensive functionality and usability tests. These units were inserted into over twenty existing internal applications, and were used in the lab to run extensive round-the-clock tests. Besides the tests of existing applications, all of the existing regression tests for the data acquisition system were performed with the board products in the configurations necessary to meet the functionality objective. During this phase a formal test was also written which was used for the duration of the project to verify the performance objective. By the time widespread testing was initiated, the performance had been improved to approximately seven times existing solutions. By further tuning the firmware, it was ultimately possible to improve this performance by another factor of two prior to the formal test phase.

We can see from this example that the FURPS quality attributes serve two purposes. First, they focus attention on producing a well-rounded quality product. Second, they encourage thinking in terms of measurable objectives. By establishing these objectives early in the project, the necessary steps were taken in time to achieve them in an orderly fashion.

11.3.1 Following Through with Assumptions

One project in our lab attempted to use the Kohoutek testing time prediction model. The project's expectation was that graphing actual defects found over time versus the model's predicted defects would enable them to know when formal QA could be ended.

This project involved moving an existing software application from one operating system and computer hardware to another, but the user interface had to be written from scratch. The Kohoutek model requires projecting an expected total number of defects found. The team used a defect density published in the literature which assumed that the defects counted did not include duplicates and enhancement requests. Unfortunately, there was no easy way at that time to query our defect tracking system to get just the number of nonduplicate, nonenhancement request defects found in the new code. So the project used total defects found, ignoring the assumptions used to create the prediction. The projected defects were based on the user interface code only, figuring that only the new code would be the source of defects. Figure 11-8 is a graph of the estimate and actual for the entire test phase.

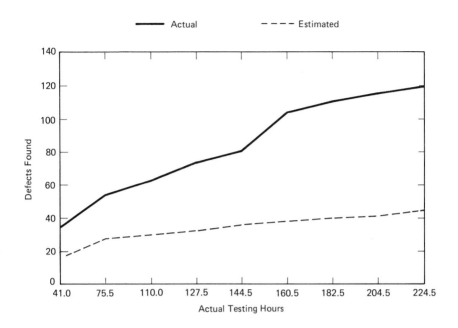

Figure 11-8   Total project defects vs. prediction model (testing activity).

After the first few weeks, it was apparent that something was wrong. It looked as though the two curves were parallel but far apart. The project manager wondered if the number of defects predicted was off by a constant of about two. After a few more weeks, they realized that it wasn't as simple as a constant multiplier. The defects were not only in the *new* code.

At the end of the project, they manually counted the number of defects that should have been plotted against the estimate. Figure 11-9 shows the new graph. Notice how closely the model predicted the actual when using the right data.

From this experience the team learned:

1. The model is good and worth using on future projects.
2. The assumption that all the defects would be in the new code was wrong. However, because the new code was for the user interface, it took no additional time to find the defects in all the other code (functionally testing the user interface exercised the corresponding program functions at the same time).

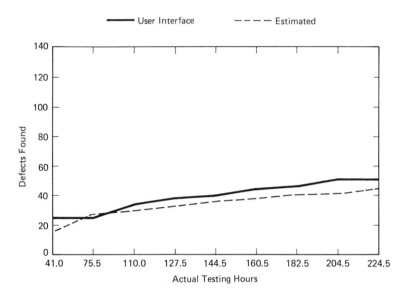

Figure 11-9   Actual defects (corrected vs. prediction model for user interface only).

3. Count defects according to the assumptions made when choosing a defect density to use in the model.

11.4 COMPARING DATA ACROSS THE INDUSTRY

Near the start of Chapter 4, we described some of the pitfalls of comparing metrics data with other companies without knowing their rules for collection. Capers Jones makes the point that there are numerous ways that one can count lines of code. Figure 11-10 is an excerpt from his recent book which illustrates this point [11]. When HP data is compared to other companies' data, it is essential to understand what definitions are being used. It might look on the surface that we are much more productive when in reality the explanation might be that we count data declarations and executable lines, whereas another company might only count executable lines.

Defect data is also difficult to compare. In order to make a fair comparison, it must be known what was counted as a defect. Traditionally, only nonduplicate program defects are reported and counted as defects. This definition is similar to reporting nonduplicate, nonenhancement requests which are found in the formal test phase. However, as we report defects earlier in the process than system test, we must be even more careful when comparing our defect data to anyone else's data. Because we are recording more defect data than most companies, our defect densities night appear higher.

Set 1: Line-Counting Variations at the Program Level
1. Count only executable lines
2. Count executable lines plus data definitions
3. Count executable lines, data definitions, and comments
4. Count executable lines, data definitions, comments, and JCL
5. Count lines as physical lines on an input screen
6. Count lines as terminated by logical delimiters
Set 2: Line-Counting Variations at the Project Level
1. Count only new lines
2. Count new lines and changed lines
3. Count new lines, changed lines, and reused lines
4. Count all delivered lines plus temporary scaffold code
5. Count all delivered lines, temporary code, and support code

Figure 11-10 Variations in software line counting methods.

The percentage of time spent in life cycle phases is also difficult to compare unless you know what activities are included in each phase. Projects using a prototyping approach have an especially hard time reporting and comparing effort by life-cycle phase, because design and implementation are so intertwined.

It was exactly these problems which existed among HP divisions that led us to establish the Software Metrics Council. The industry equivalent of our council is the IEEE working groups. The IEEE Software Reliability Metrics Standards group is currently in the balloting process. The IEEE Software Quality and Software Productivity Standards groups each have been meeting for about three years as of this writing. The industry does recognize the need for such standardization on basic metrics. It is hoped that any standards that these groups produce will resolve the issues which we have uncovered in trying to compare HP data with other companies.

11.4.1 Aiming at a Moving Target

In Chapter 9 and other sections we discussed various examples of how metrics data can help managers to more effectively estimate projects. In fact, we gave examples of how several groups at HP have changed their processes in positive ways as a result of the measurements. For "professional" estimators, this produces somewhat of a quandary, because each time the process changes, the estimator loses some of the historical basis for making accurate estimates.

During the past year, we presented some of our process-improvement experiences to a group of professional estimators. The response to the presentation was considerably less enthusiastic than we have experienced with internal groups or other external groups, and it led us to ask ourselves, "What was different about this audience?" The answer seemed to be that *it is in the best interests of professional estimators that absolutely nothing change about the software development process*, so that their ability to predict development times is always based on increasingly larger samples of consistent historical data.

Our goal, however, is to reduce software development time by using the metrics data to help guide constructive process changes. As a result, we must try experiments and constantly aim at a moving target. For us, the age of data is an important consideration. We are generally interested in how we are doing in relation to other companies' data *now*, not in relation to how they were doing ten years ago. Overestimating is costly in terms of lost bids or lost opportunity if a project is cancelled due to a predicted miss of the market window. However, overestimating is usually not a problem. We'll consider ourselves successful when overestimation occurs as a result of using a good estimate based on today's data which is too conservative due to tomorrow's process improvements shortening the cycle time.

11.5 SUMMARY

We have seen that, at this stage of maturity of software process measurement, judgment must be used in interpreting current or historical data. The software development process is not pursued with sufficient consistency that a project manager can afford to blindly trust statistical results. Fortunately, we have experienced successes already in using the limited data we have, and these successes help by showing project managers how historical data is useful.

Project measurements are a powerful means for tracking progress toward established goals. The selection of what these measurements are, and the accuracy of these measurements are under the control of the project manager. The use of FURPS to define what measures are important helps put into perspective which measures will be used to track a project.

BIBLIOGRAPHY

1. Grady R. and D. Caswell, "Understanding HP's Software Development Processes Through Metrics," *HP Software Productivity Conference* (April 1984), p. 3–49.

2. Boehm, B. W., *Software Engineering Economics.* Englewood Cliffs, N. J.: Prentice-Hall, Inc., 1981, p. 382.

3. Aron, J. D., "Estimating Resources for Large Programming Systems," *Software Engineering: Concepts and Techniques, Proceedings of the NATO Conferences,* ed. by P. Naur, B. Randell, J. Buxton, Petrocelli/Charter, New York (1976), pp. 206–217.

4. Albrecht, A. J., "Measuring Application Development Productivity," Proceedings of the Joint SHARE/GUIDE/IBM Application Development Symposium (Oct. 1979), p. 90.

5. Daly, E. B., "Management of Software Development," *IEEE Transactions on Software Engineering* (May 1977), p. 232.

6. Baker, F. T., "Chief Programmer Team Management of Production Programming," IBM Systems Journal, no. 1 (1972), pp. 56–73.

7. Conte, S., H. Dunsmore, and V. Shen, *Software Engineering Metrics and Models.* Menlo Park, Calif.: Benjamin/Cummings Publishing Co., Inc., 1986, pp. 127–134.

8. McCall, J. A., P. K. Richards, and G. F. Walters, *Factors in Software Quality* (Tech. Rep. 77CIS 02), Sunnyvale, Calif., General Electric, Command and Information Systems 1977.

9. Boehm, B., J. Brown, Lipow, M., "Quantitative Evaluation of Software Quality," *IEEE 2nd International Conference on Software Engineering,* San Francisco, Calif., (Oct. 1976), pp. 592–605.

10. HP Software Metrics Class Student Workbook, (1985).

11. Jones, C., *Programming Productivity.* New York: McGraw-Hill, 1986, p. 15.

12

GRAPHS FOR TOP-LEVEL
MANAGEMENT

The establishment of the HP-wide software metrics program generated a tremendous amount of enthusiasm among HP's management team. It provided a potential framework for better understanding software development and for increasing the involvement of top management in our software business.

12.1 DE FACTO STANDARDS

At the review meeting of the Software Metrics Council held in February of 1984, it was decided that the council would assume a process focus centered on productivity, quality, and predictability. These were the three elements which we desired to understand and control. As is typical of the HP approach, we have all tried our own approaches to using both the HP metrics, as well as more detailed metrics at individual divisions, to gain this understanding. Historically, the next step would be for several divisions to present progress reports in a particularly appealing graphical form, and one or more of them would catch management's attention and become a de facto standard.

12.2 PLANNED STANDARDS

Unfortunately, the process of adopting de facto standards can take several years. Since management was enthusiastic about the HP metrics program, we could not wait that long. We had the opportunity to take data that we already had agreed upon as the minimum set of metrics to collect, and present it in a way that would represent our productivity and quality gains. A proposal was presented at the August 1984 Software Metrics Council meeting which consisted of three graphs which present such a top-level management view. The three graphs included reports of productivity, prerelease quality, and postrelease quality. They were unanimously approved in concept; however, there was heated discussion on the details of implementation. In early September the first version of a detailed write-up of the proposal was distributed to the council. In October we received detailed critiques and some excellent refinements to the proposal. These suggestions were incorporated as much as possible into the final version of the proposal, and consensus was achieved.

12.2.1 Productivity

A divisional view of productivity must indicate whether productivity on an aggregate level is improving or not. Although input/output and revenue-oriented views of productivity exist [1], the most common representation of productivity described in software engineering literature is lines of code per person per month. With the HP metrics this is NCSS (noncomment source statements) per engineering month. The divisional graph is a scattergram by project over time, and an artificial example is illustrated in Figure 12-1.

Of the three initial graphs proposed in August 1984, this one was received the most favorably. Several changes were made which deserve discussion. First, the title refers to code volume productivity as opposed to software productivity. This emphasizes that code is just one aspect of productivity that is perhaps easier to measure than some others. Note, however, that we are not just looking at the productivity of the implementation phase. Engineering months include time spent in design, implementation, and test. There was also one division which felt very strongly that code volume should be measured in terms of logical source statements instead of NCSS. As a gross measure of productivity, there is no evidence to suggest that logical source lines would be any better at showing meaningful trends than NCSS, and it does not lend itself well to comparison with other companies. This is an area which we will investigate by upgrading our counting tools to report both logical source statements and NCSS, and each division may optionally plot either or both.

Another change in this graph was to include design, implementation, and test in the engineering month total. The intent is to emphasize the overall

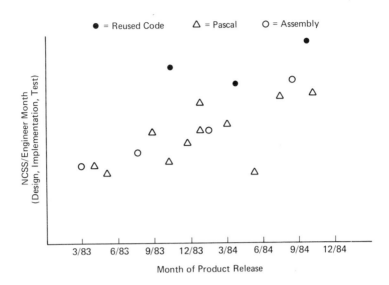

Note: Each Point Represents One Project.

Figure 12-1 Division code volume productivity.

development process more than just the coding process when measuring productivity, but to separate investigation as a slightly different process. This will probably mean that graphs of our processes will appear less productive than some which have appeared in the literature, since those seem primarily to report productivity for the coding process. By including design and test, though, it may be possible to see the influence of better design methodologies and testing techniques on our overall productivity.

Finally it was felt that different languages and possibly even different development methodologies should be shown with different symbols. Projects which have been reported for the past year and a half have followed the convention that if one language represents greater than 75 percent of the project, all the project is reported as that language. If greater than 75 percent was reused code, it is reported as all reused. Other combinations are reported as mixed.

This resulting graph seemed to provide a simple meaningful way for divisions to consistently track productivity. The following graphs which track quality are intended to prevent misuse of the productivity graph. Looking at productivity alone could encourage efforts which result in productivity improvement at the expense of quality.

12.2.2 Quality Prior to Product Release

In manufacturing areas, we have learned that steady improvement in quality both improves productivity and decreases manufacturing cycle times by eliminating excessive rework and the need for some tests. A graph which tracks defect density by product prior to release will provide an aggregate view of quality *during the development process* over time. The divisional graph includes two scattergrams showing defect densities in new projects over time, and an example of them is shown in Figure 12-2. The first scattergram shows only those defects reported during a formal test phase. This graph has the greatest likelihood of consistency in the definition of defects from division to division. The second (optional) scattergram shows all defects recorded during the development process, and the difference between the two shows how carefully a division is looking for defects prior to the test phase.

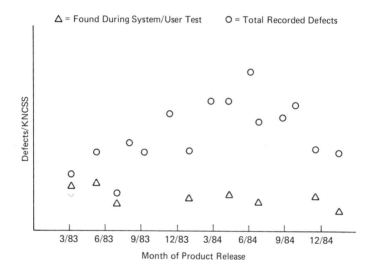

Note: Each Point Represents One Project.

Figure 12-2   Division prerelease discovered defect density.

These graphs provide a long-term check against the productivity graph. Productivity must not increase at the expense of quality, and we must not overinvest in testing instead of removing the causes of defects.

Like the graph for productivity, this one for quality also presented some problems. What really is a good trend for such a graph, up or down? Some argued that the trend should be up, since their divisions are reporting defects in greater detail than ever before in order to get at the root causes of defects. This is demonstrated as a problem when the early data in the Corporate Metrics database is examined. There is a very large variation in defect density from division to division, and even from project to project within a division. By splitting the graph into two scattergrams, we hope we have resolved the major issues. Defect densities reported during formal test should be more stable and consistent than overall defect densities.

Reported defects include documentation defects and enhancement requests, but do not count duplicate defects. We are experimenting with weighting defects by severity. For now, though, the standard graphs will not include any weighting.

Reporting and evaluating defect density prior to release is absolutely necessary if management attention is to be focused on removing the causes of defects from the software development process. For the near term this graph will be the subject of much discussion, but that is appropriate, since it is the one which probably best represents the focus of our near-term efforts to improve the process. The only important trend for this graph is the long-term trend. For the short term we must set management's expectations by predicting how many defects we expect to see based on previous projects and the level of reporting we want.

12.2.3 Quality After Product Release

For many years HP has kept very accurate records of product quality after shipment to customers because these records represent the final verdict of product quality. Therefore, a third divisional graph is necessary which can compare prerelease quality to postrelease quality. This graph is again a scattergram over time by project. See Figure 12-3.

The only problem that this graph seemed to present was what period of time after product release should be used for any given product? Some products which are small and address a broad market will produce an adequate quality sampling in three months, while large complex software packages will take much longer to sell, install, and get the users trained, and will need longer periods of customer use before we have a good indication of their quality. One possibility is a normalization factor such as an NCSS/constant multiplier which tries to adjust for these differences. This is one area that will be defined at the divisional level. The graph shown here shows six months, because that was a time mentioned by the most divisions.

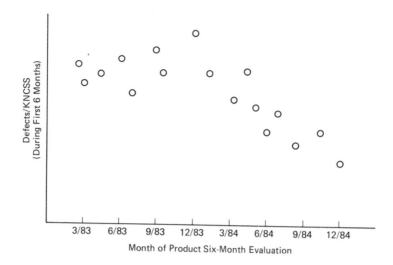

Note: Each Point Represents One Project.

Figure 12-3 Division postrelease defect density.

12.2.4 With Whom Do You Compare?

The primary goal of these graphs is to encourage all divisions to measure and improve their own software development process. This means that the most important information they can contain is trends for a division. By suggesting a standard, we can at least agree upon a common set of terminology, and we can try to emulate divisions which have success stories to tell. We already know that different companies produce many different types of software, and that these require different development techniques resulting in different levels of productivity and defects. So our suggestion is to compare with anyone, or no one, but to measure and improve your process.

BIBLIOGRAPHY

1. Basili, V., IEEE Working Group for Software Productivity Metrics, Nashua, N.H. (Sept. 1984).

13

A TRAINING PROGRAM

Tools are not effective without the appropriate levels of documentation and training. In this chapter, we describe a training program developed at HP which continues to play an important role in the success of the overall metrics program.

The Software Metrics Council's job as a sales force was to convince people to collect data and use it in decision making. These presentations included the "why," "what," and "who" aspects of software metrics. They raised the awareness that we needed software metrics, but the presentations didn't give the engineers and project managers the detailed knowledge and skills necessary to use software metrics effectively. As a result, it was decided that a class should be offered on software metrics. Such a class would also help to motivate engineers to collect and analyze data. It was designed primarily for project managers and engineers. The prerequisites were that the students must be familiar with the product life cycle and have worked for HP at least 6 months.

13.1 AN INITIAL ATTEMPT

The developer/trainer of the first draft of the new metrics class used inputs from the training group and HP experts in the field of software metrics. The first draft objective was

To provide an overview of HP's efforts in establishing meaningful measures of the software development process in order to improve quality, productivity, and predictability.

The corresponding course outline took a two-half-day seminar approach, and included guest speakers known throughout HP for their work in software metrics. This format had the advantage that the speakers were credible, and they were the best people to be presenting their own material.

There were several major problems with this format, however. First, the participants did not gain experience with data collection and analysis skills or sufficient knowledge of how to use the class documentation and automated tools available to them. Second, lab time for hands-on practice was lacking. Finally, the class outline seemed very similar to the sales presentation, except that it included testimonials by those who had used metrics successfully. We felt that the best way to convince people would be to let them experience the benefits first hand.

13.2 THE REVISED OBJECTIVE

The course objective was revised as follows:

To provide background and hands-on experience to project managers and engineers so they can immediately use software metrics in their own environment to make informed decisions in the software development process.

The course outline reflecting the new objective was three half-days with the option of a fourth half-day for material local to a particular division. It consisted of a mixture of lecture, lab, and class discussion. Since HP had been using software metrics for only a year and the industry as a whole didn't have many hard and fast rules about metrics, a format was adopted in which much of the learning came from class discussion. Lectures presented the most widely accepted theories at the time and anecdotes of how the theories were applied at HP. However, the most effective learning took place during the lab sessions where the students were asked to apply the concepts to their case study. Figure 13-1 shows the current course content.

13.3 TESTING THE WATERS

Having so many geographically dispersed divisions creates predictable problems for HP. An especially difficult problem is that many of the computer divisions are clustered, and are located nearer to corporate-based training sites, while the analytic, medical, and instrument divisions tend to be widely

Section I   Introduction
- Introduction of class participants
- Overview of course objectives and agenda

Section II   Assumptions
- Key assumptions and definitions

Section III   Software Case Study: Defect Tracking System Milestones
- Setting quality objectives as project milestones

Section IV   Analyzing a Project: Defect Tracking System (DTS)
- Estimating code and schedule
- First estimates

Section V   Introduction to Effort Estimation Tools: Using Softcost to Confirm/Refine Estimates
- Confirming/refining estimates with Softcost

Section VI   Using COCOMO to Confirm/Refine Estimates
- Confirming/refining estimates with COCOMO

Section VII   Using Code Analyzer(s) to Confirm/Refine Estimates
- Using code analyzer(s) to generate Halstead and McCabe complexity metrics

Section VIII   Establishing Testing Release Criteria
- By cost analysis
- By coverage
- By defects and defect prediction

Section IX   Case Study Postmortem

Section X   Summary

Section XI   Course Evaluation

Figure 13-1 Outline for HP software metrics course.

dispersed. Therefore, the expertise of computer systems software developers tends to be tapped more often during the development of classes. The analytical, medical, and instrument divisions tend to be skeptical that a class based heavily on inputs from the computer divisions would apply to their processes, because their software development environments are different.

In order to ensure that the software metrics course would not suffer from this problem, course outlines and implementation plans were presented to representatives from the various groups, and reactions and suggestions were sought. For the most part, the representatives liked the format of the proposed metrics class. Soliciting their opinions early in the course development helped to ensure their final acceptance. It is interesting to note that we have not seen similar acceptance from HP's information systems community. They, unlike some of these other noncomputer division engineers, were not a part of the initial class reviewers.

Later, several pilot courses were held at various sites of the noncomputer divisions. The content was generally accepted as useful and applicable to the variety of software development environments represented in the course.

13.4 CLASS DESCRIPTION

The backbone of the course is a case study of a small, relatively well-documented project. The students are broken into teams of three to five, and each is given a team name of a software metrician (for example, Boehm, Halstead, McCabe, Basili, DeMarco, and the like). Each group assumes the role of the project team responsible for producing the same case study project. They start in the investigation phase, and the teams are given only the information that the real project team had at each stage of the project. Each group is asked to estimate total engineering months and total NCSS for the project. In addition, each team is asked how they came up with the estimate and on what specific information the estimates were based.

The class teaches the Softcost [1] and COCOMO [2] estimation models with hands-on experience with tools. Making quality measurable, using Halstead and McCabe complexity measures, understanding the Kohoutek model for predicting optimal time in the QA phase, and determining branch coverage are all explained during the lecture portions at the time in the workshop when each concept would be applied on a real project. For example, the testing-time prediction model is explained at the end of the implementation phase in preparation for refining test phase estimates. In addition, at every point in the exercise, the class is provided with the data that was available to the real project team. The class is encouraged to discuss what information is available to them in real life that is not available during the class due to the artificial nature of the exercise. The intent is for the students to realize that although software development is still far from being a science, there is much information available to us which can help make it more predictable. We often fail to take advantage of it.

The class was designed so that instructors at remote locations could adapt and present the material. There is time allocated during the class for discussion of topics of local interest.

One of the problems with the class from the students' point of view has been that it didn't meet all their expectations. Some people were disillusioned to find that there is still no magic formula for software development. Evaluations of the class have shown that many people do not distinguish between what the class does not teach because of priority and time considerations and topics left out because the knowledge does not exist in the industry. To try to combat this problem, at the beginning of the class the instructor writes on a flip chart all of the expectations the students have. The instructor is advised to state explicitly which expectations the course does not intend to meet. For example, one student said, "I want to be convinced that using software metrics is worth my while." Since the course is experiential as opposed to a sales pitch, the instructor replied, "You might be disappointed, as it is my intention to teach you the facts and let you make up your own mind."

13.5 SUCCESSES

In the first year of class instruction, eight offerings of the class trained 110 people. Of the 69 students who evaluated the class, the overall average was 4.8 on a scale of 1 to 6 (6 = High). Other instructors have now also been trained to present the class at various geographical locations. The real success of the metrics class, however, is whether or not the students begin to participate in activities that support the software metrics program. Ideally, we would like to know six months after a class offering what behavioral changes resulted from the class. Although no formal canvassing has been done, the course developer/teacher has kept in contact with several of the students. These were indications of the classes' successes:

1. The section manager, a key project manager, and an engineer designated as the metrics engineer for a critical R&D project, after taking the metrics class, initiated the use of "DeMarco's methodology"[3] in their section. The entire project team was sent to training on structured analysis/design and also to the metrics class. Based on the work of the full-time metrics engineer, the project has a full set of metrics in place to track productivity, quality, and predictability.

2. The Software QA manager in the same division also took the class. He has sent data to the HP-wide database and introduced metrics collection tools to the lab. He also presented branch coverage, Halstead, and McCabe metrics concepts to the entire software section.

3. In another lab, a project manager who took the class was dissatisfied with the presentation of the COCOMO model, took her own initiative to develop the COCOMO portion of the class, and taught it the next time around. This section in the course led directly to the implementation/use of the COCOMO model for the first time in several divisions.

4. An engineer in another division was inspired to try the COCOMO model in his lab. In order to make it easier, he created a log plot of the COCOMO formula so that it could be used without a calculator. He distributed this paper tool at the last HP Software Productivity Conference, and it was enthusiastically received. This same engineer has volunteered to become a trainer of the course at his division.

Several managers who took the class early on sent their entire teams to later offerings of the class. Another indication of success is the increased size of our general metrics distribution list. We have received many more calls from people wanting to stay current on what's happening in metrics at HP since the classes were initiated.

13.6 CONCLUSION

In terms of awareness alone, we can conclude that a training class greatly contributes to the success of a software metrics program. Effective instruction in efficient measurement techniques, correct usage of data, and typical results which are experienced are skills and knowledge which can be taught. At HP, the course developer and initial trainer ensured success by keeping in contact with past students, helping them while they set up metrics programs of their own, and putting them in touch with others who could help make them successful.

Software metrics is a very broad topic; opportunities exist to measure almost every aspect of software development. Our long-term goal is to provide appropriate measures which can be taught in every engineering class that HP offers. As the use of metrics spreads and becomes as commonplace as producing PERT charts, the need for a separate class on metrics will be replaced by a project management class which teaches metrics collection and evaluation as major elements of the management job, and several software engineering classes which incorporate the use of metrics by engineers on a day-to-day basis.

BIBLIOGRAPHY

1. Tausworthe, R., "Software Specifications Document, DSN Software Cost Model," Jet Propulsion Laboratory, Pasadena, Calif., 1981.
2. Boehm, B., *Software Engineering Economics.* Englewood Cliffs, N. J.: Prentice-Hall, Inc., 1981.
3. DeMarco, T., *Controlling Software Projects.* New York: Yourdon Press, 1982.

14

THE CARE AND FEEDING
OF A METRICS PROGRAM

Early in the book, we presented a ten-step strategy for a successful software metrics program. In subsequent chapters we provided details for all of these steps, except the last one. Step ten was to establish a mechanism for changing the metrics standard in an orderly way. This chapter describes the HP Software Metrics Council and the role that its members play in monitoring and updating the strategy and in keeping momentum in the HP metrics efforts.

14.1 THE HP SOFTWARE METRICS COUNCIL

The HP Software Metrics Council is the group which has set HP's standards and charted our course. There are two distinct roles which it has played in the three years since its inception. Initially it served as a standards-making body, and while that responsibility continues, the primary role now is that of a metrics special-interest group. A year and a half after its creation, the council formalized its charter and responsibilities.

Charter:

Identify key software metrics which provide a foundation for process improvement. Promote their use by example, training, and selling.

Responsibilities:

1. Distribute information and train where necessary.
2. Propose improvements to metrics definitions.
3. Attend meetings and share results.
4. Be actively involved in process improvement activities.

In addition, it was agreed that at least two to four days per month must be allocated to metrics activities by each member of the council.

The membership of HP's Software Metrics Council has been limited to around twenty individuals. While this number prevents us from including members from all HP divisions (there are over 50 different R&D labs), it is a good size for meetings and group rapport. Initially these people were hand-picked from recommendations sought from a broad cross section of respected HP managers and engineers. A conscious effort was made to represent 75 percent of all HP software developers among the twenty representatives. This representation includes software types and geographies, as well as overall lab sizes.

The council has representatives from both the R&D and QA functions. The initial membership emphasized R&D membership, because we felt they had the greatest influence in getting measurements started and accepted by the engineers whose involvement was needed. Membership has included more QA representatives over time as metrics have become accepted and as some QA functions have demonstrated a valuable role in metrics training, tool provision, and data analysis. The on-going program clearly depends heavily on both functions.

14.1.1 Operation of the Council

The council has a "major" meeting once a year. This meeting is patterned after the first successful meeting. It starts with a Tuesday dinner (Mondays and Fridays are avoided to facilitate travel) and usually an HP speaker. It continues with an all-day Wednesday session consisting of about one-third division reports and two-thirds workshops followed by dinner and a non-HP metrics speaker. It ends on Thursday afternoon after one more workshop, more division reports, and workshop summaries. *Premeeting preparations are extensive and absolutely necessary for success.*

The council also has a "minor" meeting halfway between the major meetings which lasts just one day. The goal of this meeting is to provide necessary course corrections to decisions made at major meetings, and to ensure that momentum continues. Forms changes are usually discussed, for example. Probably the most important activity at this meeting is the information exchange and recognition of on-going efforts.

14.1.2 Behind the Scenes

If we depended only on the entire metrics council meetings, we would not succeed. There are three additional activities that go on "behind the scenes." The most important activity is that the council as a whole knows that SEL walks away from each council meeting with action items which will be resolved. This may be the single most important factor in our success. Without this in-between activity to resolve critical issues, the membership would rapidly lose faith that any progress was possible, and the very nature of many of the members' jobs is such that they have very limited time beyond the regular meetings. In addition, SEL has performed an on-going literature search and provided the members with significant articles as they were discovered, or as issues were raised.

The second activity which occurs involves review of written material generated by SEL and occasional meetings with local representatives. These reviews provide an important check and balance against SEL's going astray of the council's intentions.

The third activity does involve the entire council. They all work within their divisions to provide guidance and enthusiasm for data collection and analysis. In addition, they are the source of many valuable experiments which provide useful results to the rest of the corporation. These results have been presented at the annual HP Software Productivity Conference each of the past three years. The conferences are attended by 400 software engineers and managers each year from all parts of the company.

14.2 ISSUES A COUNCIL MIGHT ADDRESS

We have discussed the membership of HP's Software Metrics Council, its method of operation, and some of the factors which we feel were key to success in HP's environment. In this last section we will briefly summarize the primary topics investigated at HP's council meetings subsequent to the startup meeting discussed in Chapter 5. These provide some feel for progress that you might expect to make, once your own metrics program is established.

Six-month meeting: data collection forms and review of data received.

Second annual meeting: maintenance metrics and management graphs.

Eighteen-month meeting: council charter and member responsibilities.

Third annual meeting: standard categories of defects and how to reassure people that data will not be used against them.

Thirty-month meeting: standard categories of defects, continued.

A conscious effort was made to limit the focus of each of our meetings to a single, resolvable issue. Occasionally, as in the case of the management graphs, a topic was introduced to gain initial reactions. This was then followed up by work done by SEL and reviewed and discussed by the council.

14.3 CONCLUSION

Whether you start a software metrics program using a Software Metrics Council approach or some other approach, you will eventually need some mechanism to maintain your metrics standards and communicate successes and failures. Our goal in this chapter was to provide you with one approach which was successful.

In our implementation, the HP Software Metrics Council served the following needs which you must also meet:

- Final responsibility for software metric standards change and approval.
- Research and internal publication of information and results.
- On-going enthusiasm and selling of metrics concepts.
- Active involvement in home-division software process improvements.

Membership and size were controlled to ensure optimum representation and effectiveness, and the council effectiveness was facilitated by thorough preparation for meetings and activities in between meetings.

15

TWENTY-TWENTY HINDSIGHT

In the preceding chapters, we have presented the history of HP's software metrics program. Our objective in presenting our story in this way was to convince you of the value of using metrics to manage and to set your expectations for what it takes to establish a company-wide program. While the strategy to implement such a program is different for each company in its details, the ten steps we defined earlier are necessary. That isn't to say that project managers must wait until a company-wide program is in place before they collect software metrics. The greatest benefits of collecting metrics are experienced by project managers through better understanding of the process which their team is following and through measurable indications of project status.

By presenting the material in this way, we have satisfied another objective important to us. We have documented a complete historical perspective of HP's program for our own engineers. The farther we move from our initial objectives for starting the program, the easier it becomes to lose sight of our original objectives, which can lead to collecting data for the sake of data rather than for the sake of process improvement. By describing not only the details of what we collect, but also the limitations of the standard metrics and how managers have successfully extended their measurements, we hope to keep the underlying reasons for the collection clearly in the minds of our software engineering community.

The steps we followed started with research into academic and industry experience. Next, we achieved limited consensus on a basic set of metric standards, and sold these to many divisions in the company. Finally, we nurtured the program through written feedback, personal contacts, group presentations at all levels, tool development, training, and by providing forums for sharing success stories.

Before we conclude our story, there are a number of questions we would like to answer. Early in the program, they were much more difficult to answer, but now, with a clear historical perspective in mind, the questions are easier to answer, and the answers are more valuable.

15.1 WHY SHOULD ANYONE WANT TO START A METRICS PROGRAM?

Let's look at a true case history. One of HP's divisions decided to purchase and install an automated warehouse which would cost close to one million dollars. They went through the normal process of justification and determined that they would achieve a complete return on investment a year after the warehouse was operational, so the project was approved and work proceeded. What they didn't realize ahead of time was that the rigor of measuring all of the cost factors and of understanding the process well enough to adapt it to the new system led to substantial improvements by themselves. In fact, over half of the cost of the entire system was saved before one part was ever loaded into the warehouse.

One of the major reasons to measure the software development process is that it results in similar rigor and understanding. In earlier chapters we provided numerous examples of how our early metrics collection efforts quickly led to better understanding and improvements.

A second reason to start a metrics program is that the measurement activities and tools together lead to a greater level of sophistication in software engineering techniques. The success stories described in Chapter 9 are all examples of projects which used more sophisticated techniques than in past projects in order to improve their processes. This sophistication was accompanied by increased professional training and support for tools in the areas of greatest need.

Third, the use of common terminology and the sharing of success stories has led to more consistent use of the most effective development environments and tools available to our engineers. This has helped us to focus on improvements in these areas to achieve even higher short-term leverage.

Finally, we now have a way to determine our progress. As we implement change, we expect to see measurable results.

15.2 WOULD WE DO IT OVER AGAIN?

When we look at the divisions that first started taking measurements three years ago, we see without exception that both the divisions and the project managers involved are effectively using metrics on current projects. In addition, they have all supplied additional data within the last six to nine months. They're hooked.

When we look at the company-wide data, we see a similar trend. Figure 15-1 shows the HP average productivity for each year for which we have data in our database. It also shows the number of projects reporting data for each year, and this trend is definitely still rising (1986 data is only for the first half of the year). The line labeled "New Code Only" is constructed by taking the total code for each year shown (excluding projects consisting of greater than 75 percent reused code) and divided by the total engineering months for the corresponding year. The line labeled "Include Reused Code" includes the other projects. The numbers in parentheses give the total number of projects of each type.

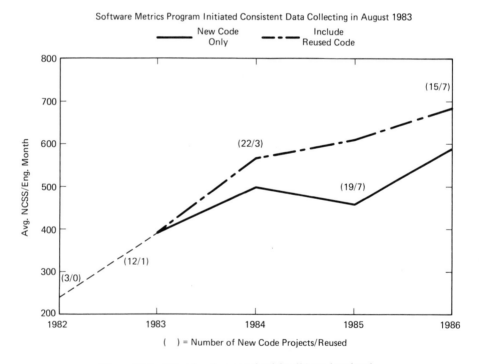

Figure 15-1   HP code volume productivity (93 total projects).

It would be nice to look at the productivity gain and say, "Wow, all we had to do was start collecting data, and our productivity improved two to three times." We have not collected data long enough yet, though, and such conclusions would be very premature. Even if we had more data and could show an impressive graph, would the gains be a direct result of collecting metrics or a result of other actions taken? In Chapter 4 we saw a graph of productivity for a Japanese company that showed no improvement for the first four years for which they had measurements. Only time will tell whether our trends will continue, or whether we will see a similar flat start-up period.

Figure 15-2 shows prerelease discovered defect density for the data collected so far. The graph includes only those defects discovered during formal test. This data is more sparse than the productivity data during the early years of HP's metrics collection.

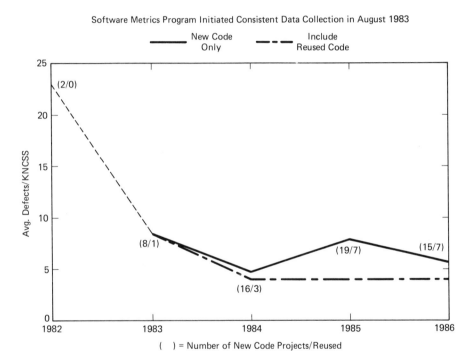

Software Metrics Program Initiated Consistent Data Collection in August 1983

Figure 15-2   HP prerelease discovered defect density (78 total projects).

Would we do it over again? Yes, and we have set a similar company-wide metrics program in place for our other engineering development processes. This program was started about a year and a half after the software-specific program was, after our initial software metrics progress showed the potential for such measurements. It was organized by individuals from many divisions with the job responsibility of "productivity manager." Their metrics were published only quite recently, and they are broken into three categories:

PROJECT/PRODUCT
    Return factor
    Project design changes
    Staff level
    Customer visits

PROCESS
    Cycle times
    Trends
    Input/output
    Productivity

PEOPLE
    Performance review delinquency
    Project completion
    Training
    Turnover

It will be interesting to follow the progress of these measurements and see how they evolve over time.

15.3 WHAT WOULD WE DO DIFFERENTLY?

There are always things you would change if you could start over. When we first set up the HP Software Metrics Council, we had no idea that we would come so far, so fast. So it is difficult to say that we would approach the overall program much differently than we did. But there are several specific areas we would emphasize differently.

First, the area where projects and divisions have been most successful so far is with quality metrics (defects, branch flow analysis, predicting testing time). Knowing this now, we probably could have pushed our original definitions farther than we did, or we could have extended them with guidelines which provided more standardization than we currently have for the definitions of defects. There continues to be considerable variation among groups in what is counted and reported for defects. While individual divisions seem capable of consistent counting, the useful exchange of information at a detailed level is greatly inhibited by the use of different terminology for similar things, or by counting or not counting the same things. For a long time HP has had standard codes for many typical hardware defects. It is likely that we need such codes for software, and we should even consider project defect reporting by groups of categories.

Second, the desire (and necessity) for tools to support metrics collection is insatiable, and we could have done more to provide these earlier in the program. This is one area where we are currently making up for lost time. As with many other product areas, our experience is that as soon as a tool is provided which solves one particular need, the user community immediately goes beyond that need to other needs which are uncovered.

The third area which we would change is more problematical, because we aren't sure how to change. We have had the least success in HP in getting metrics data collected in divisions with substantial existing software product lines. Part of the reason for this is that we did not define maintenance-related metrics until the program was a year old. These divisions have a much larger proportion of software activities involved in enhancements and maintenance than those where metrics have caught on most quickly. Even so, the maintenance metrics have not caught on as readily as those for new development did in the same time period. Another reason is that metrics already existed which characterized the nature and severity of postrelease problems, but they were not related to the development process. As a result, managers felt comfortable using the existing metrics, but these metrics provided little hope for discovering fundamental process-related changes. The coupling of the maintenance metrics which the Software Metrics Council defined to the existing postrelease metrics remains a challenge for us.

15.4 HOW FAR ALONG ARE WE?

If we considered our metrics program as a project, it probably completed its investigation phase sometime after about two years. We saw in Chapter 4 that the investigation phase of the average project is 22 percent of the total (calendar time). Extrapolating, we can say that the metrics program won't be complete for another seven years. This is a pretty sobering thought, but we interpret it as meaning that it will be some time before the measurements and their feedback are so ingrained into the process and our actions that we no longer have to discuss what to collect for each project and how to use the data.

We have good tools in place which help track defects and quality trends, and it seems likely that these will continue to provide substantial short-term gains. Whether these gains will be enough to change our development cycle times significantly and lead to the same kind of dramatic process improvements discussed in Chapter 2 for manufacturing remains to be seen. In any event, we believe that the techniques of metrics collection now in use will result in significant product improvements for our customers.

15.5 CONCLUSION

In this chapter we summarized our results up to the present (three years after the start). To us, the process followed to achieve these results was not one which was unusual or necessarily unique to our company, although our company culture certainly helped its implementation. We stated earlier that one of the primary benefits of a metrics program was the introduction of a common set of terminology. This aspect of the program is now mature, and while no measure of productivity shows orders of magnitude improvement so far, there is increasing confidence that the measures in place will lead to significant process improvements.

16

A DETAILED SOFTWARE
DEVELOPMENT PROCESS
DESCRIPTION

Much earlier, we presented a strategy to follow for the successful implementation of a company-wide software metrics program. This strategy drew heavily from the successes we experienced at HP. A natural question remains: What are we pursuing now?

In the remainder of the book, we present a vision of where we are headed. There are two chapters which deal with an overall development process description and how project managers could use metrics data automatically generated from components of the process. Some of the concepts discussed have been successfully tried by groups outside HP in limited ways, and others haven't been tried, to the best of our knowledge, except as prototypes in our labs.

16.1 DEFINITION OF THE PROBLEM

We have successfully used product life cycles at HP for many years to help us manage product development and introduction in a relatively consistent way. These life cycles included a clear definition of the product team, consisting of lab, product management, production engineering, support, and quality engineering. They stated that the management of this team was the responsibility of the lab project manager. Over time, the concepts of the hardware product life cycle were naturally extended in ways which helped to define the necessary steps for software development, but which did little to simplify them. By and large, the outputs from the intermediate steps of the software development process were prose documents describing the nature of the problem and its solution to varying levels of detail in a form considerably removed from that of the final product.

Two aspects of software development suggest that the traditional model is insufficient and needs more rigor to help project managers manage difficult software projects. The first is that the user interface to many software products is much more malleable than for past stand-alone hardware products. Where a hardware front panel used to limit the complexity of the user interface, software interfaces frequently become overly complex. This complexity has also appeared in some recent firmware-driven hardware products. Second, many of our software products interrelate with other software and hardware products, and these interrelationships tend to grow in an uncontrolled and increasingly complex manner. To complicate this second aspect even more, the interrelated software products have increasingly been responsibilities of teams dispersed over wide geographic areas. Far-reaching decisions are routinely made at very low levels within the organization. The result of these problems seems to be that, as currently defined, the job of managing software projects is significantly more complex than it was in the past.

16.2 MANAGEMENT OF COMPLEXITY

When the Software Metrics Council first defined metrics for use within HP, there were five major categories. Of the five, the categories of size, people/time/cost, and defects all provided some immediate benefits to project managers in understanding and monitoring development processes. The remaining two of difficulty (complexity) and communications were elusive, however. There was a strong feeling in the council that it was necessary to measure these last two because they both represented significant problem areas. There was little confidence in our ability to control the number of necessary communications at the project management level, but we did believe that communications and complexity correlated with longer schedules. The engineering community showed little enthusiasm for the use of these two metrics, and the lack of any appreciable data gathered in the first two years told us that some work remained.

16.2.1 Types of Complexity

In retrospect, one of the key stumbling blocks when measuring complexity is that there are many forms of complexity. For example, inherent complexity refers to the definition of the scope of a problem. The design of an operating system is clearly more complex than the design of a line-counting tool. Even an operating system can be broken down into component pieces, many of which are as simple as a line-counting tool (for example, I/O library routines). The remaining pieces remain inherently more complex, though, and the combination of them into a completed operating system is inherently complex. Early recognition of product scope that is too broad can lead to decisions to limit the scope or to solve the problem differently.

Unnecessary complexity frequently is the result of changes being made without a complete understanding of a system. The maintenance phase of mature products is particularly susceptible to introduction of unnecessary complexity, as are projects under severe time constraints.

Another type of complexity, which we will call *psychological complexity*, occurs due to the appearance of a product or set of documents. Such complexity frequently appears in the form of a "busy" transparency, where forcing too much information onto one overhead prohibits understanding by an audience. The same information on two or three overheads can be easily understood. The same problem occurs when screen interfaces are overly complicated. This type of complexity is also inherent in the book-length prose specifications that we sometimes produce.

Communications complexity is illustrated in Figure 16-1 by two possible views of communications paths we first heard Professor Vincent Shen of Purdue describe. The left figure represents a centralized project orientation, perhaps a chief designer and an implementation team, and the right figure represents a decentralized organization with technical communications necessary among all members equally. Ten necessary communications paths versus four clearly is more complicated, especially if additional organizational or distance factors are introduced.

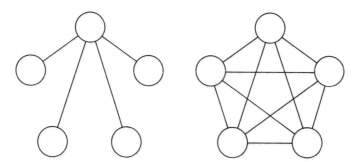

Figure 16-1   Communications paths for two different project teams.

This is not to say that all teams must be rigidly structured with formal, constrained communications. Rather, we are suggesting that early assignment of *responsibilities* for various key aspects of project completion (such as final product integration, or intermodule communications consistency) helps to limit unnecessary communications overhead and leads to better products.

The four types of complexity discussed thus far are summarized in Figure 16-2. The presence of at least four different types suggests that measuring complexity is in itself complex.

Inherent Complexity: the basic property of a problem that requires its solution to be more complex than that of another.

Unnecessary Complexity: complexity which is built into a solution that is not inherently required.

Psychological Complexity: complexity which exists solely due to the representation of a design or product, and not due to the presence of either inherent or unnecessary complexity.

Communications Complexity: complexity caused by the number of individuals involved or the method of communications required between members of a project.

Figure 16-2   Types of complexity.

With these definitions in mind, we can restate the basic problem:

> Because software is so easily changed, it tends to be changed without careful analysis or complete understanding of the impact on the internal complexity of a product or on the user-interface complexity. Furthermore, many of our software products interrelate with other software and hardware products, making it difficult to change one without requiring a change in the others.

What is needed to round out the measurements and tools already in use is a means to measure and help manage software change and complexity. The process which includes such measurements represents a development methodology which gives project managers the information necessary to simplify their jobs.

16.3 A HIGH-LEVEL PROCESS DESCRIPTION

The five major phases of the software life cycle are specifications, design, implementation, test and maintenance. Each of these can be thought of as a transformation of information about a product from one form into another. Each transformation incorporates better understanding and detail until a complete solution is achieved. Each also represents successive levels of product abstraction which are measurable.

The definition of a detailed software development process centered around metrics is based upon two premises. First, the output of each major phase can be represented partially in a graphical or pictorial form which reduces psychological complexity. Second, measurements of the product representation are possible which flag inherent or unnecessary complexity when present. Figure 16-3 shows a data flow diagram for a development methodology which includes outputs from each development transformation which are pictorially oriented and measurable, inputs which define the

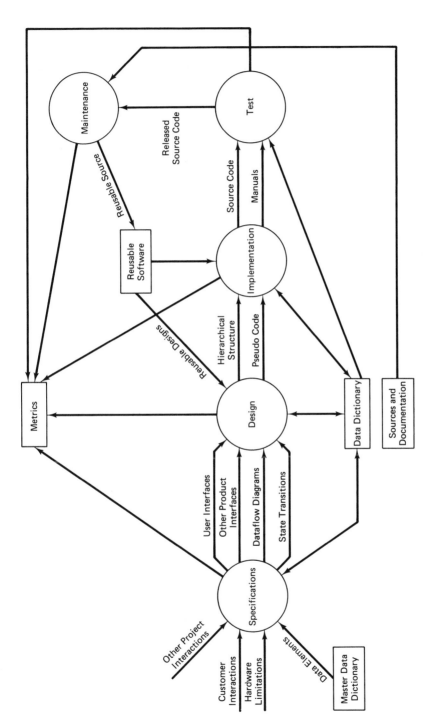

Figure 16-3 A software development methodology incorporating metrics.

195

number of communications interfaces, and databases which encourage common language and simplified communications. This diagram is intentionally simplified for purposes of illustration.

For example, the circle labeled Implementation represents a transformation. It has four input data flows. Those labeled Hierarchical Structure and Pseudo Code were outputs from another transformation. The one labeled Reusable Source comes from the database labeled Reusable Software. The remaining input is unlabeled to keep the diagram simple, and it represents data elements flowing from the database labeled Data Dictionary as well as product and support documentation flowing from the database labeled Sources and Documentation. There are four outputs, two to another transformation and two to databases.

One of the primary features illustrated in Figure 16-3 is transformations that reduce psychological complexity through the use of pictorial output. The data flows labeled User Interfaces, Data Flow Diagrams, State Transitions, and Hierarchical Structure are all assumed to be in pictorial form. A method which is gaining popularity that also helps to reduce psychological complexity is object-oriented programming. Object-oriented programming strives to hide internal operation and data structures of modules from users, and there are languages available which encourage correct usage. Such usage lends itself to the creation of reusable components. The combination of pictorial representation, correct design partitioning, and precise definition of module interfaces leads to cleaner, more maintainable systems.

A second major feature illustrated by Figure 16-3 is the measurable nature of many components of the development process. Major outputs which are measurable are shown in Table 16-1.

The Desired Measures column shows what we would like to be able to compute. For example, we would like to compare the structural complexity of two designs quantitatively, which means that we need a way of calculating structural complexity directly from measurable aspects of the hierarchy chart. The metrics column indicates some of the measurable aspects of the Outputs column. For most of the desired measures, we do not yet have a formula which relates the metrics to an overall complexity indicator.

There is little experience with many of these measures today, although several studies using complexity metrics [1,2] indicate promising results and suggest where in the software we should be investing our effort. There are two popular measures for internal software code complexity:

McCabe's cyclomatic complexity [3] indicates the number of paths through a given piece of code. It counts branching statements in order to compute the number of paths. Cyclomatic complexity can be used to predict psychological complexity; human short-term memory can retain only a limited number of paths at a time. Cyclomatic complexity can also flag the possibility of unnecessarily complex procedures. For those procedures or modules for

TABLE 16-1   Measurable Outputs of the Software Development Process

Phase	Outputs	Desired Measures	Metrics
Specifications	Data flow diagrams	Overall complexity factor, complexity of separable components, data complexity	Primitive token count, # primitive processes (bubbles)
	User Interfaces	Number of interfaces, complexity of interfaces	#screens, # required user inputs, avg. # choices/screen
Design	State transitions	Transition complexity	# states, # transitions
	Hierarchical structure	Structural complexity	# data items passed between modules, # modules
Implementation	Pseudo code	Module complexity	# branches, # procedures # variables
	Source code (including test code)	Maintainability factors	NCSS, % comments score on style analysis

which there is no clean way to reduce cyclomatic complexity, one can conclude that they are inherently complex.

The harder a module is to understand, the easier it is to make an error in writing or fixing it. Complexity measures can be used to predict error-prone modules. Given a limited budget, a project cannot afford 100 percent branch coverage or inspection coverage. It is most cost effective to simplify unnecessarily complex modules, and spend more time inspecting, reviewing, and testing those modules which are inherently more complex.

Halstead's difficulty metric [1] can have the same use as McCabe's cyclomatic complexity but uses different assumptions about what makes a module complex. Halstead believed that the ease of reading and writing software is related to the richness of the vocabulary used (unique operators and operands) as well as the number of times each variable is used. He believed that the larger the repertoire of operators used, the more difficult the algorithm would be to write and maintain. Also, the greater the average number of times each variable is used, the more difficult it is to remember the current state of the variable.

At least one study concluded that the Halstead metric is a more effective predictor of defects than McCabe's [4].* Our own experience so far has proved inconclusive. We are convinced, though, that defect-prone modules

---

* Copyright © 1979 IEEE.

are predictable by complexity analysis, but that such analysis must occur earlier in the development process than at the code level.

Besides the transformations and data flows of the methodology shown in Figure 16-3, there are five databases defined in Table 16-2, which are designed to standardize major project communications.

TABLE 16-2   Databases which Support the Software Development Process

Database	Contents
Data Dictionary	Contains data-element definitions for a project except for those in the Master Data Dictionary.
Master Data Dictionary	Contains standard data-element definitions common across all projects.
Metrics	Contains historical metrics data, project and process metrics data.
Reusable Software	Contains reusable software in the form of designs and/or source code.
Sources and Documentation	Contains all project documentation and sources (code, diagrams, and the like) in a controlled environment.

16.4 THE ROLE OF TOOLS

By examining measurable results represented in Figure 16-3, we saw several opportunities to identify complexity for project managers. It is useful to examine the software development process from the perspective of use of an integrated tool set. The circle diagram in Figure 16-4 illustrates such a description and shows tools which are used during the various development stages. The diagram does not show many aspects of development which are taken for granted: editors, compilers, file system, and the like. The combined environment would gain much of its power from the fact that the tools work together as an integrated whole. Unfortunately, such a complete *integrated* set of tools doesn't exist today other than as a long-term goal.

16.4.1 The Importance of Tools

Tools are frequently created so that some element of the software development process can be performed more quickly. Unfortunately, this has not always led to doing the job better, so we sometimes find ourselves in the position of being capable of making more mistakes faster. In presenting the data flow model in Figure 16-3, we discussed some other roles that tools can play. One primary role we have seen is minimizing psychological complexity. Sometimes this is accomplished by providing pictorial output rather than prose; other times it is by automatically dealing with necessary details. Another role they play is flagging or minimizing unnecessary complexity. For

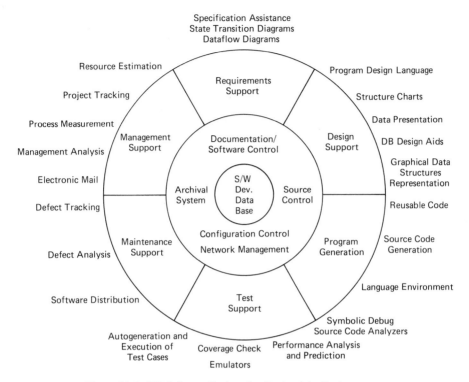

Figure 16-4   HP Software Engineering Productivity Environment.

example, source code analyzers are available which report complexity metrics. "Pretty printer" programs can actually eliminate unnecessary psychological complexity by automatically reformatting the source.

Both of these roles increase our ability to achieve a higher-quality product. A third role for tools, and perhaps the most significant, is to implement a consistent development methodology. The development methodology presented in Figure 16-3 is reinforced by the toolset of Figure 16-4 in two important ways. First, the central database(s) for documentation and software provides a common control mechanism for all important parts of a project. While depriving the project team of some freedom, such control provides important limits to unnecessary communications complexity which otherwise burdens the project manager, as well as the project team. Second, integration of the tools and the metrics which many provide gives a management view of the process through the system. This has the effect of both reinforcing the development methodology and providing the project manager with system-supplied answers to questions concerning progress.

16.4.2 Tools and Metrics

Let us look at four particular tools and the ways in which they can output complexity measures. Figure 16-5 shows a data flow representation for a part of a system. This data flow represents an expansion of a single transformation (or circle) from another, higher-level diagram. In a similar way, it is possible to decompose each circle in this diagram in more detail, until finally the problem is specified completely in terms of primitive processes with data flowing into and out of them. When data flows for an entire project are completed early in the project, there is an opportunity to determine an overall complexity factor based upon the number of transformations, data flows, unique data elements, and databases required. As the data flows are broken down into hierarchical groups of modules, these also can be analyzed for complexity if there are connections between the data flow diagramming tools and the hierarchy tool. It can be expected that complexity measures for these tools

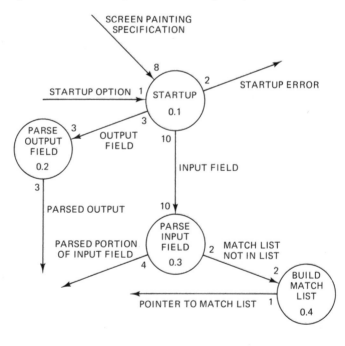

Process Name	Classification	Weight	Tokens
startup	initiation	1.0	24
parseoutputfield	separation	0.6	6
parseinputfield	separation	0.6	16
buildmatchlist	amalgamation	0.6	3

Bang: 39

Figure 16-5 Sample data flow diagram.

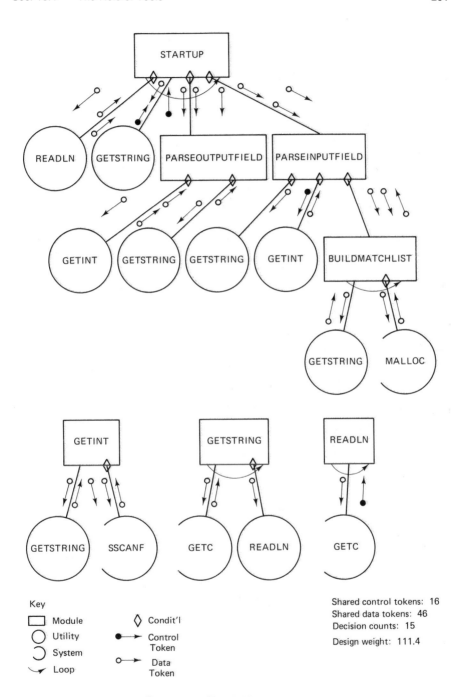

Figure 16-6 Sample hierarchy chart.

would function similarly to those at the code level using the principles described earlier of the McCabe metrics. Tom DeMarco has defined metrics of "bang" and "design weight" [5] (and their associated primitives), which we use in these examples as measures of complexity.

Figure 16-6 shows a hierarchy chart which represents a portion of the design of the system partially shown in Figure 16-5. The hierarchy tool should be able to represent the overall structural complexity by analyzing the number of modules, the number of levels, and the types of interconnects.

To illustrate pseudo code, we decompose a portion of the design shown in Figure 16-6. This representation is much simpler with a smaller complexity measure than we are likely to find in source code. These are the primary motivations for preparing pseudo code first. The thinking process steers clear of excessive detail, and fewer errors should result. If the pseudo code can be maintained (either as a part of the source for generating a program or via backward translation techniques), then the resulting product code becomes easier to maintain. The pseudo code is shown in Figure 16-7. The complexity measure is the number of branch statements including whiles, fors, and ifs.

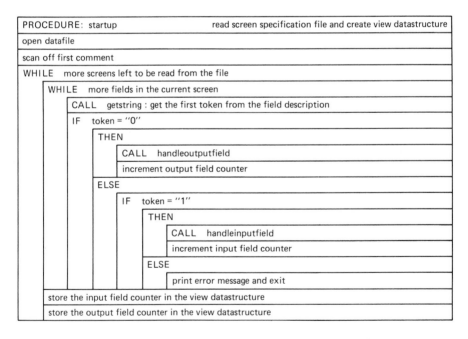

Complexity: 5
Statements: 19

Figure 16-7   Pseudo code for sample source.

Source code has been more frequently analyzed in the past than the preceding design representations. Figure 16-8 shows a fragment of the source code for a portion of the pseudo code shown in Figure 16-7 and the metrics for that fragment. Typically there are two to three times the number of source lines as pseudo code lines, and, as can be seen from this example of real source, the pseudo code is much more understandable. The summary at the end shows that the program contains 25 NCSS, 0 percent comments, and has a McCabe complexity metric of 13.

```
while ((i <= MAXSCREENS-1) & result != EF)) {
    j = 0;
    incounter = 0;
    outcounter = 0; result = OK;

    while ((j <= MAXFIELDS) & (result != EOS) & (result != EF) {

        result = getstring(delin, datafile); /* check dcl for c */
        if (result == OK) {
            if (strcmp(delim,"0") == 0) {
                result = handleoutputfield(datafile, i, outcounter);
                outcounter++;
                j++;
            }
            else
                if (strcmp(delim,"I") == 0) {
                    result = handleinputfield(datafile, incounter);
                    incounter++;
                    j++;
                }
                else {
                    printf("%s
n",MN_DATAFILE);
                }       exit();
        }
        else /* if result not OK */
            if (result != EF)

        .


        .


        .

McCabe Complexity: 13
NCSS: 25
Comments: 0
```

Figure 16-8   Sample source program.

16.4.3 Event Triggering

For complexity metrics to be of value, they must be used to create appropriate flags or trigger actions. The most important use of such a trigger is to provide immediate feedback to a software engineer concerning the complexity of a design or code. Such an early flag can lead to simplified designs or implementations. A second use of these triggers is illustrated by the way they function in a defect tracking system used at HP. When a defect occurs and is reported at an engineer's workstation, the defect report is routed automatically to the appropriate responsible engineer, and an electronic mail message alerting the recipient to its arrival is initiated as well. Similarly, steps of receipt, acceptance, forwarding, or resolution should automatically create messages. The mechanisms to create and route these messages (or alarms) play a key role in the integration of the methodological tools with the tracking and control systems of the project manager.

The examples of Figures 16-5 through 16-8 show that at each stage of development, it is possible to measure complexity. If the tools which calculate complexity make this data available, the data can be automatically compared against predefined values in order to flag potential problems. Through these, the project manager can be alerted to inherent or unnecessary levels of complexity and take appropriate actions. In combination with the more usual metrics of size, engineering time, and defects, we now have access to the information necessary to simplify the task of the software project manager.

16.5 SUMMARY

Three major points have been presented in this discussion of our vision of how metrics should be integrated into software development tools and methodologies. First, there are four forms of complexity which must be managed: inherent complexity, unnecessary complexity, psychological complexity, and communications complexity. Providing graphic outputs from various stages of the specifications and design processes help to reduce psychological complexity and make documents easier to read. Metric outputs from development tools can alert developers and/or managers to the presence of inherent or unnecessary complexity.

Second, an important key to metric usage throughout the development process is having tools that work together. As an example, we illustrated four steps of representation that went from data flow to hierarchical to pseudo code to code. This sequence represents one possible decomposition of a software problem. At each step of this decomposition, the examples showed metrics which measured the complexity of the problem representation.

Third, the concept of trigger actions was presented. This concept says that the various metrics collected by the tools of an integrated environment must play a more active role than in past metrics collection. They must interact with developers and managers as information is available. They must flag potential problems as they occur and not considerably later in the process.

Two complementary models of a modified process were presented which focused on reduction of psychological complexity and simplification of the project management task through automatic identification of various sources of complexity. By using tools to drive a measurable development methodology, it is expected that the task of software project management will be simplified. Many decisions can be virtually automatic, and others can at least be supported by quantified data.

BIBLIOGRAPHY

1. Christensen, K., G. Fitsos, and C. Smith, "A Perspective on Software Science," *IBM Systems Journal*, Vol. 20, no.4 (1981).

2. Rambo, R., P. Buckley, and E. Branyan, "Establishment and Validation of Software Metric Factors," *Proceedings of the International Society of Parametric Analysts Seventh Annual Conference* (May 1985), pp. 410–416.

3. Arthur, L. J., *Measuring Programmer Productivity and Software Quality.* New York: John Wiley and Sons, 1985, pp. 65–73.

4. Curtis, B., S. Sheppard, and P. Milliman, "Third Time Charm: Stronger Prediction of Programmer Performance by Software Complexity Metrics," *IEEE Proceedings of the Fourth International Conference on Software Engineering* (1979), pp. 356–360.

5. DeMarco, T., *Controlling Software Projects.* New York: Yourdon Press, 1982, pp. 80–91, 104–112. Reprinted by permission of Prentice-Hall, Inc., Englewood Cliffs, New Jersey.

17

THE "NEW" ROLE OF THE
SOFTWARE PROJECT MANAGER

We have looked at an overall methodology focused upon reduction of psychological complexity and measurements to flag inherent and unnecessary complexity. We then looked at how tools can support the methodology. Now let us look at the task of the project manager and see how this methodology and the associated tools can ease the burden currently placed on the project manager.

When we enumerate all of the expectations for a project manager at HP as described by our life cycle, the responsibilities are many (even though it is expected that many of the tasks are delegated) [1]:

Get product team involved	Set product specifications
Produce project data sheets	Provide project progress chart
Estimate project expenses	Manage all project resources
Produce project schedule	Produce product design
Evaluate competition and state of the art	Measure product performance
	Ensure conformance to standards
Ensure sound technical practices	Ensure serviceability
Ensure product safety	Provide project documentation
Meet reliability objectives	Provide liaison to other divisions
Communicate to appropriate groups	Oversee manual development
Set up and run checkpoint meetings	Arrange for tooling plan
Schedule and obtain project services	Arrange for product documentation
Initiate and accomplish sign-off	Provide information for support plan
Provide for field training	Ensure project follow-up

These responsibilities apply to all project managers, whether their project is software or hardware. These tasks do not include personnel-related management duties such as wage and performance reviews, recruiting, and the like. In addition, there are other responsibilities not listed which uniquely apply to hardware projects. These involve costs and planning associated with hardware prototypes, tooling, and transfer of a product into production. Now let us look at a final set of responsibilities which uniquely apply to software projects. The additions to the above list include:

Define coding standards
Define variable conventions
Select development language
Optimize product human factors
Plan for localization (adaption to foreign languages)
Arrange for backup and recovery
Arrange for quality plan
Define source, version, configuration control
Specify naming conventions
Track a changing development environment
Define design approach
Ensure common data elements and usage
Sort out enhancements versus defects
Determine strategy for multiuser systems
Plan for interfaces to other software (present and future)
Plan for target environmental considerations (output devices,
          terminals and the like)

Psychological research has shown that both the human span of absolute judgment and the span of immediate memory are limited to around seven items [2]. The prospect of picking seven items to worry about at a given time out of a list of over 40 items is overwhelming.

Having enumerated this incredible list of responsibilities, we can suggest that the basic problem for project managers is

> It is not humanly possible for them to keep track of all of their responsibilities at once. In fact, it is probable that new project managers don't even understand what some of the responsibilities entail.

Let us look at the role of the project manager from another perspective. A project manager has a split personality: the investigation personality and the development personality. During investigation the project manager is the chief contracting agent and must worry about definition of roles and responsibilities, as well as plans for how the entire project team and its activities will be coordinated. This role emphasizes controlled analysis and well-organized discussions and meetings. It is much more realistic to schedule a meeting during investigation, when all the necessary parties can conveniently attend, than during development. In contrast, the development personality (which corresponds to about eighty percent of project time, according to most data) is event- and crisis-driven. During development the project manager focuses on tracking progress and controlling the many interactions and critical project paths.

The elements of these two personalities and all of the responsibilities on the prior lists can be broken down into four major project categories: definition, estimating and scheduling, control, and tracking. Let's examine each of these, with particular emphasis on the software-specific set of responsibilities, to see how the proposed methodology and tools can help. Note that some responsibilities fall into more than one category. A simplified diagram showing each of these categories and summarizing the major flows of information is shown in Figure 17-1.

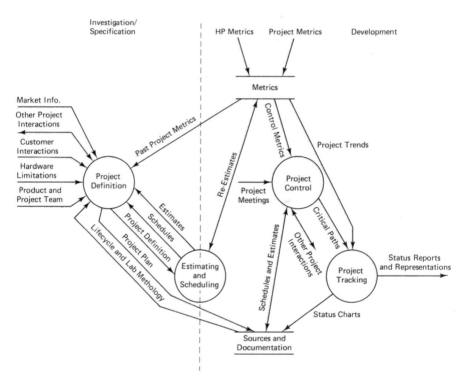

Figure 17-1   The project management process.

17.1 THE INVESTIGATION RESPONSIBILITIES

17.1.1 Project Definition

Let us define project definition *(not product definition)* as decisions which can be made or avoided, but which will generally require project management time at some point in a software project. Responsibilities in the previous list which fall under this definition include: coding standards, variable conventions, language selection, human factors, localization, backup and recovery, quality plan, and changing development environments. If these definitions are made at any point other than the very start of a project, they probably introduce unnecessary complexity to the project at the point at which they are made. This complexity may be as simple as just representing one more decision added to a plate already overflowing, or it can be even worse and represent additional work which must be done to redo earlier work. Similarly, many of the standard tasks required of the project manager can be simplified if the ground rules are defined at the very start of the project.

It is useful to define these formally in a project plan which becomes a living, working document for the duration of the project. A table of contents of a sample of such a plan is illustrated in Figure 17-2. The objective of such a plan is not to replace other documents such as the product plan or support plan. The objective of the project plan is to provide a consolidated starting point from which all members of the project team can work. Ideally this document is a summary of all necessary plans, is no longer than twenty pages, and contains many graphic and tabular summaries to minimize psychological complexity.

While such a plan is an important element in a project's success, it is typically not included in most commercially available automated project management tools. A tool which consists of a simple, but powerful guided set of questions could create a clean workable project plan with relative ease. Such a plan then could be maintained by using a common editor.

17.1.2 Estimating and Scheduling

The responsibilities of estimating and scheduling are the ones typically addressed by automated tools today. These include estimating project expenses and schedule and laying out a project progress chart (usually PERT or Gantt or both). These tools generally do not simplify the project management job, because they do not provide for automated inputs to the continual updates of schedules or progress charts. Today's tools are passive. They are driven solely by inputs from the project manager, when the project manager has the time and motivation to use them, with whatever information is currently known through discussions with team members. Estimating packages generally have no feedback paths from the development process to

Introduction

Product identification, name, mnemonic, number, team, abstract, objectives

Product Description

Product environment, definitions and features, target users, localization, human factors, user manuals

Project Standards

Coding standards, naming conventions, language(s), backup and recovery, design standards, configuration management plan

Product Development Plan

Form of reporting status, reviews, meetings, documents, metrics, quality objectives, and means of verification (FURPS)

Product Support Plan

Documentation, training, verification, manufacturing/distribution, maintenance projections, installation/support, feedback, postimplementation review

Resource Requirements

Hardware, tools, people expertise

Schedule

Code estimates, milestones, Gantt chart, PERT chart, contingency plans

Issues

Technical, organizational, phased releases

Figure 17-2   Sample outline for a project plan.

trigger reestimation, yet significantly more is known about the project at every step. As a minimum, the start of each new phase should trigger such a reestimation via electronic mail to the project manager. It, in turn, ought to automatically lead to revised project progress charts. Other situations which should trigger reestimation include schedule slips greater than some defined percentage, or design or module size estimations off by more than a defined percentage.

17.2 THE DEVELOPMENT RESPONSIBILITIES

17.2.1 Project Control

The elements of project control from our earlier list include: source, version, configuration control, naming conventions, changing development environment, design approach, common data elements and usage, human factors (user interfaces), changing personnel assignments and responsibilities, and overall quality. Some of these responsibilities are significantly simplified by specific tools. For example, source, version, and configuration control problems are largely removed from the realm of real-time project manager worries by systems which require all team members to check in and out all documentation and software under development and insure conformity to an agreed-upon set of rules.

Other elements, such as design approach, common data elements and usage, and overall quality can be helped through automated flags and measurements taken by various tools involved in the transformations shown in Figure 16-3. For example, as the specification of a product using data flow diagrams and screens approaches completion, complexity metrics both at overall levels and different levels of breakdown could flag potential problem areas. With these flags available early in the process, the project manager has the opportunity to deal with potential problems, thus reducing the overall complexity of the project and its management.

17.2.2 Project Tracking

Let us define project tracking as the project management task of providing visible forms of project progress for the team and other interested parties. Project tracking and project control have interrelated needs, but it is useful to address the subject of tracking separately, because the demands for tracking are generally from people outside the project team (like upper management and other departments), and the form of output is generally less detailed than for control alone. As with many of the responsibilities included in project control, these tasks are also aided by both the outputs of the tools described earlier and by tracking the more standard metrics of size, engineering hours, and defects.

Typical reports which aid tracking are completion trends of code versus estimates, completion status of software by individual responsibility or module grouping, test coverage trends, trends of amount of code integrated, and trends of defect detection. Elements which could be automated are status summaries from the data flow diagrammer, the hierarchical chart drawer, the pseudo code tool, and the compilers used by the project.

17.3 A DECISION SUPPORT APPROACH

We see that it is possible to minimize the difficulty of the project management job by using tools and data. The form of this solution, though, must take into account the high-pressure, interrupt-driven environment in which the software project manager works. Next, we will describe a set of tools which form the basis for a project management Decision Support System (DSS). Some parts of the description relate to existing tools, while other parts relate to tools or capabilities of tools which currently do not exist.

There are generally four major elements of a DSS. First, it has a very friendly user interface. (It is easy to use, and very little training or documentation is necessary.) Second, it contains a very flexible database (typically relational), so it is possible to easily add, delete, or manipulate data (including "what if" questions). Third, accurate information gathering from diverse sources is supported and facilitated. Fourth, graphic outputs play a major role.

In addition to these properties, it is desirable that the communications role of the project manager be enhanced by any automated solutions. In particular, both input data and messages, as well as outputs communicating decisions and background information, must be readily accessible to the project and product teams.

17.3.1 The Investigation Activities

Two responsibilities of the project manager discussed earlier are executed primarily during project investigation: project definition, and estimating and scheduling. As suggested earlier, a set of guided questions could lead to an organized output. Figure 17-3 illustrates a small section of the project plan outlined in Figure 17-2.

Ideally, a second automatic output could consist of a set of overheads which are suitable for management presentations corresponding to the major sections of the project plan.

Two aspects of building an automated project planning tool are important to remember. First, in order for a question-driven approach to be useful to a project manager, it must be quickly reentrant at various points. This is because a project plan is not a document done sequentially in a quiet room. The major task of its preparation essentially consists of getting numerous inputs and commitments from busy people of the involved groups. Second, at some point it becomes far easier for project managers to simply deal with documents by using their favorite editor, so any special formatting characters used to make the document appear nice (to minimize psychological complexity) must be relatively obvious and easy to use.

Figure 17-2 addressed many of the organizational aspects of the project, and attempted to encourage all of the early communication and "contract negotiation" with groups outside the immediate development group necessary for a successful project. Another major activity done by the development team during the investigation is the initial estimating. The following excerpts from an internal estimating package used at HP, called Softcost, shows an illustration of how the process is facilitated (refer to page 213):

Guided Questions

Section 5 - Product Support

Who will produce the following documents? $\boxed{\text{RETURN}}$ means not required, "?" means not yet defined)

Who will write user manual?   **technical writer**

Who will write installation guide?   **?**

Who will write quick reference guide? $\boxed{\text{RETURN}}$

Who will write systems administrators guide?   **development team**

Will internal product documentation be supplied to customer (Y/N)?   **N**

Are any other customer support documents required?   **Configuration guides**

Who will write the configuration guides?   **technical writer**

Describe the levels of customer training which will be supplied. **Training will consist of three levels ...**

.

.

.

Output

5.0 PRODUCT SUPPORT

5.1 Documentation Plan

The final product will include a user manual, an installation guide, and a systems administrators guide. These manuals will be produced by:

User manual - technical writer

Installation guide - ?

Systems administrators guide - development team

Configuration guides - technical writer

5.2 Training Plan

Training will consist of three levels ...

Figure 17-3   Excerpt from tool-assisted project plan.

11. Overall   implementation   personnel   qualifications   and   motivation?   (Response)

    1. n/a   2. low   3. medium   4. high   3

12. Percentage of programmers doing both functional design and development?

    1. n/a   2. <25   3. 25-50   4. >50   4

13. Previous programmer experience with application of similar or greater size and complexity?

    1. n/a   2. minimal   3. moderate   4. extensive   3

14. Previous experience with operational computer to be used?

    1. n/a   2. minimal   3. moderate   4. extensive   4

15. Previous experience with programming language(s) to be used?

    1. n/a   2. minimal   3. moderate   4. extensive   3

16. Use of top-down methodology?

    1. n/a   2. low   3. medium   4. high   3

The total number of questions asked is forty-six, but like the questions in the project plan example, *the power of the tool is derived from the process of forcing the project manager to consider the many possibilities.* One of the outputs of this process is that shown in Figure 17-4 [3].

Revised Estimated Overall Parameters (Average)	
Esitmated size (KNCSS):	41
Effort (person-months):	67
(kilo-dollars):	532
Productivity (NCSS/person-month):	615
Duration (months):	18
Average staff (persons):	3.7
Expected maximum staffing at:	12 months from start

Figure 17-4   Softcost report on budgeted resources.

We would prefer to use an estimating example which is not driven by lines of code, because lines of code are not well-known early in the investigation phase. At some HP divisions, though, Softcost is producing reasonable results. Other groups are using manual estimating techniques based upon more accurate functional analysis of the problem. Nevertheless, the cost factors explored by questions such as those shown in this example must be considered when any estimating technique is used. Putting the estimates and their means of derivation *into the project plan* provides a reminder and a reason to reestimate later in the project as more accurate information is known (our assumption is that the project plan is revised at each of the transitions from investigation/specification to design to implementation to test).

Many project managers use automated tools to produce PERT charts which include project plan components (estimates, deliverables) and product components (code, documentation). PERTs provide a link between the investigation activities and the development activities. A section of one is shown in Figure 17-5.

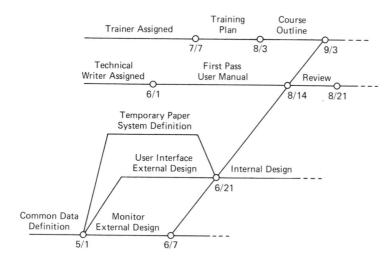

Figure 17-5   Portion of a project PERT chart.

The three activities of project plan, estimation, and PERT chart normally proceed in parallel and closely interrelate. Together they represent a reasonably complete decision support system during investigation which helps to simplify the project management task later during development.

17.3.2 The Development Activities

During development, the project manager is much more interrupt-driven. At this point the primary concerns are project control and project tracking. While a project PERT chart is typically an important tool for project control, access to information which drives it is difficult. One element of a DSS which can significantly help is an automated project management status table which consists of data from a combination of design tools, source control tools, defect tracking tools, and weekly reports by the software engineers. Figure 17-6 illustrates such a table.

Project Management Status Table

Module	Function	Resp. Eng.	Est. NCSS	Actual NCSS	Current Complexity	Defects	Status	Compiles
DISPLAY		D.C.	390	442		21	T	30
	MATCH			73	8	6*		
	GETUSERSTRING			100	42*	2		
	GETADDEDIT			64	25*			
	GETMAININPUT			56	23			
	GETDELETEINPUT			53	23			
	GETONELINE			36	11			
	GETPLOTMENU			60	25*			
ARC		M.G.	60*	112	28*	4*	D	
SUM		M.G.	180	209	57*	3	C	5
CRL		S.B.	215	221	52*	1	D	
SUB		D.D.	250	279	81	4	T	2

Figure 17-6 Project management status table.

Earlier, the subject of event triggering was discussed in the context of complexity metrics. From Figure 17-6, it can be seen that all of the other major status elements also lend themselves to setting flags on the report or to triggering mail messages under certain conditions. The example of Figure 17-6 contains asterisks (*) by various items in the table. These represent boundary conditions defined by the project manager which have been violated.

Items on the PERT chart are equally appropriate for triggering messages. For example, status meetings or document completions should be flagged some period of time prior to the event. These, particularly, should trigger mail messages to reenforce their importance.

In addition to the automated status table and the PERT chart, an important visible tracking mechanism that the project manager uses during development is graphs of project trends. Figures 17-7 and 17-8 illustrate two graphs which are produced from data collected for the project tracking. These help to demonstrate project progress and status to the various groups who are impacted.

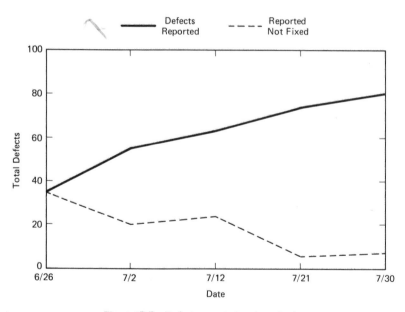

Figure 17-7   Defects reported and resolved.

As in the investigation phase, we see three activities which closely interrelate to help organize the many parallel activities of the project management job: the project management status table, graphs of project trends, and the PERT chart. In the development phase, the information is much more heavily driven by metrics data than during the investigation phase, but it is likely to

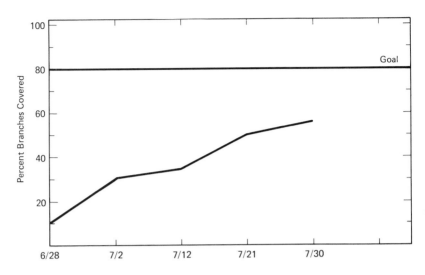

Figure 17-8   Percentage of branch coverage by tests.

be more effective when most of the data is automatically provided in a DSS framework.

17.4 SUMMARY

We examined the job of software project management. It was broken down into forty different responsibilities and then into the categories of definition, estimating and scheduling, control, and tracking. By describing a Project Management Decision Support System coupled with a development methodology, we proposed a way to provide help to the overburdened project manager. The DSS would:

1. Interact with the manager to produce a project plan. It would remind the manager what decisions must be made, help with estimates and PERT representation of schedules, and automatically format a project planning document.
2. Act as an early warning system for complexity in the software under development and provide visible means for demonstrating progress.
3. Handle some of the necessary communications automatically.

The DSS which was described would deal with many of the key responsibilities of project managers during the investigation and development activities of a project. Managing the development activity is particularly facilitated by metrics captured by various development and support tools which then automatically forward data to the Project Management DSS.

Most of the measures and tools shown in the examples here have already been successfully used to better understand, simplify, and improve the development processes at HP. What remains is to automate the collection of the remainder of the metrics and to network the information to a more complete Project Management Decision Support System.

BIBLIOGRAPHY

1. *Hewlett-Packard Software Product Lifecycle*, 5955-1756 (February 1983), pp. A 2.1-2–A 2.1-4.

2. Miller, G., "The Magical Number Seven, Plus or Minus Two: Some Limits on Our Capacity for Processing Information," *The Psychological Review*, Vol. 63, no. 2 (March 1956), p. 92.

3. *Softcost: Software Cost Estimation Tool*, User Guide for Version A.00.07, Hewlett-Packard (Nov. 1984), p. 9-3.

18

THE FINAL CONCLUSION

In Chapter 3, we defined a ten-step strategy to follow in implementing a metrics program. We followed with details of how we have proceeded with each step in HP. It has been our goal to present these steps through historical narrative and numerous graphic examples in a way that is at once persuasive and useful. The many success stories alone should be enough to persuade the most skeptical project manager that there is value to collecting some metrics. Based upon our experience, the primary obstacles to widespread usage of software metrics are clear communication of these successes and overcoming the fear of measurement.

18.1 THE ADVANTAGES

Just in case anyone is still unconvinced about the value of a software metrics program after plowing their way this far, we'll try one final time to summarize the advantages.

Software metrics will help you to:

- Understand software development processes better.
- Measure progress.

- Provide common terminology for key controlling elements of the process.
- Identify complex software elements.
- Make software management more objective and less subjective.
- Enable your engineers and managers to estimate and schedule better.
- Better evaluate your competitive position.
- Understand where automation is needed.
- Identify engineering practices which lead to the highest quality and productivity.
- Make critical decisions earlier in the development process.
- Eliminate fundamental causes of defects.
- Encourage the use of software engineering techniques by your engineers and managers.
- Encourage the definition of a long-term software development strategy based upon a measured understanding of current practices and needs.
- Be more competitive.

18.2 ONE LAST WORD

After three years of commitment to HP's metrics program, we are not totally objective about metrics. The successes are infectious, and the techniques of measurement are rapidly becoming accepted by both managers and engineers. We wish that we had more stories to present now, but the ones included give a broad sampling from which you can leverage your own metrics program. We hope they have helped, and we wish you luck as you "measure the beginning."

A

DEFINITIONS OF METRICS
USED IN HP

Throughout this book, we have discussed many different metrics. Some of these are widely used and we have had good experience with them. Others have been used at only one or two divisions, and we have little experience with them. The combination of these two categories still represents a small fraction of the hundreds of software metrics which have been defined and proposed in the literature.

In this appendix, we present the definitions for the metrics which we are using at HP. The definitions are divided into three parts: primitive metrics, computed metrics, and other important definitions. Let us start with definitions for primitive metrics and computed metrics.

Primitive metric: a metric which is directly measurable or countable.

Computed metric: a mathematical combination of two or more primitive metrics.

A.1 PRIMITIVE METRICS

When we began the HP Software Metrics Program, it was difficult to know what the best metrics would be for HP, since there were so many. What we did know is that the primitive metrics we selected were driven by two requirements. First, they had to demonstrate useful management potential in the form of a computed metric. Second, either automation of their measurement had to be relatively easy, or the return on investment for their measurement had to be high. The selection of a complete set of primitive metrics was a critical decision. By selecting the right set of primitive metrics, we would be able to experiment with a variety of computed metrics to determine which were most meaningful. This was particularly the case when automated tools were created to provide either primitive and/or computed metrics. For example, the primary primitives which were selected for code size were NCSS and comments (including blank lines). Our code counters also count blank lines, compiler directives, data declarations, as well as primitives used to compute complexity. These additional primitives are then automatically available for individual divisions to run experiments. The only primitives we list here are the ones that we know someone at HP has specifically measured and experimented with.

Branch: any executable statement that results in a choice of which statement to execute next.

Calendar month: time elapsed between specific project checkpoints. The total calendar time must equal the sum of the calendar times for individual activities. A project which started in January and ended in March of the same year took three calendar months independent of the actual effort expended.

Comment line: a line in which only comments (as defined by the source language) appear.

Control token: a data element used to determine the control flow of a function.

Data token: a data element which is really used as data instead of for control.

Defect: any flaw in the specification, design, or implementation of a product.

Difficulty: a number computed by Softcost which depends upon the answers to 45 specific questions (see Appendix B).

Engineering Months: the sum of calendar payroll months attributed to each project engineer, including people doing testing, adjusted to exclude extended vacations and extended leaves. This does not include time project managers spend on management tasks.

LOD: lines of documentation not included in program source code.

NCLS: noncomment logical source statements count statements, ignoring whether they physically occupy more than one line in a program.

NCSS: noncomment source statements which include compiler directives, data declarations, and executable code. Each physical line of code is counted once. Each include file is counted once. Print statements are noncomment source statements.

Overtime (or undertime):   engineering time over/under the 40-hour engineering week averaged over the duration of a project. Percentage of over/under time can be used as a normalization factor for engineering months.

Procedure: a logical and physical grouping of statements which can be compiled independently of the rest of the program, has local data, and can be called from other parts of a program by a well-defined interface.

Source checkout: the withdrawal of a specific source module from a source control system.

Total operands: the total number of occurrences of operands in a program (Halstead's N2).

Total operators: the total number of occurrences of operators in a program (Halstead's N1).

Unique operands: a unique variable or constant within a program (Halstead's eta2).

Unique operators: a unique language construct which affects the value or ordering of operands within a program (Halstead's eta1).

A.2 COMPUTED METRICS

Computed metrics are used as management indicators for some aspect of software development which is of particular interest. Throughout this book we have shown many graphs of computed metrics. Frequently the primitives which compose the computed metrics are plotted against each other in an attempt to characterize a trend (such as NCSS over time, or defects fixed over time). Other times they are further broken down in an attempt to subdivide a problem area (such as defects/KNCSS broken down by module). In addition to the most widely used metrics listed here, refer to Figure 11-8 for a large number of other computed metrics which are useful for ensuring specific project goals.

Average fixed defects/working day: self-explanatory.

Average engineering hours/fixed defect: self-explanatory.

Average reported defects/working day: self-explanatory.

Bang: "a quantitative indicator of net usable function from the user's point of view" [1]. There are two methods for computing Bang. Computation of Bang for function-strong systems involves counting the tokens entering and leaving the function multiplied by the weight of the function. For data-strong systems it involves counting the objects in the database weighted by the number of relationships of which the object is a member.

Branches covered/total branches: when running a program, this metric indicates what percentage of the decision points were actually executed.

Defects/KNCSS: self-explanatory.

Defects/LOD: self-explanatory.

Defects/testing time: self-explanatory.

Design weight: "Design weight is a simple sum of the module weights over the set of all modules in the design" [1]. Each module weight is a function of the token count associated with the module and the expected number of decision counts which are predicted based on the structure of data.

NCSS/engineering month: self-explanatory.

Percent overtime: average overtime/40 hours per week.

(Phase) engineering months/total engineering months: self-explanatory.

A.3 OTHER IMPORTANT DEFINITIONS

There are other definitions which are critical to the use of the metrics defined as primitive or computed. Many of these definitions could be considered as primitive metrics which assume a true or false value, but it is more useful to separate them into this third category than it is to keep them with the primitive metrics and make the primitive list seem excessively long.

Applications software: software that operates on top of and uses systems software. Applications software also generally solves a generic class of problems for a narrow set of customers and needs.

Defect (critical):   the customer is unable to use the product, resulting in a critical impact on their operation. This problem requires an immediate solution.

Defect (serious):   the customer is able to use the product, but is severely restricted. A temporary solution should be supplied.

Defect (medium):   the customer can use the product with limitations that are not critical to overall operations.

Defect (low):   the customer can circumvent the problem and use the product with only slight inconvenience.

Defect (unclassified):   a defect which has been reported but has not yet been analyzed to determine severity or difficulty to fix.

Design phase: start of the Internal Specification (IS) through start of coding for final product.

Firmware: software generally designed to execute from ROM (Read Only Memory) or RAM (Random Access Memory) under control of a microprocessor.

Implementation phase: start of coding for final product through start of system (formal, public) testing.

Investigation/external specification phase: start of investigation through approval of the external specification (ES) document.

Maintenance phase: starts after release of the product and continues until its obsolescence.

(Phase) activity: an activity relates engineering hours to actions performed rather than to the formal project phase currently in progress. Thus, engineering hours spent performing design during the implementation phase should be counted as design hours.

Recycled software: software incorporated into a product that was either used intact or highly leveraged from a different product or another part of the same product.

Reused software: software incorporated into a product that was used intact from a different product or another part of the same product.

Systems software: software generally designed to execute from the memory of minicomputers. It functions as the framework for developing and executing other software.

Test phase: start of system testing through product release.

Testing time: time spent on all activities relating to system (formal, public) testing. This includes writing test plans, writing test code, system and integration testing, and finding and removing defects found during test activities.

BIBLIOGRAPHY

1. DeMarco, T., *Controlling Software Projects.* New York: Yourdon Press, 1982, pp. 89, 109. Reprinted by permission of Prentice-Hall, Inc., Englewood Cliffs, New Jersey.

B

THE EVOLUTION OF HP'S
SOFTWARE METRICS FORMS

This appendix includes the first two versions of HP's software metrics forms. These should be useful, because they illustrate some of the pitfalls of collecting historical information. In each case we describe what problems were encountered with the forms and the steps we have taken to avoid them in the future.

B.1 FIRST RELEASE

We were pretty idealistic with the first forms and thought that we had reduced them to a simple enough set of inputs so that it would be easy to get all of the information. This was definitely not the case. With the first forms we began to see patterns of input, however, which helped us to better understand the most significant problems people faced.

The forms which follow were those first forms. (The difficulty survey questions were reproduced from the original Softcost questions [1].)

HEWLETT PACKARD	**PEOPLE/TIME/COST**	**SOFTWARE METRICS FORM**

PRODUCT _____ PHASE _____ DATE _____

AVERAGE (FULLY BURDENED) LABOR RATE _____

	EFFORT IN ENG. MO.	CALENDAR MO.
INVESTIGATE/SPEC		
DESIGN		
IMPLEMENT		
TEST		
TOTALS		

CODING INSTRUCTIONS:

1) EFFORT IS MEASURED BY ENGINEERING MONTH. 1 ENGINEERING MONTH IS EQUAL TO 40-50 HOURS PER WEEK WITH NO ADJUSTMENTS FOR VACATIONS OR SICK LEAVE. EFFORT DOES NOT INCLUDE TIME PROJECT MANAGERS SPEND ON MANAGEMENT TASKS.

2) THE TOTAL FOR CALENDAR MO. DOES NOT NECESSARILY REPRESENT THE SUM OF THE TIMES FOR PROJECT PHASES. SOME PROJECT PHASES MAY OVERLAP.

3) THE MEASUREMENT POINTS ARE DELINEATED AS FOLLOWS:

      INVESTIGATE/SPEC - ENDS WHEN ERS APPROVED
      DESIGN   - ENDS WHEN CODING STARTS FOR FINAL PRODUCT
      IMPLEMENTATION   - ENDS WHEN SYSTEM TEST STARTS
      TEST   - ENDS AT MR

HEWLETT PACKARD	**SIZE**			**SOFTWARE METRICS FORM**		

PRODUCT _____ PHASE _____ DATE _____

	DELIVERED PRODUCT			SUPPORTING CODE/DOC		
	NEW1	NEW2	REUSED CODE	NEW1	NEW2	REUSED CODE
COMPILER DIRECTIVES						
DATA DECLARATIONS						
EXECUTABLE CODE						
SUBTOTAL (NCSS)						
COMMENTS						
BLANK LINES						
TOTAL LINES OF CODE						
BYTES OF OBJECT CODE						
LINES OF DOC.						

CODING INSTRUCTIONS:

1) LANGUAGE NAMES MUST BE ENTERED IN SHADED AREAS IN NEW CODE CATEGORIES OF THE DELIVERED PRODUCT AND SUPPORTING CODE/DOC CLASSIFICATIONS. LANGUAGE IS NOT TRACKED FOR REUSED CODE. ADDITIONAL FORMS MUST BE COMPLETED IF MORE THAN TWO LANGUAGES ARE USED FOR THE PRODUCT.

2) INPUT TO ALL CELLS IS NUMBER OF LINES, WITH THE EXCEPTION OF BYTES OF OBJECT CODE.

3) LINES OF DOC. INCLUDES MESSAGE FILES AND VIEW SCREENS FOR DELIVERED PRODUCT AND INTERNAL DOC. FOR SUPPORTING CODE/DOC.

HEWLETT PACKARD	DEFECTS		SOFTWARE METRICS FORM

PRODUCT _____ PHASE _____ DATE _____

	KPR INTRODUCED	KPR FOUND	KPR CORRECTED
INVESTIGATE/SPEC			
DESIGN			
IMPLEMENT			
TEST			
POST RELEASE			
TOTALS			

CODING INSTRUCTIONS:

   1) INPUT TO ALL CELLS IS A CUMULATIVE KPR (KNOW PROBLEM REPORT)
      COUNT.

   2) THE MEASUREMENT POINTS ARE DELINEATED AS FOLLOWS:

           INVESTIGATE/SPEC - ENDS WHEN ERS APPROVED
           DESIGN   - ENDS WHEN CODING STARTS FOR FINAL PRODUCT
           IMPLEMENTATION   - ENDS WHEN SYSTEM TEST STARTS
           TEST   - ENDS AT MR
           POST RELEASE   - ENDS AT OBSOLESCENCE

```
┌─────────────────────────────────────────────────────────────────────────┐
│  [hp] HEWLETT                    COMMUNICATIONS              SOFTWARE      │
│       PACKARD                                             METRICS FORM     │
│                                                                           │
│   PRODUCT _____  PHASE _____  DATE _____    │
│                                                                           │
├─────────────────────────────────────────────────────────────────────────┤
│                                                                           │
│                                                                           │
│                                                                           │
│      PLEASE RESPOND WITH A NUMERIC ANSWER FOR EACH OF THE FOLLOWING        │
│      QUESTIONS:                                                           │
│                                                                           │
│           1) HOW MANY ENGINEERS ARE ON YOUR PROJECT TEAM:       ____      │
│                                                                           │
│           2) HOW MANY PEOPLE ARE ON YOUR PRODUCT TEAM:          ____      │
│                                                                           │
│        HOW MANY INTERFACES/INTERDEPENDENCIES DO YOU HAVE WITH             │
│                                                                           │
│           3) OTHER LAB PROJECTS:                                ____      │
│                                                                           │
│           4) OTHER LOCAL ENTITIES:                              ____      │
│                                                                           │
│           5) OTHER REMOTE ENTITIES:                             ____      │
│                                                                           │
│           6) NON-HP ENTITIES:                                   ____      │
│                                                                           │
│                                                                           │
│                                                                           │
│                                                                           │
│                                                                           │
│                                                                           │
│                                                                           │
│                                                                           │
└─────────────────────────────────────────────────────────────────────────┘
```

```
┌────────────────────────────────────────────────────────────────┐
│                  │SOFTWARE PROJECT HISTORY QUESTIONNAIRE│        │
│                                                                  │
│  *** NOTE:  THIS FORM SHOULD TAKE NO MORE THAN 20 MINUTES TO FILL OUT *** │
│                          Project Identification                  │
│  Project Title:_____             │
│                                                                  │
│  Project ID:_____             │
│                                                                  │
│  Version:_____             │
│                                                                  │
│  Project Manager:_____             │
│                                                                  │
│  Product Number:_____             │
│                                                                  │
│  Manufacturing Release Date:_____             │
│                                                                  │
│  Project Authorization Date:_____             │
│                                                                  │
│                                                                  │
│                          General Information                     │
│                                                                  │
│  1.  Indicate the type of software created                       │
│                                                                  │
│        _____ Firmware                                            │
│        _____ Operating System                                    │
│        _____ I/O Subsystem                                       │
│        _____ Data Communications                                 │
│        _____ Data Base Manager                                   │
│        _____ Compiler                                            │
│        _____ Subsystem, e.g., Graphics Package, Report Writer, etc. │
│        _____ Instrument Controller                               │
│        _____ End-User Application, e.g., Payroll, Cost Accounting, etc. │
│        _____ Process Control System                              │
│        _____ Other (Please Specify)_____               │
│                                                                  │
│  2.  Indicate type of development.                               │
│                                                                  │
│        _____ New system                                          │
│        _____ Rebuild using most of the existing specifications   │
│        _____ Rebuild using substantially new specifications      │
│        _____ Conversion                                          │
│        _____ Other (Please Specify)_____               │
│                                                                  │
│  3.  What language(s) was used for development?                  │
│                                                                  │
│        _____       │
│                                                                  │
│                                                                  │
│  Revision Date:  10/22/84                                        │
│                                                                  │
└────────────────────────────────────────────────────────────────┘
```

Software Project History Questionnaire (Continued)
Page 2

4. Indicate the development computer.

_____ HP 3000   _____ Series 200   _____ HP 64000
_____ HP 1000   _____ Series 100   _____ Other (Specify Below)
_____ HP Series 500   _____ Series 80   _____

5. Indicate the development operating system.

_____ MPE
_____ RTE
_____ UNIX
_____ PASCAL/OS
_____ BASIC/OS
_____ Other (Please Specify)_____

6. Indicate the target computer.

_____ HP 3000
_____ HP 1000
_____ HP 9000
_____ Series 200
_____ Series 100
_____ Series 80
_____ HP 64000
_____ Other (Please Specify)_____

7. Indicate the target operating system.

_____ MPE
_____ RTE
_____ UNIX
_____ PASCAL/OS
_____ BASIC/OS
_____ Other (Please Specify)_____

Revision Date: 10/22/84

```
Software Project History Questionnaire (Continued)
Page 3

                        Life Cycle Information


Life Cycle General Definition

For the purpose of this document, the software life cycle is divided into four
phases:

- Investigation/Specification
- Design
- Implementation
- Test

Each phase is delineated by the following milestones:

Investigation/Specification--Start of investigation through approval of the
                  External Specification (ES) document.

Design--Start of the Internal Specification (IS) through start of coding for
                  final product.

Implementation--Start of coding for final product through start of system
                  testing.

Test--Start of system testing through manufacturing release.

Any of these phases can potentially overlap, for this reason the total elapsed
time of the development effort will not necessarily equal the sum of the elapsed
time for each phase.


Investigation/Specification Phase

1.  Indicate the three top project objectives with 1 as highest priority;
    then indicate whether they were met to your satisfaction.

    Priority 1-3    Objective Met?

    _____          _____          Extensive Functionality
    _____          _____          Maximum Usability
    _____          _____          High Reliability
    _____          _____          High Performance
    _____          _____          Easily Supportable
    _____          _____          Time to Market
    _____          _____          Portability
    _____          _____          Compatability
    _____          _____          Other #1 _____
    _____          _____          Other #2 _____
    _____          _____          Other #3 _____

Revision Date:  10/22/84
```

Software Project History Questionnaire (Continued)
Page 4

2. Indicate which of the following methodologies were used.

_____ Modeling/Simulation
_____ Prototyping
_____ Diagrammatic Representation
_____ Other (Please Specify)_____
_____
_____
_____

3. Indicate which of the following tools were used.

_____ Modeling/Simulation Aids
_____ Prototyper
_____ Specification Language
_____ Other (Please Specify)_____
_____
_____
_____

4. Percent of the specification on which formal design reviews were held?

_____

5. In your estimation, what percent of any project schedule overrun was due to unstable requirements?

_____

Design Phase

1. Indicate the number of people on the team who used the following methodologies.

_____ Yourdon
_____ Jackson
_____ Warnier-Orr
_____ Myers Composite Design
_____ HIPO
_____ SADT
_____ Stepwise Refinement
_____ Other (Please Specify)_____
_____
_____
_____

Revision Date: 10/22/84

Software Project History Questionnaire (Continued)
Page 5

Design Phase (Continued)

2. Percent of the detail design on which formal design reviews were held?

    _____

Implementation Phase

1. Indicate which of the following methodologies were used?

    _____ Structured Programming
    _____ Coding Standards
    _____ Top Down Development
    _____ Bottom Up Development
    _____ Software Libraries
    _____ Phased Integration
    _____ Other (Please Specify)_____
    _____
    _____
    _____

2. Indicate which of the following tools were used?

    _____ Source Code Generators
    _____ Data Dictionaries
    _____ Screen/Form Generators
    _____ Symbolic Debuggers
    _____ Syntax Directed Editors
    _____ Standard Text Editors
    _____ Version Control System
    _____ Cross-Referencing Utilities
    _____ Other (Please Specify)_____
    _____
    _____
    _____

Revision Date: 10/22/84

Software Project History Questionnaire (Continued)
Page 6

Test Phase

1. Indicate which of the following test methodologies were used?

   _____ Written Test Plans
   _____ Test Activities Pert Chart
   _____ Top Down Testing
   _____ Bottom Up Testing
   _____ Test Teams
   _____ Alpha Sites
   _____ Beta Sites
   _____ Other (Please Specify)_____

   _____
   _____
   _____

2. Indicate which of the following test tools were used?

   _____ Test Drivers
   _____ Automated Test Packages
   _____ Path Flow Analyzers
   _____ Test Data Generators
   _____ Test Comparators
   _____ Other (Please Specify)_____

   _____
   _____
   _____

Project Management

1. Indicate which project management techniques were used?

   _____ Project Notebook
   _____ Algorithmic Modeling Estimation
   _____ Expert Judgement Estimating
   _____ Top Down Estimating
   _____ Bottom Up Estimating
   _____ Pert Charting
   _____ Gantt Charting
   _____ Resource Planning
   _____ ROI Planning
   _____ Other (Please Specify)_____

   _____
   _____
   _____

Revision Date: 10/22/84

Software Project History Questionnaire (Continued)
Page 7

Project Management (Continued)

2. Indicate which of the following tools were used?

    _____ Time/Resource Estimators
    _____ Pert Chart Generators
    _____ Gantt Chart Generators
    _____ Other (Please Specify)_____

    _____
    _____
    _____

3. Indicate which of the following project documents were created?

    _____ Investigation Report
    _____ External Specification
    _____ Internal Specification
    _____ Internal Maintenance Specification
    _____ Quality Plan
    _____ Test Plan
    _____ Other (Please Specify)_____

    _____
    _____
    _____

4. Indicate which of the following project standards were used?

    _____ Design Standards
    _____ Coding Standards
    _____ User Interface Standards
    _____ Other (Please Specify)_____

    _____
    _____
    _____

5. Specify the percent of staff turnover during the project (e.g., staff of
    10 with loss of 5 = 50 percent).

    _____

6. Was formal training of the development staff undertaken?

    _____ Yes   _____ No

    If yes, list the types of classes attended:

    _____
    _____
    _____

Revision Date: 10/22/84

Software Project History Questionnaire (Continued)
Page 8

Softcost Difficulty Calibration

This section contains questions about the difficulty of the project and its
environment.

Difficulty Survey #1

1. What percent of the programming task is in Assembly language?_____

2. What percent of the new or modified code must be storage-optimized?_____

3. What percent of the new or modified code must be timing-optimized?_____

4. What percent of the total programming task is "hard"?_____

5. What percent of the total programming task is "easy"?_____

6. What percent of the total program requirements will be established
   and stable before design, and will not be altered before delivery?_____

7. What percent of the requirements are likely to change slightly
   before delivery, but will do so under project control?_____

8. What percent of the requirements are likely to change more drastically
   before delivery, but will do so under project control?_____

   NOTE: 100 percent minus the answers to questions 6-8 equals the
   percentage of requirements changed freely before delivery beyond
   control of the project. What percent was this?_____

9. What is the average staff experience, in years (from work similar
   to the task being estimated)?_____

Revision Date: 10/22/84

```
Software Project History Questionnaire (Continued)
Page 9


Difficulty Survey #2

(CIRCLE ONE)

1.  Expected percentage of code developed to be actually delivered?

    a.  Not Applicable
    b.  0-90
    c.  91-99
    d.  100

2.  Complexity of data flow?

    a.  Not Applicable
    b.  High
    c.  Medium
    d.  Low

3.  Overall complexity of program and data structure architecture?

    a.  Not Applicable
    b.  High
    c.  Medium
    d.  Low

4.  Complexity of internal logical design?

    a.  Not Applicable
    b.  High
    c.  Medium
    d.  Low

5.  Complexity of functional requirements (external specs)?

    a.  Not Applicable
    b.  High
    c.  Medium
    d.  Low

6.  Expected user involvement in requirements definition?

    a.  Not Applicable
    b.  Much
    c.  Some
    d.  None




Revision Date:  10/22/84
```

Software Project History Questionnaire (Continued)
Page 10

7. Customer experience in application area?

    a. Not Applicable
    b. Much
    c. None
    d. Some

8. Customer/implementor interface complexity?

    a. Not Applicable
    b. High
    c. Medium
    d. Low

9. Interfaces with other software development projects or organizations?

    a. Not Applicable
    b. Many
    c. Few
    d. None

10. Efficiency of implementing organization?

    a. Not Applicable
    b. Poor
    c. O.K.
    d. Good

11. Overall implementation personnel qualifications and motivation?

    a. Not Applicable
    b. Low
    c. Medium
    d. High

12. Percent of programmers doing both functional design and development?

    a. Not Applicable
    b. Less than 25
    c. 25-50
    d. Greater than 50

13. Previous programmer experience with application of similar or greater size
    and complexity?

    a. Not Applicable
    b. Minimal
    c. Moderate
    d. Extensive

Revision Date: 10/22/84

Software Project History Questionnaire (Continued)
Page 11

14. Previous experience with operational computer to be used?

    a. Not Applicable
    b. Minimal
    c. Moderate
    d. Extensive

15. Previous experience with programming language(s) to be used?

    a. Not Applicable
    b. Minimal
    c. Moderate
    d. Extensive

16. Use of top-down methodology?

    a. Not Applicable
    b. Low
    c. Medium
    d. High

17. Use of structured "chief programmer" team concepts?
    (Librarian; strong technical leader)

    a. Not Applicable
    b. Low
    c. Medium
    d. High

18. Use of Structured Programming?

    a. Not Applicable
    b. Low
    c. Medium
    d. High

19. Use of design and code inspections?

    a. Not Applicable
    b. Low
    c. QA
    d. Peer

20. Classified security environment for computer?

    a. Not Applicable
    b. Yes
    c. Unknown
    d. No

Revision Date: 10/22/84

Software Project History Questionnaire (Continued)
Page 12

21. Hardware under concurrent development?

    a. Not Applicable
    b. Much
    c. Some
    d. None

22. Percent of work done at primary development site?

    a. Not Applicable
    b. Less then 70
    c. 70-90
    d. Greater than 90

23. Development computer access mode?

    a. Not Applicable
    b. Remote
    c. Scheduled
    d. Demand

24. Percent of development computer access availability?

    a. Not Applicable
    b. Less than 30
    c. 30-60
    d. Greater than 60

25. Quality of software development tools and environment?

    a. Not Applicable
    b. Poor
    c. O.K.
    d. Good

26. Maturity of system and support software?

    a. Not Applicable
    b. Buggy
    c. O.K.
    d. Good

27. Overall adverse constraints on program design?

    a. Not Applicable
    b. Severe
    c. Average
    d. Minimal

Revision Date: 10/22/84

Software Project History Questionnaire (Continued)
Page 13

28. Is the program real-time or multi-task?

    a. Not Applicable
    b. Much
    c. Some
    d. None

29. Software to be adaptable to multiple computer configurations?

    a. Not Applicable
    b. Yes
    c. Unknown
    d. No

30. Adaptation required to change from development to operational environment?

    a. Not Applicable
    b. Much
    c. Some
    d. Minimal

LIST ANY OTHER FACTORS OR EVENTS WHICH HAD A SIGNIFICANT POSITIVE OR NEGATIVE
IMPACT ON PRODUCTIVITY OR PRODUCT QUALITY.

_____

_____

_____

_____

Revision Date: 10/22/84

B.2 SECOND RELEASE

One problem with the first forms was that, even though we thought we had selected well-understood terms, it was still necessary to define them in detail on the forms.

Another problem we discovered was that some people were reluctant to fill them out because they seemed long. We attempted to overcome this concern by adding a cover sheet which provided estimates for how long the process of filling them out should take.

In addition, there was confusion about when to fill in the forms and when to send them. Although we intended that the forms would be used locally throughout the development process and that people would only send the final numbers to us at the end, many managers sent us a set of forms after each phase completion. Thus, we added information about where and when the forms should be sent to us.

B.2.1 People/Time/Cost

This form seemed to present few problems. The only real change was the clarification that testing times for all people involved in test were to be included.

B.2.2 Size

The size form underwent major changes. We recognized that very few projects consisted of 100 percent new code. We wanted to be explicit about how to count reused code. Whereas all the data was expected to fit on one form before, one sheet per language became necessary with the new form. We continued to collect information about code which is not delivered to customers (supporting code), although we now expected separate forms to be filled out.

The most important change, perhaps, was the addition of the line counter name or degree of confidence if no automated counter was used. This helped us identify local line counters that we could distribute to others in similar development environments, identify environments where line counters did not exist, and helped us to know which data to trust and which not to trust.

B.2.3 Defects

We changed terminology from "KPR" to "defect." KPRs were tracked by our postrelease system, STARS, and did not include any enhancement requests, whereas defects include those enhancement requests which would eventually be implemented.

B.2.4 Communications

It was very difficult for projects to precisely count communications, especially because the required communications changed throughout the life cycle. We believed that communications overhead had a profound impact on schedules, and we also learned that a project manager could not control the dependencies of the project. As a result, few people filled out the communication form, and it was eliminated.

B.2.5 Difficulty

The difficulty questionnaire was not changed.

B.2.6 Maintenance

We extended our metrics standard to include software maintenance activities, the major omissions in the definitions from the previous summer. The Maintenance form contains questions pertaining to engineering time, source size changes, defects reported and corrected during the current quarter, and personnel characteristics of the maintenance team. The form is intended to be filled out each fiscal quarter to reflect maintenance activities in the previous quarter. We concluded that the collection and analysis of the new metrics should help to answer the following types of questions critical to management:

- How should we plan for staffing maintenance of a software product family?
- When is a product stable?
- Is Mean Time Between Failures (MTBF) for a software product really a meaningful measure of software quality [2]?
- In which development phase should tool and training investments be made?

And for development teams:

- How does documentation improve supportability?
- How many defects can we expect to find in a project of a given size?
- What relationships exist between defects found prior to release and those found after release?

And for the CPE (Current Product Engineering—CPE teams at HP provide enhancements and defect fixes for major released software products) team:

- What, if any, is the relationship between the size of a product and the average time to fix a defect?
- What is the average time to fix a defect?
- How much testing is necessary to ensure a fix is correct?
- What percentage of defects are introduced during maintenance? During enhancements?

HP SOFTWARE METRICS COLLECTION FORMS

Form	Estimated Time to Fill Out
PEOPLE/TIME/COST	5 Minutes per month
SIZE	3 Minutes using automated tool
DEFECTS	Depends on defect tracking system in use
COMMUNICATIONS	Optional
DIFFICULTY	20 Minutes
MAINTENANCE	10 Minutes

INTRODUCTION

Every software development project has resources allocated to it: schedule, staffing, capital equipment, tool & test development. Everyone in the corporation benefits from the optimum allocation of these resources. Not until we quantify the inputs and the outputs of the software development process can we begin to optimize our investments in software development and maintenance.

From an engineer's point of view, the data will point to life cycle phases which are time consuming and defect prone as well as phases where not enough time is allocated. Once identified, these phases can become the focus of tool and test development. Keeping track of engineering months in terms of 40 hour weeks leads to more accurate records of development effort, which in turn should lead to more accurate estimates and reasonable expectations.

The project manager can use the metrics on these forms to predict whether or not the schedule can be met. For example, several project managers are now able to predict the time that will be required by the formal QA phase and are able to establish objective release criteria. By tracking estimates versus actuals and revising estimates continually during the development of a product, project managers will gain the practice and expertise in estimating effort.

PROCEDURE

The forms are intended for use locally throughout the lifecycle of a product. In addition, the final project data is to be sent to Corporate Engineering upon release for archiving. This data is available for analysis by divisions and facilitates learning from divisions with similar development practices.

PEOPLE/TIME/COST: should be revised at the end of each life-cycle phase.

DEFECTS: should be updated at the end of each life-cycle phase.

SIZE: should be filled in before the formal test phase and again at release in order to track the amount of rework required in the test phase. Only the final size is to be sent to Corporate Engineering.

COMMUNICATIONS: This form is suggested as a local experiment only and is not intended to be sent to Corporate Engineering. It tries to quantify the amount of effort expended on communication and coordination activities.

DIFFICULTY: This project profile questionnaire should be filled in at the very beginning of a new project. Answers should be revised as the project progresses and better information becomes available. At release, the latest answers should be sent to Corporate Engineering with the other forms.

MAINTENANCE: After a product releases, the maintenance form should be filled out and mailed to Corporate Engineering on the first day of the fiscal quarter.

HEWLETT PACKARD	**PEOPLE/TIME/COST**	**SOFTWARE METRICS FORM**

PRODUCT _____ PHASE _____ DATE _____

AVERAGE (FULLY BURDENED) LABOR RATE _____

	EFFORT IN ENG. MO.	**CALENDAR MO.**
INVESTIGATE/SPEC.		
DESIGN		
IMPLEMENT		
TEST		
TOTALS		

PROCEDURE

1. ASK YOUR LAB MANAGER FOR THE FULLY BURDENED LABOR RATE.

2. FILL OUT THE APPROPRIATE ROW AT THE END OF EACH LIFE CYCLE PHASE.

3. UPON PRODUCT RELEASE, SEND THE COMPLETED FORM TO:

    Debbie Caswell
    Hewlett-Packard Company
    M/S 43UA
    19420 Homestead Road
    Cupertino, CA 95014

Revision Date: 10/22/84

PEOPLE/TIME/COST INSTRUCTIONS

DEFINING THE TERMS:

ENGINEERING MONTH:	40–50 hours per week with no adjustments for vacations or sick leave. Effort includes time of R&D engineers and all people doing testing but does not include time project managers spend on management tasks.
INVESTIGATION/ EXTERNAL SPEC:	Start of investigation through approval of the External Specification (ES) document.
DESIGN:	Start of the Internal Specification (IS) through start of coding for final product.
IMPLEMENTATION:	Start of coding for final product through start of system testing.
TEST:	Start of system testing through manufacturing release.

> NOTE: The total for calendar months does not necessarily represent the sum of
> the times for project phases. Some project phases may overlap.

HEWLETT PACKARD | SIZE | **SOFTWARE METRICS FORM**

PRODUCT _____ PHASE _____ DATE _____

Language _____ Delivered or Supporting Code
(circle one)
Name of line counter or other technique used (indicated confidence level if a guess was used):

_____

	New Code	Reused Code			
		Unchanged	Added	Deleted	Modified
Compiler Directives					
Data Declarations					
Executable Code					
NCSS (Subtotal)					
Comments					
Blank Lines					
TOTAL LINES					
# Procedures					
Bytes of Object Code					
Lines of Documentation					

PROCEDURE

1. USE AN AUTOMATIC LINE COUNTER IF ONE IS AVAILABLE. IF NO TOOL IS AVAILABLE, LOOK AT THE
COMPILED LISTING TO GET THE NUMBER OF EXECUTABLE STATEMENTS. IF YOU MUST GUESS, INDICATE
NCSS, TOTAL LINES, & LINES OF DOCUMENTATION, PLUS YOUR CONFIDENCE LEVEL.
2. FILL OUT THE FORM AT THE END OF THE IMPLEMENTATION PHASE AND AGAIN AFTER THE TESTING PHASE.
UPON RELEASE, SEND THE LATEST COUNTS ON THIS FORM TO DEBBIE CASWELL, AT HEWLETT–PACKARD:

Building 43UA
19420 Homestead Road
Revision Date: 10/22/84   Cupertino, CA 95014

SIZE INSTRUCTIONS

DEFINING THE TERMS:

DELIVERED   Refers to those lines of code which go into the product delivered to
PRODUCT: the customer.

SUPPORTING   Refers to test code, special tooling, and internal documentation needed
CODE/DOC.:   in support of developing the delivered product.

NCSS: Non–commented source statements which includes compiler directives, data
                   declarations, and executable code.

COUNTING RULES:

1.   Don't double count:

     A. Each line of code counted once.
     B. Each include file counted once.

2.   A commended executable line is counted as executable code, not as a comment.

3.   Notes on lines of documentation:

     A. Lines of documentation are those not included in the source code.
     B. Any documentation or messages in file that are not source files are lines of documentation.

4.   Print statements are lines of code.

![hp] HEWLETT PACKARD	DEFECTS		SOFTWARE METRICS FORM
PRODUCT _____ PHASE _____ DATE _____			

	DEFECT INTRODUCED	DEFECT FOUND	DEFECT CORRECTED
INVESTIGATE/SPEC			
DESIGN			
IMPLEMENT			
TEST			
TOTALS			

PROCEDURE

1. AT THE END OF EACH PHASE, FILL IN THE APPROPRIATE ROW ON THE FORM. IN THE "INTRODUCED" COLUMN, ADD THE RESULTS OF YOUR DEFECT ANALYSIS TO THE TOTALS ALREADY THERE. FOR EXAMPLE, IF DURING THE IMPLEMENTATION YOU FOUND X DESIGN DEFECTS, ADD X TO THE CURRENT TOTAL OF DESIGN INTRODUCED DEFECTS.

2. AT RELEASE, SEND THE COMPLETED FORM TO:

Debbie Caswell
Hewlett-Packard Company
M/S 43UA
19420 Homestead Road
Cupertino, CA 95014

Revision Date: 10/22/84

DEFECTS INSTRUCTIONS

DEFINING THE TERMS:

DEFECT: A defect includes any deviation from the specification and also errors
                        in the specification. Once the product specification is accepted, any
                        new features added or old features deleted are defects introduced inthe
                        I/S phase.

DEFECT
INTRODUCED: Problems can be introduced in the current phase or previous phases only.

DEFECT
CORRECTED: Problems can be corrected in the current phase only.

EXAMPLE DEFECTS FOR THE FOLLOWING PHASES ARE:

Investigation/   A. Defects found in formal review of documents produced; e.g., ERS, Marketing Plan.
External Spec:
                        B. Defects found in the design, implementation, test, or post-release phases which
                            are attributed to a flaw in the output of the investigation/external spec. phase.

                        All enhancements which are identified after completion of this phase and
                        implemented prior to manufacturing release are considered defects.

Design: A. Defects found during design inspections or through modeling.

                        B. Defects found during the implementation test, or post-release phases which
                            areattributed to a flaw in the design.

Implementation: A. Defects found during code inspections, unit test, and debug.

                        B. Defects found during test or post-release phases which are attributed
                            to a flaw in the implementation.

Test: Defects introduced in the test phase include undesired side effects of fixes for other
                        defects. Testing defects can be found during the testing phases or post-release.

NOTE: Question to ask yourself, "Are you ready for formal review?" If so, defects can be found,
       counted, and recorded.

HEWLETT PACKARD |MAINTENANCE| **SOFTWARE METRICS FORM**

PRODUCT _____ QUARTER _____ DATE _____

REVISION # _____ NUMBER OF ENGINEERS _____

AVERAGE (FULLY BURDENED) LABOR RATE _____ ENGINEERING HOURS _____

UNCLASSIFIED DEFECTS _____

NUMBER OF DEFECTS INTRODUCED

INVEST/SPEC	DESIGN	IMPLEMENT	TEST	POST-RELEASE
[ ]	[ ]	[ ]	[ ]	[ ]

TOTAL DEFECTS FOUND AFTER RELEASE [ ]
TOTAL DEFECTS CORRECTED AFTER RELEASE [ ]

	DELIVERED	SUPPORTING
	ADDED [ ]	ADDED [ ]
NCSS*	DELETED [ ]	DELETED [ ]
	MODIFIED [ ]	MODIFIED [ ]
* LINE COUNTERS RUN ONCE	LANGUAGE _____	LANGUAGE _____

(USE BACK OF FORM FOR OTHER LANGUAGES)

AVERAGE PERCENTAGE OF MAINTENANCE TEAM WHO WERE ON DEVELOPMENT TEAM [ ]

AVERAGE NUMBER OF YEARS EXPERIENCE FOR THE MAINTENANCE TEAM [ ]

PERCENT FIXES FOR WHICH PEER DESK CHECKS OR WALK-THROUGHS WERE HELD [ ]

YOUR NAME _____

PROCEDURE
SEND THIS FORM TO DEBBIE CASWELL AT CORPORATE ENG. ON THE FISCAL QUARTER:
Hewlett-Packard Company
M/S 43UA
19420 Homestead Road
Cupertino, CA 95014

Revision Date: 10/22/84

MAINTENANCE INSTRUCTIONS

THIS FORM IS TO BE USED FOR CURRENT PRODUCT ENGINEERING ONLY. THE DEVELOPMENT
SET OF FORMS SHOULD BE USED WHEN A NEW PRODUCT NUMBER IS ASSIGNED AND NEW
REVENUE IS GENERATED.

DEFINING THE TERMS:

QUARTER: Fiscal quarter.

NUMBER OF   Total number of R&D and Q&A engineers contributing time to maintaining the product.
ENGINEERS:

ENGINEERING HRS: ACTUAL hours worked on a problem. Does not include overhead.

UNCLASSIFIED
SERVICE REQ.:   Service requests received but not diagnosed.

NUMBER DEFECTS   Include known problems at release. Defects introduced in the post–release phase are bad
INTRODUCED: fixes or side effects.

NCSS: Non–commented source statements. A line counter is typically run once at MR.
                      For few changes, it will be easier to track lines that have changed
                      and update the last size count accordingly.

NOTE: All information supplied on this form summarizes the current state of the product, not the changes
      since the last report on the last form.

B.3 THIRD RELEASE

The second forms were much more successful than the first set, and we found that we received more data and that we had to answer fewer questions. One continuing problem was that when we received data, there were frequently one or two important items missing. We would follow up with a phone call to the project manager, and they generally could supply the desired information. We concluded that people collecting the data were probably collecting the correct things, but that the length of the forms was still intimidating.

We decided to separate the forms into two parts: the necessary information in four pages and the optional information in a separate packet. Even the necessary forms have optional, shaded fields (refer to Chapter 5 for the four-page forms).

B.3.1 The Project Questionnaire

Despite supplying the estimated time to complete the form, the project questionnaire was often not completed and returned with the other, more crucial data. This meant that vital project information such as project manager, release date, and start date was not supplied. (The other forms didn't ask for it.) With the third release forms, it is easier to see what information is required. Also, the crucial data is now separate from the Softcost questionnaire.

B.3.2 People/Time/Cost

The Fully Burdened Labor Rate had been included originally in order to compare the real dollar cost of an engineer for each division. Since our divisions are located throughout the world, the cost of running a lab is very different among divisions.

Very few project managers or engineers knew what their fully-burdened labor rate was. In fact, much to our surprise, this was not a common term to lab managers, many of whom asked which costs to add into the total and which not to. In addition, there were never any requests to use the data. As a result, the newest forms don't ask for it.

B.3.3 Size

Although the emphasis on reused code was ideal, there were practical problems with it. Most projects were not using a source control system which counted lines added, deleted, and modified. A program which is the same size at check-in and check-out might have had the same number of lines added as deleted. That information was not captured in an automated way. The new forms simply ask for a percentage of reused code.

The amount of supporting code information had been sparse, so it was relegated to the optional collection forms.

B.3.4 Defects

The only change was to make the defect introduced column optional.

B.3.5 Maintenance Metrics

Although the forms were agreed upon in August 1984, as of May 1985 we had not received any completed forms. There clearly was not as much enthusiasm for tracking maintenance activities as there was for development activities. One reported point of difficulty was that size data was difficult to determine accurately without a sophisticated tool which would keep track of lines added versus changed and deleted.

BIBLIOGRAPHY

1. Tausworthe, R., "Deep Space Network Software Cost Estimation Model," Jet Propulsion Laboratory, JPL Publication 81-7, Pasadena, Calif. (1981).
2. Littlewood, B., "How to Measure Software Reliability, and How Not to...," *IEEE Third International Conference on Software Engineering* (May 1978), pp. 37–45.

C

BIBLIOGRAPHY

Our feeling is that a simple list of all the software metrics references with which we are familiar would not be especially useful by itself. As a result, this bibliography is organized into two sections. The first section presents a limited list of those references which have most influenced our thinking while setting up our program. Where we feel that other articles that have come to our attention present the material more concisely or more effectively, we have listed them in addition to the original articles which influenced us. In addition to this summary section, there is a complete alphabetical listing which includes all the references in this book, as well as other references which might be of interest.

We have organized our bibliography somewhat differently, also. Rather than just a simple alphabetical listing, we have grouped the first section by general topical area so that it is easier to look for additional information about a particular subject in which you might be interested. Finally, we have given you in this first section a short description of what each particular article or book helped us with the most. We hope these comments and method of organization are useful.

C.1 GENERAL REFERENCE

1. B. W. Boehm, *Software Engineering Economics.*, Englewood Cliffs, N. J.: Prentice-Hall, Inc., 1981.

   This book is certainly one of the most complete reference books on the subject of software metrics on the market. It contains descriptions of what and how to measure elements of software engineering with quite a few useful graphs of real data. The book has a heavy focus on estimating and the use of statistics to refine metrics knowledge and the estimating process. Boehm describes one of the more popular estimating models, COCOMO, in detail. Much of the data is based on experiences at TRW. The only drawback of the book is that it is very long and difficult to read through, but it has influenced our thinking extensively.

2. T. DeMarco, *Controlling Software Projects.* New York: Yourdon Press, 1982.

   DeMarco's delightfully readable book offers motivation for why software data collection and analysis is essential to the success of any software producer. He offers a software methodology which must be followed (although it is general enough that he recommends tailoring it to the needs of each individual project) in order to use the metrics he proposes. One of the points we like the most about the book is that it advocates measures during all of the major stages of development, and not just overall measures. Unfortunately, these are not backed up with a lot of data or graphs, so it is difficult to pick any set as a starter set with the belief that you are starting at the highest leveraged point.

C.2 SIZE

3. A. Albrecht and J. Gaffney, "Software Function, Source Lines of Code, and Development Effort Prediction: A Software Science Validation," *IEEE Transactions on Software Engineering*, Vol. SE-9, no. 6 (Nov. 1983), pp. 639–648.

   We have not used function points (that we know of) at HP, and this article helped convince us initially not to. It does a good job of explaining what they are, relating them to some of Halstead's metrics, and showing that they can be used effectively to estimate software size and effort. There are two reasons we steered clear of function points initially. First, their calculation and measurement violated our ease-of-use criteria, because the whole process seemed complicated to teach and use. Second, we had reservations over whether they would apply equally well outside the EDP or applications areas due to the way they were defined and the projects to which they had been applied.

4. C. Jones, *Programming Productivity: Issues for the Eighties.* IEEE Computer Society Press, 1981, pp. 5–8.

   This short excerpt presents an extremely important caution on tracking productivity using lines of code. It shows how comparing high-level language usage to low-level language usage can be misleading. The book also contains various other metrics articles of interest, including ones by Curtis, Basili, Walston/Felix, and several others by Jones.

C.3 DEFECTS

5. B. Curtis, S. Sheppard, and P. Milliman, "Third Time Charm: Stronger Prediction of Programmer Performance by Software Complexity Metrics," *IEEE Proceedings of the Fourth International Conference on Software Engineering* (1979), pp. 356–360 (also contained in the Jones referenced book).

   This article discusses the usefulness of LOC, Halstead's E, and McCabe's v(G) in predicting defect-prone software modules.

6. A. Endres, "An Analysis of Errors and Their Causes in System Programs," *IEEE Transactions on Software Engineering*, Vol. SE-1, no. 2 (June 1975), pp. 140–149.

   This article contains an excellent breakdown of defect types. It also presents thorough data which supports the importance of studying the development process through analysis of defects, their categorization, and their causes.

7. H. Kohoutek, "A Practical Approach to Software Reliability Management," 29th EOQC Conference on Quality and Development, Estoril Portugal (June 1985), pp. 211–220.

   This article presents an empirical model developed at one division of HP which is used to determine when testing is complete on a project. Its popularity has spread within HP, and the concept seems quite useful.

8. R. Rambo, P. Buckley, and E. Branyan, "Establishment and Validation of Software Metric Factors," *Proceedings of the International Society of Parametric Analysts Seventh Annual Conference* (May 1985), pp. 406–417.

   This recent article from General Electric contains some interesting results of how they are trying to use complexity measurement to reduce defects. One conclusion presented lists eight possible threshold values which statistically showed a relationship to fewer than a nominal error rate. Another conclusion was that the maximum number of decision statements is 14 to optimize reliability. This conclusion was specifically related to the use of McCabe metrics. Finally it goes on to list five specific variables which contributed to error updates in their study.

9. V. Y. Shen, S. M. Thebaut, and L. R. Paulsen, "Identifying Error-Prone Software–An Empirical Study," *IEEE Transactions on Software Engineering*, Vol. SE-11, no. 4 (April 1985), pp. 317–323.

   This article discusses statistical analysis of five IBM projects to explore the use of several metrics in predicting software defects. It concludes that metrics related to the amount of data and to the structural complexity of programs appear useful in identifying error-prone modules at an early stage. It also sheds some interesting light on errors in new versus modified or translated code.

C.4 COMPLEXITY

10. L. J. Arthur, *Measuring Programmer Productivity and Software Quality*. New York: John Wiley and Sons, 1985, pp. 65–73.

    This book contains the best brief explanation of McCabe's metrics that we have seen (with the exception of the third flow graph in Figure 4.8, which should have a complexity number of 3 instead of 4).

11. K. Christensen, G. Fitsos, and C. Smith, "A Perspective on Software Science," *IBM Systems Journal*, Vol. 20, no. 4 (1981), pp. 372–387.

    This article contains a thorough, excellent description of Halstead's metrics along with statistical results relating to their application to projects measured at IBM.

12. N. F. Schneidewind, and H. M. Hoffmann, "An Experiment in Software Error Data Collection and Analysis, *IEEE Transactions on Software Engineering*, Vol. SE-5, no. 3 (May 1979), pp. 276–286.

    This article reports on an experiment which correlates probability of defects with complexity. The four projects studied were small, but the research seems thorough and encourages us to measure complexity.

C.5 STYLE ANALYSIS

13. M. J. Rees, "Automatic Assessment Aids for Pascal Programs," *SIGPLAN Notices*, Vol. 17, no. 10 (October 1982), pp. 33–42.

    This article discusses a program which was written to compare Pascal programs written by students. Different elements of "style" are measured, such as average line length, use of comments, use of indentation, length of identifiers, use of labels and gotos, and the like. The concept of feeding style analysis back to programmers as a means to improving program maintainability was intriguing to us, and we have experimented, using a program like the one described.

14. A. H. Jorgensen, "A Methodology for Measuring the Readability and Modifiability of Computer Programs," *BIT*, Vol. 20 (1980), pp. 394–405.

    This article provides a useful discussion of style analysis based upon experimental results and statistical analyses. Evaluation of style based upon results given by "computer science experts" is compared with automated analyses.

C.6 DESIGN METRICS

(refer to DeMarco, *Controlling Software Projects*, above, under general reference.)

DeMarco's book is the best reference of the few we found which propose metrics pertinent to design activities.

15. S. Henry, and D. Kafura, "Software Structure Metrics Based on Information Flow," *IEEE Transactions on Software Engineering*, Vol. SE-7, no. 5 (Sept. 1981), pp. 510–518.

16. S. Henry, and D. Kafura, "The Evaluation of Software Systems' Structure Using Quantitative Software Metrics," *Software—Practice and Experience*, Vol. 14, no. 6 (June 1984), pp. 561–573.

Even though the metrics in these articles are evaluated in the context of code as opposed to design, a very good case is made for their application at the design level. Analysis of UNIX system source code is performed and correlated to procedure changes, and complexity as measured by their metrics is related to need for change in the sources. In the second article, the dramatic effect of restructuring a software system is illustrated through the use of their information-flow metrics.

17. D. Troy, and S. Zweben, "Measuring the Quality of Structured Designs," *The Journal of Systems and Software* (June 1981), pp. 113–120.

A study involving 21 metrics taken from software design documents was performed on a single project. These metrics measured coupling, cohesion, complexity, modularity, and size. Within the limited context of the study, the coupling metrics seemed most important and the complexity metrics second.

C.7 MAINTENANCE

18. E. Daly, "Management of Software Development," *IEEE Transactions on Software Engineering* (May 1977), pp. 229–242.

The Daly article is one of the better articles we could find which included some detailed metrics data for the maintenance process. It discusses percentage efforts required for maintenance versus development, design methods which enhance maintainability, relative costs for defect discovery at different points in the process, the correct personnel makeup of a maintenance team, and general guidelines for how many postrelease changes to expect and how frequently they should occur.

19. B. P. Lientz, and E. B. Swanson, *Software Maintenance Management*. Reading, Mass.: Addison-Wesley 1980.

This book is certainly the most complete analysis of maintenance factors that we have seen. We prefer data based upon specific measurements, though, and this book is based upon a survey of close to 500 data processing managers. The fact that it is a book means that you have to dig some for what you might want. Finally, it is important to keep in mind that results for R&D organizations will be different from those for data processing organizations.

20. H. D. Rombach, "Impact of Software Structure on Maintenance," *IEEE Conference on Software Maintenance* (Nov. 1985), pp. 152–160.

This article was one of the most recently written which discussed some metrics for maintenance. It dealt with 50 experiments carried out by six graduate research assistants. These experiments were designed to measure maintainability, comprehensibility, locality, modifiability, and reusability. While the results are difficult to generalize to all kinds of software, the measures seem useful, and the approach is consistent with the practical approach to other metrics that we have taken in HP. The entire proceedings in which this particular article was contained was also quite useful.

C.8 DOCUMENTATION

21. V. R. Basili, and D. M. Weiss, "Evaluation of a Software Requirements Document By Analysis of Change Data," *Proceedings of the Fifth International Conference on Software Engineering* (March 1981), pp. 253–262.

    This article discusses an in-depth study of changes to a specifications document. It presents the metrics collected and a useful breakdown of the data into graphic form.

C.9 ESTIMATION

(Refer to Boehm, *Software Engineering Economics*, above, under general reference.)

Barry Boehm's COCOMO is one of the best and most popular estimating models in the software business. He actually presents several models in his book, each of which requires more inputs and gives more accurate results than the previous one. Quite a few entities at HP use the COCOMO model.

22. H. Dunsmore, V. Shen, and S. Conte, "A Comparison of a Few Effort Estimation Models, " Department of Computer Sciences, Purdue University.

    This paper presents a very good overview into the basis for most popular cost estimation models for software. It also explores the accuracy of several specific models against a database of 189 commercial projects gathered at Purdue. These results show that the state of the art of cost estimation is still quite young.

23. R. Tausworth, "Software Specifications Document, DSN Software Cost Model," Jet Propulsion Laboratory, JPL Publication 81-7, Pasadena, Calif. (1981).

    This is the paper which describes in detail the Softcost model which HP adopted for internal use early during our metrics program. It explains the inputs, the model itself, and the outputs. The model borrows heavily from other popular models and was calibrated using published industry data, as well as JPL data. The paper describes the parameters which can be changed to calibrate for a specific environment.

C.10 PEOPLE FACTORS

24. W. Bridges, "Managing Organizational Transitions" (not published - material from this paper is contained in the other Bridges paper listed in the alphabetical listing).

    This article explores human responses to change. Bridges introduces the concept of transition as the natural period after change and goes into good detail about how people can be expected to react and the underlying reasons for their actions. The article is excellent reading for all managers, and the material is appropriate to far more than metrics situations.

25. F. P. Brooks, *The Mythical Man-Month*. Reading, Mass.: Addison-Wesley, 1975.

    This book is a classic. While it doesn't contain a great deal of information specifically of a metrics nature, it is still one of the best sources of input regarding large software projects and the particular problems they face. Brooks does show several graphs and tables of productivity and defect data, and while the data is now old, it is still probably as good as any available for large projects. We categorize this book with the "human factors" group because it is best read for that specific topic as related to large projects.

26. A. J. Thadhani, "Factors Affecting Programmer Productivity During Application Development," *IBM Systems Journal*, Vol. 23, no. 1 (1984), pp. 19–35.

    This article discusses the effects of computer services, terminal response times, breakdowns of programmer time expenditures, productivity issues of experienced versus inexperienced programmers, and introduces the concepts of intrinsic complexity and perceived complexity. It gives some valuable insight into how equipment utilization can leverage productivity either positively or negatively, and into how important a factor response time is. The concepts of intrinsic and perceived complexity are also important notions that started us thinking about complexity factors.

27. T. Tuttle, and D. Sink, "Taking the Threat Out of Productivity Measurement," *National Productivity Review* (Winter 1984–1985), pp. 24–32.

    This short article discusses fears generated by productivity measurement and proposes dealing with them through the use of "force-field analysis." An excellent article for anyone about to introduce metrics either at the project or company level.

28. G. Weinberg, and E. Schulman,, "Goals and Performance in Computer Programming," *Human Factors* Vol. 16, no. 1 (1974), pp. 70–77.

    This article describes an experiment conducted with six different programming teams given different objectives for the same program. It provides great insight into the dilemma all software managers face when presented with the challenge of which factors matter the most, and how programming teams respond to specifications for the job.

C.11 MISCELLANEOUS

29. K. H. Kim, "A Look at Japan's Development of Software Engineering Technology," *Computer* (May 1983), pp. 26–37.

    This article contains no specifics regarding metrics other than a productivity graph from Toshiba going back to 1972, but the graph itself and the length of time they have been measuring impressed us a great deal. It does present a good overview of work that is being done in Japan in both industry and universities.

30. D. Tajima, and T. Matsubara, "The Computer Software Industry in Japan," *Computer* (May 1981), pp.89–96.

    This article is primarily a survey of computer and software suppliers in Japan. It also contains several interesting graphs of data from Hitachi showing cost estimate accuracy and defect analysis.

31. J. Vosburgh, et al., "Productivity Factors and Programming Environments," *IEEE 7th International Conference on Software Engineering* (March 1984), pp. 143–152.

    This relatively recent article presents the results of in-depth measurements of 44 projects at ITT since 1980. It contains some interesting results concerning hardware constraints, customer participation, and specifications. It shows an impressive correlation of productivity against modern programming practices, and an interesting breakdown of programming environments into categories of real-time, nonreal-time, and business applications.

C.12 COMPLETE ALPHABETIC LISTING

Articles described earlier are marked with "**" in front of the authors' names.

1. Abdel-Hamid, Tarek K. and S. E. Madnick, "The Dynamics of Software Project Scheduling," *Communications of the ACM* (May 1983), Vol. 26, Number 5, pp. 340–346.

2. Abe, Joichi, K. Sakamura, and H. Aiso, "An Analysis of Software Product Failure," *Proceedings of the Fourth International Conference on Software Engineering* Munich, (Sept. 1979).

3. ACM Sigmetrics, "Performance Evaluation Review," Vol. 11, no. 3, (Fall 1982), pp. 49–67.

4. Aho, A. and J. Ullman. *Principles of Compiler Design.* Reading, Mass.: Addison Wesley, 1977.

5. Akiyama, F., "An Example of Software System Debugging," *Proceedings of the 1971 IFIP Congress* Amsterdam: North-Holland, 1971, pp. 353–359.

6. **Albrecht, Allan J. and J. Gaffney**, "Software Function, Source Lines of Code, and Development Effort Prediction: A Software Science Validation," *IEEE Transactions on Software Engineering* Vol. SE-9, no. 6 (Nov. 1983), pp. 639–647.

7. Albrecht, A. J., "Measuring Application Development Productivity," *Proceedings of the Joint SHARE/GUIDE/IBM Application Development Symposium* (Oct. 1979), pp. 83-92.

8. Allen, T. J., "Communications in the Research and Development Laboratory," *Technology Review* (Oct./Nov. 1967).

9. Allen, T. J. and A. R. Fusfeld, "Design for Communication in the Research and Development Lab," *Technology Review* (May 1976), pp. 65–71.

10. Altmayer, L. and J. DeGood, "A Distributed Software Development Case Study," *HP Software Productivity Conference Proceedings* (April 1986), pp. 1-54 – 1-62.

11. Aron, J. D., "Estimating Resources for Large Programming Systems," *Software Engineering: Concepts and Techniques, Proceedings of the NATO Conferences* (Ed. by P. Naur, B. Randell, and J. Buxton), New York: Petrocelli/Charter, 1976, pp. 206–217.

12. **Arthur, L. J.**, *Measuring Programmer Productivity and Software Quality.* New York: Wiley and Sons, 1985.

13. Bailey, J. W. and V. R. Basili, "A Meta-Model for Software Development Resource Expenditures," *5th International Conference on Software Engineering* (March 1981), pp. 107–116.

14. Baker, F. T., "Chief Programmer Team Management of Production Programming," *IBM Systems Journal*, no. 1 (1972), pp. 56–73.

15. Balza, J., "Improving the Methods of Software Project Estimation at CNO," *HP Software Productivity Conference Proceedings* (April 1986), pp. 1-2-1-18.

16. Basili, V. R. and R. W. Selby, "Metric Analysis and Data Validation Across Fortran Projects," *IEEE Transactions on Software Engineering*" Vol. SE-9, no. 6 (Nov. 1983), pp. 652–663.

17. **Basili, V. R. and D. M. Weiss**, "Evaluation of a Software Requirements Document by Analysis of Change Data," *Proceedings of the Fifth International Conference on Software Engineering* (March 1981), pp. 314–323.

18. Basili, V. R., "Changes and Errors as Measures of Software Development." *IEEE EH0167-7/80/0000-0062* (July 1980) pp. 62–64.

19. Basili, V. R. and R. W. Reiter, "Evaluating Automatable Measures of Software Development," *Proceedings, Workshop on Quantitative Software Models* (Oct. 1979), pp. 107–116.

20. Basili, V. R. and R. W. Reiter, "An Investigation of Human Factors in Software Development," *Computer* (Dec. 1979), pp. 21–38.

21. Basili, V., IEEE Working Group for Software Productivity Metrics, Nashua, N. H. (Sept. 1984).

22. Basili, V., "A Methodology for Collecting Valid Software Engineering Data," *IEEE Transactions on Software Engineering* Vol. SE-10, no. 6 (Nov. 1984), pp. 728–738.

23. Belady, L. A. and M. M. Lehman, "The Characteristics of Large Systems," *Research Directions in Software Technology* (Ed by P. Wegner) Cambridge, Mass.: MIT Press, 1979, pp. 106–142.

24. Belford, P. C. and R. A. Berg, "Central Flow Control Software Development: A Case Study of the Effectiveness of Software Engineering Techniques," *IEEE Proceedings of the Fourth International Conference on Software Engineering* Munich (Sept. 1979), IEEE CH 1479-5/79.0000-0378, pp. 85–93.

25. Berry, R. and B. Meekings, "A Style Analysis of C Programs," *Communications of the ACM*, Vol. 28, no. 1 (Jan. 1985), pp. 80–88.

26. Blair, S., "A Defect Tracking System for the UNIX© Environment," *HP Journal*, Vol. 37, no. 3 (March 1986), pp. 15–18.

27. **Boehm, Barry W.**, *Software Engineering Economics*. Englewood Cliffs, N. J.:Prentice-Hall, Inc., 1981.

28. Boehm, Barry W., "Software Engineering Economics," *IEEE Transactions on Software Engineering* Vol. SE-10, no. 1 (Jan. 1984), pp. 4–21.

29. Boehm, B. W., J. R. Brown, H. Kaspar, M. Lipow, G. MacLeod, and M. J. Merritt, "Characteristics of Software Quality," *TRW Series of Software Technology*, Vol. 1. Amsterdam: TRW and North-Holland Publishing Company, 1978.

30. Boehm, B. W., "An Experiment in Small-Scale Application Software Engineering," *IEEE Transactions on Software Engineering* Vol. SE-7, no. 5 (Sept. 1981), pp. 482–493.

31. Boehm, B. W., J. R. Brown, M. Lipow, "Quantitative Evaluation of Software Quality," *IEEE 2nd International Conference on Software Engineering* San Francisco, Calif. (Oct. 1976), pp. 592–605.

32. Boehm, B. W., M. H. Penedo, R. D. Stuckle, R. D. Williams, A. B. Pyster, "A Software Development Environment for Improving Productivity," *Computer* (June 1984), pp. 30–42.

33. Boehm, B. W., J. F. Elwell, A. B. Pyster, E. D. Stuckle, and R. D. Williams, "The TRW Software Productivity System," *Proceedings 6th International Conference on Software Engineering* (Sept. 1982), pp. 148–156.

34. Bridges, W., "How to Manage Organizational Transition," *Training* (1985).

35. **Bridges, William**, "Managing Organizational Transitions," presentation at Pajaro Dunes, Calif. (Feb. 1985).

36. Britcher, B. and J. Craig, "Upgrading Aging Software Systems Using Modern Software Engineering Practices," *IEEE Conference on Software Maintenance* (Nov. 1985), pp. 162–170.

37. **Brooks, F. P.**, *The Mythical Man-Month*. Reading, Mass.: Addison-Wesley, 1975.

38. Brooks, F. P., "The Mythical Man-Month," *Datamation* (Dec. 1974), pp. 304–311.

39. Brooks, W. Douglas, "Software Technology Payoff: Some Statistical Evidence," *Structured Programming, The Journal of Systems and Software 2*, (1981), pp. 3–9.

40. Bugarin, J., "CNO Process Measures," (March 1984).

41. Carper, I. L., S. Harvey, and J. C. Wethesbe, "Computer Capacity Planning: Strategy and Methodologies," *Data Base* (Summer 1983), pp. 3–11.

42. Chen, E. T., "Program Complexity and Programmer Productivity," *IEEE Transactions on Software Engineering* Vol. SE-4, no. 3. (May 1978), pp. 187- 194.

43. **Christensen, K, G. P. Fitsos, and C. P. Smith**, "A Perspective on Software Science," *IBM Systems Journal*, Vol. 20, no. 4 (1981), pp. 372–387.

44. Conte, S., H. Dunsmore, and V. Shen, "Software Effort Estimation and Productivity," *Advances in Computers* (Ed. by M. C. Yovits), Vol. 24. Academic Press, Inc., 1985, pp. 1–60.

45. Conte, S., H. Dunsmore, and V. Shen, *Software Engineering Metrics and Models*. Menlo Park, Calif.: Benjamin/Cummings Publishing Co., Inc., 1986.

46. Cook, Michael L., "Software Metrics: An Introduction and Annotated Bibliography," *ACM Sigsoft, Software Engineering Notes*, Vol. 7, no. 2 (April 1982), pp. 41–60.

47. Coulter, N., "Software Science and Cognitive Psychology," *IEEE Transactions on Software Engineering* Vol., SE-9, no. 2 (March 1983), pp. 166–171.

48. Curtis, B., S. B. Sheppard, P. Milliman, M. A. Borst, and T. Love, "Measuring the Psychological Complexity of Software Maintenance Tasks With the Halstead and McCabe Metrics," *IEEE Transactions on Software Engineering* Vol. SE-5, no. 2 (March 1979), pp. 96–104.

49. **Curtis, B., S. B. Sheppard, and P. Milliman**, "Third Time Charm: Stronger Prediction of Programmer Performance by Software Complexity Metrics," *Proceedings of the Fourth International Conference on Software Engineering* (July 1979), pp. 356–360.

50. **Daly, Edmund B.**, "Management of Software Development," *IEEE Transactions on Software Engineering* (May 1977), pp. 229–242.

51. Datapro Research Corporation, "Estimating Application Software Life-Cycle Development Costs," Jan. 1980.

52. Deardorff, E., "Projection of Project Cost and Project Duration at Waltham," *HP Software Productivity Conference Proceedings* (April 1986), pp. 1-70–1-85.

53. DeMarco, Tom, "An Algorithm for Sizing Software Products," *SigMetrics Performance Evaluation Review*, Vol. 12, no. 2 (Spring/Summer 1984) pp. 13–22.

54. **DeMarco, Tom**, *Controlling Software Projects*. New York: Yourdon Press, 1982.

55. DeMarco, T. and T. Lister, "Programmer Performance and the Effects of the Workplace," *IEEE Proceedings of the Eighth International Conference on Software Engineering* London (Aug. 1985), pp. 268–272.

56. DiPersio, T., D. Isbister, and B. Shneiderman, "An Experiment Using Memorization/Reconstruction as a Measure of Programmer Ability," *International Journal of Man-Machine Studies*, no. 13, (1980), pp. 339–354.

57. Dniestrowski, A., J. M. Guillaume, R. Mortier, "Software Engineering in Avionics Applications," *IEEE Proceedings of the Third International Conference on Software Engineering* Atlanta (May 1978), pp. 124–131.

58. Doerflinger, C. and V. Basili, "Monitoring Software Development through Dynamic Variables," *IEEE Transactions on Software Engineering* Vol. SE-11, no. 9 (Sept. 1985), pp. 978–985.

59. Drake, D., "A Pre-Release Measure of Software Reliability," *HP Software Productivity Conference Proceedings* (April 1986), pp. 2-58–2-71.

60. **Dunsmore, H., V. Shen, and S. Conte**, "A Comparison of a Few Effort Estimation Models," Department of Computer Sciences, Purdue University.

61. Dunsmore, H. E. and A. S. Wang, "A Step Toward Early Software Size Estimation for Use in Productivity Models," *1985 National Conference on Software Quality and Productivity* (March 6-8 1985), pp. 1–9.

62. **Endres, Albert**, "An Analysis of Errors and Their Causes in System Programs," *IEEE Transactions on Software Engineering* Vol. SE-1, no. 2 (June 1975), pp. 140–149.

63. Fagan, M. E., "Advances in Software Inspections," *IEEE Transactions on Software Engineering* Vol. SE-12, no. 7 (July 1986), pp. 744–751.

64. Fagan, M. E., "Inspecting Software Design and Code," *Datamation*, Vol. 23, no. 10 (Oct. 1977), pp. 133–144.

65. Fagan, M. E., "Design and Code Inspections to Reduce Errors in Program Development," *IBM Systems Journal*, Vol. 15, no. 3 (1976), pp. 182–210.

66. Felix, G. H. and J. L. Riggs, "Productivity Measurement by Objectives," *National Productivity Review* (Autumn 1983), pp. 386–393.

67. Feuer, A. R., and E. B. Fowlkes, "Relating Computer Program Maintainability Software Measures," *AFIPS National Computer Conference Expo Conference Proceedings*, Vol. 48 (June 4-7 1979), pp. 1003–1012.

68. Finch, B., Presentation to Second Annual HP Software Metrics Conference (August 1984).

69. Fuget, C., "Using Quality Metrics to Improve Life Cycle Productivity," *HP Software Productivity Conference Proceedings* (April 1986), pp. 1-86–1-93.

70. Gaffney, John E., "Estimating the Number of Faults in Code," *IEEE Transactions on Software Engineering* Vol. SE-10, no. 4 (July 1984), pp. 459–465.

71. Gilb, T., "Evolutionary Delivery Versus the 'Waterfall Model'," *Software Engineering Notes (ACM SIGSOFT)* July 1985.

72. Gordon, R., "Measuring Improvements in Program Clarity," *IEEE Transactions on Software Engineering* Vol. SE-5, no. 2 (Mar. 1979) pp. 79–90.

73. Grady, B. and D. Caswell, "Understanding HP's Software Development Processes through Software Metrics," *HP Software Productivity Conference Proceedings* (April 1984), pp. 3-38–3-54.

74. Grady, B. and D. Caswell, "Tools for Collecting and Analyzing Software Metrics," *HP Software Productivity Conference Proceedings* (April 1985), pp. 1-52–1-67.

75. Grady, B. and D. Caswell, "Establishing Standards," (Sept. 1985).

76. Grady, B. and D. Caswell, "Graphs for Top-Level Management," Letter from Chuck House to all HP R&D managers (April 18 1985).

77. Grady, B. and D. Caswell, "The Use of Software Metrics to Improve Project Estimation," *Proceedings of the International Society of Parametric Analysts Seventh Annual Conference* (May 1985), pp. 129–144.

78. Grady, B. and D. Caswell, "The Human Element," (Dec. 1985).

79. Grady, B. and E. Brigham, "A Survey of HP Software Development," *HP Software Productivity Conference Proceedings* (April 1986), pp. 1-126–1-141.

80. Gremillion, L., "Determinants of Program Repair Maintenance Requirements," *Communications of the ACM*, Vol. 27, no. 8 (Aug. 1984), pp. 826–832.

81. Gustafson, D., A. Melton, and C. Hsieh, "An Analysis of Software Changes During Maintenance and Enhancement," *IEEE Conference on Software Maintenance* (Nov. 1985), pp. 92–95.

82. Hamilton, G., "Improving Software Development Using Quality Control," *HP Software Productivity Conference Proceedings* (April 1985), pp. 1-96–1-102.

83. Hamilton, P. and J. Musa, "Measuring Reliability of Computation Center Software," *Third International Conference on Software Engineering* (May 1978), pp. 29–36.

84. Harrison, W., K. Magel, R. Kluczny, and A. DeKock, "Applying Software Complexity Metrics to Program Maintenance," *Computer* (Sept. 1982), pp. 65–79.

85. Henry, S. and D. Kafura, "The Evaluation of Software Systems' Structure Using Quantitative Software Metrics," *Software-Practice and Experience*, Vol. 14 (6) (June 1984), pp. 561–573.

86. Henry, S., and D. Kafura, "Software Structure Metrics Based on Information Flow," *IEEE Transactions on Software Engineering* Vol. SE-7, no. 5 (Sept. 1981), pp. 510–518.

87. *Hewlett-Packard Software Product Lifecycle*, 5955-1756 (February 1983).

88. HP Software Metrics Class Student Workbook (1985).

89. Hill, Gregory P., "Controlling the Maintainability of PL/I and PL/I-Like Software," *IEEE Conference on Software Maintenance* (Nov. 1985), pp. 106–110.

90. Hutchens, D. H. and V. R. Basili, "System Structure Analysis: Clustering with Data Bindings," *IEEE Transactions on Software Engineering* Vol. SE-11, no. 8 (Aug. 1985), pp. 749–757.

91. *IEEE Standard Glossary of Software Engineering Terminology*, IEEE Std 729-1983, New York (1983).

92. Ishikawa, K., *Guide to Quality Control*. Tokyo: Asian Productivity Organization, 1976.

93. Jensen, Randall W., "Projected Productivity Impact of Near-Term ADA Use in Software System Development," *Proceedings of the International Society of Parametric Analysts Seventh Annual Conference* (May 1985), pp. 42–55.

94. Jensen, Randall W., "A Macro-Level Software Development Cost Estimation Methodology," *IEEE CH1625-3/80/0000/0320* (March 1980), pp. 320–325.

95. Jones, C., Letter (July 25 1986).

96. Jones, C., "Measuring Programming Quality and Productivity," *IBM Systems Journal*, Vol. 17, no. 1 (1978), pp. 39–63.

97. Jones, C., "Measuring Software Productivity With Function Points," submitted to *Computerworld* for publication (Oct. 1984).

98. Jones, C., Presentation to Hewlett Packard (June 1985).

99. Jones, C., *Programming Productivity*. New York: McGraw-Hill Book Co., 1986.

100. **Jones, C.**, *Programming Productivity: Issues for the Eighties*, IEEE Computer Society Press (1981), pp. 5–8.

101. Jorgensen, A. H., "A Methodology for Measuring the Readability and Modifiability of Computer Programs," *BIT*, Vol. 20 (1980), pp. 394–405.

102. Juran, J., F. Gryna, and R. Bingham Jr., *Quality Control Handbook,* 3rd ed. New York: McGraw Hill, 1974.

103. Kenyon, D., "Implementing a Software Metrics Program," *HP Software Productivity Conference Proceedings* (April 1985), pp. 1-103–1-117.

104. Kenyon, D., Presentation to Second Annual HP Software Metrics Conference (August 1984).

105. **Kim, K. H.**, "A Look at Japan's Development of Software Engineering Technology," *IEEE Computer* (May 1983), pp. 26–37.

106. **Kohoutek, Henry J.**, "A Practical Approach to Software Reliability Management," *Proceedings of the 29th EOQC Conference, Quality and Development*, Vol. 2 (June 1985), pp. 211–220.

107. Lambert, G. N., "A Comparative Study of System Response Time on Program Developer Productivity," *IBM Systems Journal*, Vol. 23, no. 1 (1984), pp. 36–43.

108. Lawrence, M., "Programming Methodology, Organizational Environment, and Programming Productivity," *The Journal of Systems and Software* (Sept. 1981), pp. 257–269.

109. Lebowitz, L., Presentation to Second Annual HP Software Metrics Conference (August,1984).

110. Lientz, B. P. and E. B. Swanson, "Software Maintenance: A User/ Management Tug-Of-War," *Data Management* (April 1979), pp. 26–30.

111. **Lientz**, B. P. and E. B. Swanson, *Software Maintenance Management*. Reading, Mass.: Addison-Wesley, 1980.

112. Lipow, M., "Number of Faults per Line of Code," *IEEE Transactions on Software Engineering* Vol. SE-8, no. 4 (July 1982), pp. 437–439.

113. Littlewood, B., "How to Measure Software Reliability, and How Not To . . . ," *Proceedings of the Third International Conference on Software Engineering* (May 1978), pp. 37–45.

114. Littlewood, B., "Validation of a Software Reliability Model," *IEEE Second Software Life Cycle Management Workshop* (Aug. 1978), pp. 146–152.

115. Lundberg, D., "A Method of Predicting the Software Release Date Based Upon Source Code Changes," *HP Software Productivity Conference* (April 1984), pp. 1-67–1-73.

116. McCabe, Thomas J., "A Complexity Measure," *IEEE Transactions on Software Engineering* (Dec. 1976), pp. 308–320.

117. Merlini, M., "Is Big Blue Big Brother," *Datamation* (March 1984), pp. 52–61.

118. Miller, G. A., "The Magical Number Seven, Plus or Minus Two: Some Limits on Our Capacity for Processing Information," *The Psychological Review*, Vol. 63, no. 2 (March 1956), pp. 81–97.

119. Monray, J., "How Two Engineers Made the Difference," *HP Software Productivity Conference Proceedings* (April 1986), pp. 1-19–1-28.

120. Munson, J. B. and R. T. Yeh, "Report by the IEEE Software Engineering Productivity Workshop," (March 8-9 1981), San Diego, Calif., CH1702-0/81, pp. 329–359.

121. Munson, J. B., "Software Maintainability: A Practical Concern for Life-Cycle Costs," *Computer*, Vol. 14, no. 11 (Nov. 1981), pp. 103–109.

122. Musa, J. D., "The Measurement and Management of Software Reliability," *Proceedings of the IEEE*, Vol. 68, no. 9 (Sept. 1980), pp. 1131–1143.

123. Musa, J. D., "Measuring Reliability of Computation Center Software," *IEEE Proceedings of the Third International Conference on Software Engineering* (May 1978), pp. 29–36.

124. Musa, John D., "Software Reliability Measurement," *The Journal of Systems and Software*, Vol. 1 (1980), pp. 223–241.

125. Nielson, L., "Using NCSS as a Tool to Estimate Effort and Schedule," *HP Software Productivity Conference Proceedings* (April 1986), pp. 1-94–1-105.

126. Nichols, P, D. Herington, and R. Lipp, "A Software Testing Methodology Using Branch Analysis," *HP Software Productivity Conference Proceedings* (April 1986), pp. 2-72–2-82.

127. Ohba, Mitsuru, "Software Reliability Analysis Models," *IBM J. Res. Develop.*, Vol. 28, no. 4 (July 1984), pp. 428–443.

128. Ohba, Mitsuru, "Software Quality = Test Accuracy X Text Coverage," *IEEE 0270-5257/82/0000/0287* (1982), pp. 287–293.

129. Osborne, K., "An Experiment in Programming Methodologies," *HP Software Productivity Conference Proceedings* (April 1984), pp. 1-18–1-23.

130. Paige, Michael, "A Metric for Software Test Planning," *Proceedings of the Fourth International Conference on Computer Software and Application.* Chicago, Ill.: Oct. 27-31, 1980, pp. 499–504.

131. Peercy, D., "A Software Maintainability Evaluation Methodology," *IEEE Transactions on Software Engineering* Vol. SE-7, no. 4 (July 1981), pp. 343–351.

132. Peters, T. and R. Waterman, *In Search of Excellence.* New York: Harper & Row, 1982.

133. Petschenik, Nathan H., "Practical Priorities in System Testing," *IEEE Software* (Sept. 1985), pp. 18–23.

134. Putnam, L. H., "SLIM, A Quantitative Tool for Software Cost and Schedule Estimation (A Demonstration of a Software Management Tool)," *Proceedings of the NBS/IEEE/ACM Software Tool Fair* (March 1981), pp. 49–57.

135. Putnam, L. I., "A General Empirical Solution to the Macro Software Sizing and Estimating Problem," *IEEE Transactions on Software Engineering* Vol. SE-4, no. 4 (July 1978), pp. 345–361.

136. Putnam, L. H., and A. Fitzsimmons, "Estimating Software Costs," *Datamation* (Sept. 1979), pp. 312–315.

137. Ramamoorthy, A., W. Tsai, and Y. Usuda, "Software Engineering: Problems and Perspectives," *Computer* (Oct. 1984), pp. 191–207.

138. **Rambo, R., Dr. P. Buckley, and E. Branyan**, "Establishment and Validation of Software Metric Factors," *Proceedings of the International Society of Parametric Analysts Seventh Annual Conference* (May 1985), pp. 406–417.

139. **Rees, Michael J.**, "Automatic Assessment Aids for Pascal Programs," *SIGPLAN Notices*, Vol. 17, no. 10 (Oct. 1982), pp. 33–42.

140. Roberts, E. B., "Generating Effective Corporate Innovation," *Technology Review* (Nov. 1977), p. 29.

141. Rombach, H. D., "Design Metrics for Maintenance, NASA, Goddard Space Flight Center, Greenbelt, MD, (Nov. 1984), pp. 100–135.

142. **Rombach, H. D.**, "Impact of Software Structure on Maintenance," *IEEE Conference on Software Maintenance* (Nov. 1985), pp. 152–160.

143. Rubey, R. J., J. A. Dana, and P. W. Biche, "Quantitative Aspects of Software Validation," *IEEE Transactions on Software Engineering* Vol. SE-1, no. 2 (June 1975), pp. 150–155.

144. Rubin, Dr. Howard A., "Macro-Estimation of Software Development Parameters: The Estimacs System," *IEEE CH1919-0/83/0000/0109* (1983), pp. 109–113.

145. Sakai, B. and S. Davey, "Spectrum Metrics Collection Program," *HP Software Productivity Conference Proceedings* (April 1986), pp. 1-113–1-125.

146. Schaefer, H., "Metrics for Optimal Maintenance Management," *IEEE Conference on Software Maintenance* (Nov. 1985), pp. 114–119.

147. **Schneidewind, N. F., and H. M. Hoffman,**, "An Experiment in Software Error Data Collection and Analysis," *IEEE Transactions on Software Engineering* Vol. SE-5, no. 3 (May 1979), pp. 276–286.

148. Scott, B. and D. Decot, "Inspections at DSD - Automating Data Input and Data Analysis," *HP Software Productivity Conference Proceedings* (April 1985), pp. 1-79–1-89.

149. **Shen, V. Y., T. Yu, S. M. Thebaut, and L. R. Paulsen**, "Identifying Error-Prone Software — An Empirical Study," *IEEE Transactions on Software Engineering* Vol. SE-11, no. 4 (April 1985), pp. 317–323.

150. Shen, V. Y., "The Relationship Between Student Grades and Software Science Parameters-" *IEEE CH1515-6/79/0000-0783* (June 1979), pp. 783–785.

151. Shooman, M. L., "Types, Distribution, and Test and Correction Times for Programming Errors," *IEEE Proceedings of the 1975 Conference on Reliable Software*, Los Angeles, Calif. (April 1975), pp. 347–357.

152. Sieloff, C., "Software TQC: Improving the Software Development Process Through Statistical Quality Control," *HP Software Productivity Conference Proceedings* (April 1984), pp. 2-49–2-62.

153. Silverman, B., "Software Cost and Productivity Improvements: An Analogical View," *Computer* (May 1985), pp. 86–95.

154. Silverstein, A., "Some QA Metrics Support Tools," *HP Software Productivity Conference Proceedings* (April 1986), pp. 1-106–1-112.

155. Sink, D. S., "Strategic Planning for Successful Design, Development, and Implementation of Productivity Management Programs," *IEEE 1984 Fall Industrial Engineering Conference Proceedings* (Fall 1984), pp. 391–397.

156. Stanley, M., "Software Cost Estimating," *Royal Signals & Radar Establishment Memorandum no. 3472*, U.S. Department of Commerce National Technical Information Service (May 1982).

157. Sunazuka, T., M. Azuma, and N. Yamagishi, "Software Quality Assessment Technology," *IEEE, Proceedings of the Eighth International Conference on Software Engineering* London (August 1985), IEEE CH2139-4/85/0000/0142, pp. 142–148.

158. Sunohara, T., A. Takano, K. Uehara, and T. Ohkawa, "Program Complexity Measure for Software Development Management," *IEEE CH1627-9/81/0000/0100* (Sept. 1981), pp. 100–106.

159. **Tajima, D. and T. Matsubara**, "The Computer Software Industry in Japan," *Computer*, Vol. 14, no. 5 (May 1981), pp. 89–96.

160. Tajima, D. and T. Matsubara, "Inside the Japanese Software Industry," *Computer* (March 1984), pp. 34–43.

161. Tanik, Murat M., "A Comparison of Program Complexity Prediction Models," *ACM SIGSOFT, Software Engineering Notes*, Vol. 5, no. 4 (Oct. 1980), pp. 10–16.

162. Tausworthe, R., "Software Specifications Document, DSN Software Cost Model," Jet Propulsion Laboratory, JPL Publication 81-7, Pasadena, Calif., (1981).

163. **Thadhani, A. J.**, "Factors Affecting Programmer Productivity During Application Development," *IBM Systems Journal*, Vol. 23, no. 1 (1984), pp. 19–35.

164. Thayer, T., M. Lipow, and E. Nelson, *Software Reliability: A Study of Large Project Reality.* Amsterdam: North-Holland, Inc., 1978.

165. Troy, Douglas A., "Measuring the Quality of Structured Designs," *The Journal of Systems and Software 2* (June 1981), pp. 113–120.

166. **Tuttle, Tomas C. and Scott D. Sink**, "Taking the Threat out of Productivity Measurement," *National Productivity Review* (Winter 1984-85), pp. 24–32.

167. U. S. Social Security Administration, "Productivity Measurement in Software Engineering," (Participants include Brown, B. R., H. Herlich, M. D. Emerson, C. L. Williamson, M. V. Greco, W. Sherman,), *U. S. Department of Commerce National Technical Information Service* (June 1983), pp. 1–57.

168. Vessey, V. and R. Weber, "Some Factors Affecting Program Repair Maintenance: An Empirical Study," *Communications of the ACM*, Vol. 26, no. 2 (Feb. 1983), pp. 128–134.

169. Vomocil, Dave, "Locating Suspect Software and Documentation by Monitoring Basic Information About Changes to Source Files," *Pacific Northwest Software Quality Conference Proceedings* (Sept. 1985), pp. 264–275.

170. ****Vosburgh, J., B. Curtis, R. Wolverton, B. Albert, H. Malec, S. Hoben, and Y. Liu**, "Productivity Factors and Programming Environments," *IEEE 0270-5257/84/0000/0143* (1984), pp. 143–152.

171. Walker, W., "Practical Management of the Software Test Phase," *HP Software Productivity Conference Proceedings* (April 1986), pp. 2-92–2-106.

172. Walsh, Thomas J., "A Software Reliability Study Using a Complexity Measure," *Proceedings of the 1979 National Computer Conference.* New Jersey: AFIPS Press (1979), pp. 761–768.

173. Walston, C. E., and C. P. Felix, "A Method of Programming Measurement and Estimation," *IBM Systems Journal*, no. 1 (1977), pp. 54–73.

174. Walters, Gene F., "Software Quality Metrics for Life-Cycle Cost-Reduction," *IEEE Transactions on Reliability*, Vol. R-28, no. 3 (Aug. 1979), pp. 212–219.

175. Ward, J., "Using Quality Metrics for Critical Application Software," *HP Software Productivity Conference Proceedings* (April 1985), pp. 1-39–1-51.

176. ****Weinberg, G. M., and E. L. Schulman**, "Goals and Performance in Computer Programming," *Human Factors* Vol.16, no. 1 (1974), pp. 70–77.

177. Weinberg, Gerald M., "The Psychology of Improved Programming Performance," *Datamation* (Nov. 1972), pp. 82–85.

178. Weinberg, G., *Psychology of Computer Programming.* New York: Van Nostrand Reinhold Co., 1971.

179. Weiss, D. M. and V. R. Basili, "Evaluating Software Development by Analysis of Changes: Some Data from the Software Engineering Laboratory," *IEEE Transactions on Software Engineering* Vol. SE-11, no. 2 (Feb. 1985), pp. 157–168.

180. Whitworth, M. and P. Szulewski, "The Measurement of Control and Data Flow Complexity in Software Designs," *IEEE CH1607-1/80/0000-0735* (Jan. 1980), pp. 735–743.

181. Yau, S. and J. Collofello, "Design Stability Measures for Software Maintenance," *IEEE Transactions on Software Engineering* Vol. SE-11, no. 9 (Sept. 1985), pp. 849–856.

182. Yin, B. H., and J. W. Winchester, "The Establishment and Use of Measures to Evaluate the Quality of Software Designs," *Proceedings of the Software Quality and Assurance Workshop*, New York: Association for Computing Machinery, 1978, pp. 45–52.

183. Young, J., Letter to all general managers, management council, and QA managers (April 1986).

184. Young, J., Presentation to HP managers (1982).

185. Yuen, Chong Hok, "An Empirical Approach to the Study of Errors in Large Software Under Maintenance," *IEEE CH2219-4/85/0000/0096* (April 1985), pp. 96–105.

INDEX

INDEX

V

Variable conventions, 209
Version control, 210

W

Walkthroughs:
    code, 105
    design, 105
Weight, 200
Weinberg, 20
Weiss, David, 26
What if?, 212

Y

Young, John, 14, 79